DEMOCRACY
AND WHY IT WILL FAIL IN AMERICA

JOHN L. BOWMAN

DEMOCRACY
AND WHY IT WILL FAIL IN AMERICA

The cover art is a portion of the oil-on-canvas painting scene at the Signing of the Constitution of the United States by Howard Chandler Christy, now on display along the east stairway of the House of Representatives wing of the Capitol building in Washington D.C. It depicts the signing of the Constitution at Independence Hall in Philadelphia on September 17, 1787.

The painting represents the birth of democracy in America.

Cover and interior design by Kathryn Banks.

CONTENTS

SECTION III
The Reasons Democracy Fails

SECTION IV
Democracy in America

PREFACE

This book was inspired by Francis Fukuyama's book *The End of History and the Last Man*, in which he predicted democracy is the end of human political development. This bold assertion sparked an interest that precipitated my long journey into democracy. I started this book not knowing its conclusion. Having lived my life in a democracy, my first reaction was that he was right; but as I studied and thought more on his thesis, my mind changed. My unfortunate conclusion is that it will fail, and this book is about why. I now believe democracy goes through a natural lifecycle and ultimately fails.

Certainly, I am not prescient; I could be wrong. Indeed, the very concept of history being cyclical rather than progressive is controversial. I could well be, as R. G. Collingwood pointed out, like one of those from the past, wrongly judging the future from their time's perspective. Posterity may well judge me wrong. For me, however, if one admits defeat before one tries, one would never try. So, I mined my knowledge and experience and wrote this book presenting my story.

My views come from a variety of sources, including what I learned in my education, which included degrees in philosophy and history; my readings; and my personal observations, experience, and intuition, syllogistically connecting causes with consequences and reflection. I was particularly influenced in my views by the failure of past democracies, like Athens and France after the French Revolution, and by historic authors like Solon, Aristotle and Alexis de Tocqueville. Many of my views on history were derived from Collingwood and on political philosophy from Georg Wilhelm Friedrich Hegel, Friedrich Nietzsche and John Locke. Many seemed to support my views in one way or another, which made the lonely road of prediction more endurable. One of the most enlightening chapters for me to write is chapter three, which is about these historic thinkers' views, particularly their arguments against democracy. These are arguments that may well explain why, in the early twenty-first century, history's longest existing democracy — America — fails, and Fukuyama is wrong. See it as you will, reader, but it seems to me that we can infer the wind from the movement of the trees.

In spite of my thesis, I should say that I am an advocate for democracy. I have spent a long and happy life living in one — it can be a great political system. In its early idealistic phase, it could well be the best political system devised by humans. In this, I am in agreement with Fukuyama. However, democracy naturally segues into something it is not. In this respect, this book is a clarion call to return to an earlier, purer form of democracy. It is an extended argument to revivify the true spirit of democracy, particularly in America. I believe Locke was right when he wrote that in nature we are free but in continual danger. For Locke, the proper alternative to the natural state is not political dictatorship or tyranny, but rather a democratically elected government and the effective protection of the basic human rights to life, liberty and property, under the rule of law. I believe early democracy, with a few notable exceptions, provided these.

This book is not a scholastic work with interminable quotations, citations and references. I wanted to keep it simple and write a story, rather than build a case. Citations are important, but they disturb my flow of thought. Thus, I did not put many quotes in quotation marks but instead, in order to avoid plagiarism and acknowledge the source of the quote, endeavored to credit the comment to the author in context or preface it with the words 'paraphrased' or 'verbatim' in parenthesis. I will repeat, for example, what Frank C. Bourne or Tocqueville wrote, and either say they wrote it or preface the quote with (verbatim) or (paraphrased), depending on which one it is. All quotes were taken from assumedly reliable sources.

This is my view on the future of democracy. I hope you enjoy my effort.

John Bowman

PORTLAND, OREGON · 2016

INTRODUCTION

Historically, democracy has not been a popular political philosophy. With few exceptions, the ancients despised democracy. Plato believed despotism comes out of democracy, and Cicero, who was particularly disdainful, criticized the ancient philosopher Heraclitus's pro-democratic sentiment that there shall be no distinctions bestowed by the people. Friedrich Nietzsche derided democracy, and in *On the Genealogy of Morals,* he wrote that democracy heralds symptoms of life in decline. Thomas Carlyle attacked democracy as an absurd social ideal, and early seventeenth-century French historian and statesman François Guizot wrote that democracy brings chaos. Early American patriot John Winthrop opposed unconstrained democracy, calling it the meanest and worst of all forms of government. Founding Father John Adams said that democracy never lasts long—it soon wastes, exhausts and murders itself. Elbridge Gerry, another American statesman and member of the Constitutional Convention, warned that evils flow from excess democracy, and Brooks Adams, an early American historian, described democracy as an infinite mass of conflicting minds and interests. Russian writer Leo Tolstoy detested democracy, and Winston Churchill called it only the best of the worst kinds of political systems. American contentious newspaper pundit H. L. Mencken wrote that democracy is the most expensive and nefarious kind of government ever heard of on Earth and that it threatens the two greatest intellectual possessions of modern man—personal freedom and the limitation of government. Contemporary American writer Kenneth Minogue, in *Politics*, criticized democracies for catering to the poor.

Fukuyama's Claim

In *The End of History and the Last Man*, Francis Fukuyama has a different view—he extols democracy's virtues and claims that it is the end of human political development. He persuasively weaves an attractive theory in defense of democracy, describing the reasons it evolved and why it will prevail. His involved theory uses German philosopher Georg Wilhelm Friedrich Hegel's famous dialectic that ostensibly leads to human freedom. Briefly, Fukuyama argues that two pillars of history, economics and recognition on one hand and freedom and equality on the other, interact as thesis and antithesis, and the result is a synthesis that inexorably ends in liberal democracy. For Fukuyama, the democracies we live in today are the best form of government humans are capable of conceiving—we can't do better. So, who is right?

The Appeal of Democracy

Democracy has tremendous appeal. There is a reason immigrants flocked to fledging democratic America, the majority of citizens in the world today live in democracies and over half of the world's governments are democratic. Democracy offers freedom, equality, justice and opportunity for both the enterprising and oppressed. Alternative historic political systems like dictatorships, oligarchies, plutocracies and theocracies cater to a limited few, whereas democracy is for all. Democracy is like a backdrop that accommodates many projections—a flexible framework within which numerous systems can function. Economically, capitalism and socialism, business and labor can coexist and function within a democracy. Extreme political systems like communism and fascism tolerate little variety within their ideologies.

But, in some ways democracy is like Phidias's statue—it only looks good at a distance. The ancient Athenians wanted to erect a statue of Minerva on a high pillar, so they engaged two sculptors, Phidias and Alcamenes, to create them. Alcamenes crated a wonderful likeness of the goddess, and Phidias made her deformed, with lips wide open and nose out of order. At first, the Athenians were horrified with Phidias's effort, but they quickly changed their minds when it was hoisted up on the pedestal. Distance had erased her distortions and enhanced her appearance. Democracy, like Phidias's statue, looks good at a distance, but on closer examination, many of her flaws become apparent.

Phidias's Democracy

So what are democracy's flaws? Perhaps its greatest flaw arises from its attraction—freedom. There is a reason Hegel believed freedom was humans' enduring aspiration; historically, under various governmental systems, most people had no freedom. In the Classical and Middle Ages, most people were oppressed; the result was a certain resignation to fate. Democracy changes this, and in many ways, it removes our historic Rousseauian chains and sets us free.

But freedom under democracy is an illusion—we still have to deal with fate. As the ancient Stoics said about fate: we are like a dog on a leash, and we have control over only that within the length of the leash. Further matters, like death and our natural abilities, are beyond our control. Democracy becomes many people's spiritual effort to escape their fates or to metaphorically cut the leash that holds them. It is from this illusion most of democracies' fundamental flaws arise.

The aspiration to cut the leash and be free is good, but the unintended consequences too often are pernicious. This book is about those consequences — the loss of freedom, injustice, inequality and immorality. Democracy brings a kind of unreal, artificial worldview that detaches people from nature, which results in divisiveness. Democracy engenders a kind of Protagorean man that is the measure of all things and emphasizes nurture over nature — we are not what we are because of our human nature, but rather our environment.

But freedom entails responsibility, self-restraint and, above all, rationality, which apparently are characteristics beyond the ability of most of humanity. In many ways, humans cannot handle the freedom democracy brings. They cannot because humans are driven by passion — their emotions do their thinking. Emotions are good, as we would not be human without them, but when they govern us all in the form of a political system, many things go wrong. Try as we may to cut the leash, we cannot escape our human natures.

Democracy's Future

We can only know so much from our present perspective, and what we know today becomes obsolete tomorrow with the advancement of human knowledge on so many fronts. In history, it seems wrong to claim that one political system is the end of history — a claim many past thinkers have said of their own once-successful, now-extinct political systems. Human political systems evolve and change, and many are extinct — they are like a fragile pane of glass that is easily broken. Fukuyama's claim that democracy is the end of human political history is one of those panes.

Democracy is popular now, but history tells us that democracies are rare, contentious, and short-lived — and they usually end in some kind of dictatorship. My contention is they go through a natural life cycle where their characteristics unleash certain forces that militate against them. It is these very forces that propel democracies over time to extremist political philosophies that gradually segues power to one sect. It works only until its extremes emerge. It is a political philosophy that carries the seeds of its own destruction. Fukuyama's human need for recognition does not account for the more fundamental survival instinct and need for humans to honor a social contract — civilization rests on the latter and not the former. The future is opaque, and truth is an alluring mirage that always recedes when you approach her, like Phidias's statue. Humans do rightfully aspire to freedom, but that freedom is lost in democracy to the majority. Being in the minority in a modern democracy is no different than being a helot in ancient Sparta or a serf in the feudal Middle Ages.

Why Is This Important?

Preserving democracy is important because it has the fundamentals of a good and just political system. Democracies can be great to live in. We all can benefit by living in a good democracy, and the benefits it brings such as freedom, rights, prosperity and peace. If democracy becomes unstable and anarchistic, we all face civil strife, uncertainty and danger if civil war ensues. If history is a good teacher, we also face the prospect of a dictatorship or other form of narrow rule.

The loss of a democratic form of government should be particularly concerning to those who have gained the most under its aegis. Those who have historically been repressed or ignored, such as women, minorities, the poor and the disabled, are those who stand to lose the most. It is in everyone's interests to preserve a form of democracy that accommodates all sects of people.

Book Outline

The first chapter of this book endeavors to define democracy — we must fix in our minds a correct description of the topic. This is particularly important because democracy has been described many ways and contains many characteristics. Defining democracy is a process of discerning whether it meets certain fundamental criteria and then analyzing its characteristics to see where it fits on a democratic continuum. For example, there are different kinds of democracies, such as direct, representative and constitutional. Because most democracies are representative, I use it as the usual representative of a democratic system.

Direct democracy is probably the purest form of democracy, but it has its problems, including inefficiency and sometimes chaos due to rule by the mob. Representative democracy solves many of the problems of direct democracy, but it can be less than democratic. Representatives who do not vote their constituents' interests, gerrymandering, political party influence and rules of order are all ways the people's interests can be thwarted.

Alternative forms of government are not discussed in this book, although it would be interesting and could illuminate many of democracy's vices and virtues when compared to other systems. Dictatorships are the furthest from democracy but often efficient; monarchies and aristocracies represent a chosen few but leave the majority out of power; plutocracies represent the rich and leave out the poor; oligarchies represent an elite and their supporters but leave opposing interests without representation; theocracies advance religious interests, but not those of nonbelievers. Democracy is the only political system that endeavors to represent all the people.

Chapter two traces the history of democracy from ancient Greece to the present. Particularly cogent for this book is sixth-century Athenian lawmaker Solon's effort to enhance democracy and reconcile the eternal war between the rich and poor. His solutions resonate through time. Democracy was rare in the Middle Ages with a few exceptions, which are described later. Much of this chapter deals with modern democracy arising from the French and American revolutions. These events and the thinkers, like John Locke and Montesquieu, by and large define our present conception of democracy.

Perhaps one of the most interesting chapters in this book is two, because it deals with the historic arguments against democracy. From a modern perspective, some are clearly wrong and self-serving, while others are quite prescient. The arguments were broken down into those without merit, those with some merit but that are not fatal and those with merit. It is instructive to observe how the historic arguments with merit play out in this book.

Fukuyama's book *The End of History and the Last Man* is the topic of chapter three. Fukuyama makes the rather audacious claim that democracy is the end of human political development, or the end of history. His theory and reasons for believing this are evaluated in this chapter. Chapter five deals with the nature of democracy itself and how it naturally evolves. Numerous sources, including history, tell us that democracy is not a static political system but rather a dynamic one that evolves due to its very nature. For organizational purposes, I identified three stages of democracy—early, mature and late.

Chapters six through eleven delineate my reasons why democracy ultimately fails. Chapters six through eight are perhaps the most controversial. In them, the reasons democracy naturally leads to loss of freedom, inequality and injustice are presented. Freedom, equality and justice are defined different ways by different people, hence the potential for disagreement. Few would disagree with the contention in chapter nine—the concentration of power occurs—but more might disagree with the contention that it is a problem. Similarly, few would disagree that any society that is immoral is in decline, but some could disagree with my assertion in chapter ten that democracy leads to relative morality. People have different ideas of what it means to be moral. Disagree as they may, few would disagree with my assertion in chapter eleven that democracy leads to divisiveness—all they have to do is observe America today.

Chapter twelve is my effort to relate the themes developed in this book to America today. In it, I endeavor to apply the assertions about democracy developed in this book to contemporary America. The arguments against democracy are evaluated, and how the stages of democracy match American history and the manifestations of democracy's fatal flaws in contemporary America are illustrated. My conclusion is that democracy will fail in America, and in the conclusion I explain why—It turns out the real problem is us.

SECTION I

The Definition and History of Democracy

Chapter One

DEFINING DEMOCRACY

I once took a class on the philosophy of religion, and the professor spent the first class — fifty minutes — asking everyone to define religion. He wrote students' ideas on the blackboard and had thirty different definitions by the end of the class. He asked the class how we could possibly have an intelligent conversation about religion when few agree on what it means? Like religion, people have different ideas of democracy's definition. So to understand what this book is about, this chapter will endeavor to define democracy.

Francis Fukuyama defined democracy as the right held universally by all citizens to have a share of political power, individuals' right to vote and participate in politics and to choose their own government through periodic secret ballot voting within multi-party elections on the basis of universal and equal adult suffrage. This is a good definition of democracy, but it is more than this. A comprehensive definition should include rule by majority, as well as democracy's conditions and characteristics, and a description of the kinds of democracies and certain limiting factors in democracy.

The root definition of democracy is derived from its etymology. It was coined in the fifth century BCE from the Greek words *demos*, which means "people," and *kratos*, which means "power" or "rule," hence *demokratía* or the "rule of the people." It is the upward control of government by the people, government from and by the people and government where supreme power resides in the people. It is, as Abraham Lincoln famously said, a government of the people, by the people and for the people. The appeal of democracy was perhaps instigated by John Locke, who believed that the only legitimate governments are those that have the consent of the people — and can be overthrown without it. This is a common, timeless sentiment that was expressed by the Dutch in 1581 in their Oath of Abjuration, proclaiming independence from Spain's hegemony and two hundred years later by Thomas Jefferson in the Declaration of Independence, declaring American independence from England's various transgressions.

Democracy generally involves voting by citizens who make decisions based on majority rule and sometimes elect representatives who administer society. Democracies often involve assemblies that perform various functions. Universal voting is a sign of pure democracies, where all voters participate freely and fully in the life of their society. In contrast to other forms of government, a key definition of democracy is the ability of the people to control its leaders. It offers the ability to oust leaders without revolution.

Conditions

There are certain conditions that must exist for a true democracy to exist — those without them are pseudo democracies. A prerequisite of any democracy is the rule of law. Nobody, including leaders, lawmakers and judges, is above the law;

otherwise the will of the people could be thwarted. Likewise, there must also exist adherence to written law, because if any individuals can alter the law, they become the lawgivers and not the people. There must exist citizen political equality, because if sects of citizens are excluded from the voting, the people are not represented. Significantly, there must exist equal treatment under the law or equality before the law. It is inconsistent with the spirit of democracy's demand for equality to treat people unequally under the law. Many of these conditions for democracy are embodied and protected by constitutions that establish democratic principles. Finally, there must exist civil society outside of government. Democracy cannot exist in anarchy or civil war—circumstances its very nature intends to avert. Conditions for democracy that have changed include racial and gender voting restrictions and a property qualification to vote. Historic quasi-democracies did exist with these conditions, but their existence highlighted the contradiction and tension between two of democracy's ideals—freedom and equality. A condition for true modern democracy is universal suffrage.

Characteristics

There are certain aspirational characteristics of democracy that add to its allure but are not necessary for its existence. The principal ones are equality and freedom. Equal citizenship, equal social status, equal treatment and rights under the law, freedom from oppression, freedom of expression and freedom from intrusive government are perhaps the most significant and alluring characteristics of democracy. Indeed, equality and freedom militate for access to education and being adequately informed so citizens can vote their will. These are characteristics, however, because democracy can exist with some inequality, such as in wealth and circumscribed freedoms—e.g. taking the right to vote away from a felon.

Alexis de Tocqueville mentioned two additional characteristics of democracies, the first of which is their tendency to promote the welfare of the greatest possible number. This is only a natural consequence because those whose welfare is at stake in a democracy are those who vote. The second is that democracy brings the notion of rights to the humblest citizens. Rights protect individual citizens from tyrannical government, which is in keeping with the spirit of authority from below and not above. This, for Tocqueville, is one of democracy's greatest strengths.

Constitutions are a characteristic of democracy because they frame the democratic political system, describe the source of political power, eliminate the dictator giving laws by fiat and often proscribe the power of government. The limitations on governmental power, usually called negative rights, are a key characteristic of constitutional democracies. These constitutionally created human rights, or civil rights and liberties, often include due process, the right to petition elected officials for redress of grievances, freedom of political expression, freedom of speech and freedom of the press. Certain other characteristics of democracy include majority rule, depending on whether there is universal suffrage; direct voting in a pure democracy and representative voting in a republican democracy; general parliamentary sovereignty; judicial independence and judicial review, where courts can nullify unconstitutional legislation; and the separation of powers, often in legislative, judicial and executive spheres of power, each with checks on the other.

Democracies sometimes characteristically give rise to political parties that coalesce sects of citizens' views in order to influence government and law. Not all democracies, including early America, had political parties, so they are not part of the definition or condition of democracy. Omnipotent single-party political systems, such as in the former U.S.S.R., call themselves democracies, but they are not because those outside the party have no political power. Universal suffrage and majority rule, key components of democracy, are made irrelevant when there is only one candidate to vote for. Libertarians did not run for office in the former communist Soviet Union.

Types

It should be noted that these definitions, conditions and characteristics of democracy are general because there are different kinds of democracies. The two basic kinds are direct and representative, but there also exists parliamentary democracy (where government is ruled by representatives), presidential democracy (where a president or leader is elected by voters), constitutional democracy (where elected representatives exercise power subject to a constitution and hybrid democracies (that mix some of the various democratic systems, often along with a referendum system). The constitutional democratic system often emphasizes the rights and freedoms of individual citizens against the will of the majority — they tend to protect the minorities' civil liberties. Generally, many consider direct democracy, where the people are the true governors, characteristic of true democracy. The further democracy is adulterated by alternate systems, the more its definition and legitimacy becomes problematic.

It should be noted that a democracy is not necessarily the same as a ptochocracy, as some claim. A ptochocracy is rule by the poor rather than by the people. It is the opposite of a plutocracy, or rule by the wealthy, which should not be confused with a plutocratic government, which is one that existed previously. The question of whether democracies naturally segue into ptochocracies will be examined in chapter seven.

Limiting Factors

Generally in democracy, rule by the people means rule by rational people. Infants, some criminals and those who are insane are not full participants in a democracy because they cannot or will not abide by the rule of law. This raises an interesting question: If people under the age of eighteen are considered incompetent to vote, why are those over eighteen who are ignorant allowed to vote? In democracy, there is not always equality or universal suffrage.

This discussion of the definition of democracy raises an important point, which is that democracy is a continuum. Every democracy contains some of the definitions, conditions, characteristics and descriptions of democracy, but not all of them. There never has been a perfect democracy. At what point do you call a political system a democracy? Some states, for example exhibit only some of democracy's characteristics and are given the appellation democracy. This is important because, as we shall see in chapter five on the cycles of democracy, its definition on that continuum changes with time, and it becomes less democratic. Therefore, this book is about many different kinds of democracies that fall on that continuum of democracies. Further, it seems that people's definition of democracy alters as it progresses, which further complicates a clear definition. Thus, the real question in this book is about what form of democracy will prevail or fail.

Chapter Two

THE HISTORY OF DEMOCRACY

H istory does not tell us much about democracies. From it we learn that they are rare, usually fail, often end in dictatorships and are usually adulterated with oligarchic influence or minimal suffrage. Recent history tells us most of the world aspires to be democratic, and that democracy may well be the wave of the future.

Research indicates that Francis Fukuyama's claim that before 1776 there had been no democracies anywhere in the world, including Pericles's Athenian democracy, is true. Indeed, past democracies were really not democracies. Most historic "democracies" had a few characteristics of true democracy, such as assemblies, elections and representation; however, the power rarely resided in the people but rather in a small portion of the population. In virtually all historic democratic governments, citizenship consisted of an elite class, which was only changed with the enfranchisement of all adult citizens during the suffrage movements of the nineteenth and twentieth centuries.

Ancient Democracy

As early as 700 BCE, ancient Sparta had a hybrid political system that contained some democratic characteristics. The rulers consisted of two kings; rich elder *gerontes*; five *ephors* that controlled the legislative, judicial and financial branches; and the *apella*, or *demos*, which was an assembly of citizens that held meetings once a month. Male citizens thirty and older could participate in the *appela*, which voted on measures that were decided by the majority—the votes were crudely counted by shouting. The Spartan system contained some checks and balances, elections, voting, assemblies and rule by majority.

Most sources cite Athenian democracy as the earliest, which arose in the ancient Greek polis in the fifth century BCE. This democracy occurred intermittently over three hundred years, from early 500 to late 322 BCE, when the Macedonians suppressed it. It was a direct democracy, where individual citizens rather than representatives voted on issues, which required a simple majority to pass. About one hundred officeholders were elected, who were subject to scrutiny before their election and could be removed at anytime by the assembly and penalized after their term of office for poor performance. Citizens could propose laws, speak to and make suggestions to the assembly and initiate lawsuits. In 403 BCE, it was decreed that laws voted by the assembly were subject to being annulled by jury review and the courts. There was tremendous citizen involvement in governing under Athenian democracy. Indeed, citizens were derided for not participating in politics—the word "idiot" is derived from the Greek word that means a private person not actively interested in politics.

From a historic perspective, a failure of the Athenian and Spartan democracies was that only adult male Athenian citizens who had completed military training could vote. Women, slaves, foreigners, non-landowners and males under twenty years old were excluded. It has been estimated that only 20 percent of Athens's population was eligible to vote. Neither Athens or Sparta had a universal democracy. In spite of this, it is generally considered that Athenians under democracy enjoyed unprecedented liberty, which is why their democracy is lauded by its modern observers as the first example of a working direct democracy. Some Athenian institutions survived Macedonian conquest in the late second century BCE, but whether they represented real democracy is questionable.

The principle architects of the Athenian democracy were Solon, Cleisthenes, Ephialtes, Pericles and Eucleides. I will go into detail on Solon for three reasons: He demonstrates the difficulty of achieving compromise in a democracy. He envisioned perhaps the best achievable balance between rich and poor—a compromise democracy obliterates. Lastly, he did this timelessly more than 2,500 years ago. I will return to Solon and his ideas often in this book.

Solon (c. 640–after 500 BCE) was a sixth-century Athenian poet and lawmaker famously described by Plutarch in *The Rise and Fall of Athens*. His philosophies of life were eclectic; he was a lover of knowledge and no great admirer of wealth, as he considered wealth an unstable force in human affairs. He believed human life is subject to fortune, which forbids us to take pride in the good things of the present. He thought that no man should be proclaimed happy until he is dead (because fortune might turn on the happiest of men and make them miserable); thus, declaring a man happy is like making an athlete the victor before the race is decided. Solon's realistic views are significant because they reveal his inner misgivings that the rich and poor could be reconciled and that creating a constitution to reconcile them would be fraught with perils.

Around 594 BCE, there was turmoil in Athens between the rich and poor, and revolution was possible — many poor were in debt to a few rich. Solon, due to his reputation for wisdom, was chosen to draft an Athenian constitution that intended to reconcile this eternal war by easing the suffering of the poor while avoiding offending the oligarchs and creating tyranny. So they asked Solon to create a new constitution, which he agreed to with reservation. The rich liked him because they thought he would base equality on merit and achievement, and the poor liked him because they thought he would base equality on quantitative equality. Many of his reforms were compromises that laid the groundwork for the future developments in Athenian democracy by creating a free peasantry and restricting the oligarchy. For his efforts, some consider him the true father of democracy.

Solon knew that it is hard to please everybody, so to mitigate the risk of dividing Athenian society into haves and have-nots, he created a sliding scale of privilege that contained something for everyone. He wanted to mitigate the revolutionary sentiments of the poor but also protect the rights of the elite to their property. He distinguished between two types of poor: the truly needy and the lazy. He believed there existed a duty to help those in real need, but he did not want to encourage the idle. On one hand, for example, he believed that if people were in true need of water, they could use their neighbor's well. On the other hand, though, an inquiry should be made into their means of livelihood; those who can show no occupation shall be punished. He both freed those who were enslaved due to debt and also punished those who could not support themselves. Regarding the wealthy, he decried the selfishness of the rich but was committed to defending their rights to their land and preeminent positions in government. His constitution, for example, tied political privilege to income in order to appease the rich. In the end, he left the government mostly in the hands of the rich but gave the masses some say.

Solon forged his Athenian constitution by laying down laws, or axioms, that were intended to last one hundred years. Above all, he established the principle that Athenian laws would be made by the body of Athenian citizens and not foreigners. He repealed all Draconian laws, or laws written by Draco in blood and not ink, which punished many minor offenses like idleness with death. He addressed the suffering of the poor in many ways. One of his first acts was to free those who had been enslaved by debt, mostly by reducing interest on debt. He also fixed the value of the mina, which had the effect of devaluing the currency, thus making it easier to repay loans. He eventually abolished all debts. He brought back exiled citizens who had been seized for debt and set them free. Disenfranchised citizens were given their rights, except those who did not take sides in civil war. Solon wanted people to be involved in their society—he did not want people sitting back waiting to see which side would win. He also allowed for the right of popular appeal, which increased the power of the courts and gave the common people the right to go to court on behalf of someone else in order to protect the common man. He formed a second chamber of government, which consisted of four hundred men, thus creating two councils in order to mollify the people. In justice, Solon allowed indictments to be brought against anybody by anyone, which took the justice system out of the hands of the powerful families and put it into the hands of the state—which at that time consisted only of voting males. The result was to further transfer the dispensation of justice from the family to the state. Finally, he allowed the right of popular appeal, which further increased the power of the courts.

Collaterally, Solon addressed the interests of the rich. He left government in their hands and strengthened the laws protecting the right to private property. He was concerned about the disparity of wealth, so he allowed childless men to adopt children, which mitigated the concentration of wealth through family inheritance, and he allowed a man with no children the right to bequeath his property to anybody. This had the effect of strengthening private property. Unlike many socialistic systems today, Solon also encouraged the art of manufacturing. He required that no son be obligated to support his father unless he has been taught a trade, and he granted Athenian naturalization only to foreigners who practiced a trade.Solon's prescience of female suffrage under democracy was mixed. On one hand, his laws provided that a heiress whose husband is impotent may marry his closest of his kin so her child could belong to the same family, and he abolished dowries. He believed marriage should not be a profit-making venture. On the other hand, he promulgated laws regulating women's appearances in public, limited fines for rape to one hundred drachmae and, most significantly, did not include slaves or women in his democracy. He even made it illegal for a man to sell his daughter or sister unless it was discovered they were no longer virgins. Irrelevantly, he made it illegal to speak ill of the dead (as if they cared).

Predictably, Solon's laws did not please either side—the rich were angry for being deprived of their securities, and the poor upset because he did not redistribute the land or impose a strict equal form of living on everybody. One critic, Anacharsis, said in response to Solon's laws that it is folly to assume that injustice and greed could be kept within bounds by law. They were like spiders' webs in which the small fly gets entangled and torn to pieces by the rich and powerful. Solon's response was to say simply that it is to everybody's advantage to abide by the law. According to Plutarch, Solon himself lamented that, in great affairs such as creating a democracy, you cannot please all parties. Ironically, he left Athens after his laws were created to escape criticism of his legislation. He was later iconicized and venerated by the Athenians, who kept his laws for hundreds of years.

Cleisthenes, born approx. 570 BCE, was a noble Athenian and the uncle of Pericles. He created a constitution in 508–7 BCE that established a democratic form of government that had the effect of increasing the power of the Athenian assembly and reducing the power of the nobility. This is considered by some the first true democracy, which is why Cleisthenes is sometimes referred to as the father of Athenian democracy. He was exiled from Athens but recalled to assume Athenian leadership, which gave him the opportunity to bring about change. He established legislative bodies run by individuals chosen by lottery, which was a semblance of democracy and reorganized the boule, which proposed laws for assembly voters to accept, reject or amend. Cleisthenes's policies had the effect of devolving a significant portion of Athens's political power to the people.

Ephialtes was an Athenian politician in the late 460s BCE who continued Solon and Cleisthenes's devolution of power to the Athenian people by diminishing the influence of the powerful conservative oligarch Areopagus. Some consider this the true beginning of Athenian democracy. He had the assembly pass reforms that limited the oligarchs' power by dividing their powers and transferring them to the democratic council of the *boule* and the courts. In 461 BCE, Ephialtes was assassinated, probably by the resentful oligarchs he had reduced.

Pericles (c. 495–429 BCE) was perhaps the most famous of the Athenian statesmen who advanced democracy. His time is iconically referred to as the Age of Pericles (approx. 461–429 BCE), during which the historian Thucydides considered him the first citizen of Athens. Pericles was a statesman, solider, promoter of arts and, significantly, an advocate of Athenian democracy. He created the Athenian empire, he was the greatest and longest lasting democratic leader of Athens and he led his country during the early period of the Peloponnesian war. His democratic initiatives involved further mitigating the power of the rich and powerful oligarchs, enacting legislation opening political power to the lower classes and making public offices available to more citizens. After his death, Athenian democracy was twice briefly interrupted by oligarchic revolutions around the end of the

Peloponnesian War but, in the end, restored. In his funeral oration, he was cited for bringing democracy to Athens, creating a government from the many, bringing equal justice and promoting advancement that depended on merit.

Eucleides was a fifth-century BCE Athenian *archon* who promoted democracy like the others: by challenging the reigning oligarchic power. His reign occurred during the democratic revival of Athens in 403–402 BCE after the reign of the thirty tyrants. He was known for reconciling enemies, inaugurating harmony in Athenian politics, preaching tolerance toward those who committed atrocities under the thirty tyrants and restoring democracy to Athens. The Athenian story of democracy is very much a history of these democratic leaders gradually wresting away power from the rich and landed Athenian hereditary oligarchic aristocracy and giving it to the people.

Ancient Rome initially had some democratic characteristics, which were mitigated as it segued into an oligarchic empire. The Roman Republic had a senate in which a chosen class of citizens voted laws; it was a system with checks and balances. During Cicero's time, for example, there existed both the senate and general assembly. Although the real power of government rested in the senate, the general assembly endeavored to represent the plebeians, along with the tribunes, whose charge was to protect their interests. Roman government also included censors and proconsuls, who had the effect of balancing senatorial power. The early Roman Republic, and certainly the later Roman Empire, directed by emperors, was not a democratic system, per se. The Republic was, rather, a system based on compromise intended to prevent one citizen from gaining too much power. Indeed, in early Roman history a dictator could be appointed only for six months. In many respects, modern democracies mimic the Roman Republic model of democracy rather that the Greek model because the Romans had elected representatives, an elected leader and checks and balances.

The republican form of Roman democracy ended with the ascendancy of Octavian to the leadership of Rome after the Battle of Actium in 31 BCE. His ascendancy to Emperor Augustus heralded the beginning of the Roman Empire, governed by all-powerful emperors. This later period is best described as a dictatorship with occasional tyranny.

Democracy in the Middle Ages

The political concept of democracy was rare during the feudal Middle Ages. There were some governments that involved elections and assemblies, but they were not true universal democracies because there was no universal suffrage; power resided within a few, and assemblies could usually be dismissed by a monarch. It was, rather, a time of kings, popes, princes, nobility and hereditary rights. Land was the ultimate source of wealth, and those who possessed it were the rulers. Power followed from the land and those who owned it. It was a period in which property legally passed through families from generation to generation, which the majority vote in a democracy usually resists. Like most historic democracies, it was a "democracy," where a few privileged people voted, controlled power and exercised power. There were, however, a few exceptions.

Middle Age Scandinavian *things* were assemblies of the free men that legislated and elected a leader, which in theory was based on the rule of one man, one vote. It was a place where all free men came together for legislative reasons, usually to deal with existing laws. The traditions of these *things* are seen today in the parliaments of Scandinavian countries like Norway (the *Storting*) and Denmark (the *Folketing*). One of the oldest parliamentary institutions was Iceland's *Althing*, which was founded in 930 CE. In it, constituencies elected members and parties allocated seats based on proportional voting, which enabled a parliament that was generally proportional to its electoral support. However, like most historic "democracies," the *Althing* was dominated by influential clans, and the one man with one vote invariably came from a wealthy family.

In the eleventh century in small areas of Switzerland, there evolved some forms of government similar to Athenian direct democracy. There were small communities where adult males who able to walk to an assembly could cast a vote. Such meetings were called district communities, or *Landsgemeinde*, the earliest one occurring in 1249 CE. These district assemblies became the legislative authorities within many Swiss federations.

The experience of democracy in Italy during the Middle Ages is perhaps one of the best examples of democracy's development during the Middle Ages. Northern Italy in the eleventh through thirteenth centuries prospered but was insecurely bound by imperial Germany on the north and the Papal States to the south, so they endeavored to control their own destiny by creating mediaeval communes. Many of the cities in this area such as Pisa, Siena, Florence and Milan created municipal communal councils. These fledging communes grew in wealth and gradually became independent governments. Initially they exhibited some democratic characteristics where every male citizen could participate in an assembly; however oligarchies gradually emerged to control these early assemblies which were dominated by rich, noble and merchant families. Predictably, the wealthy noble families constantly feuded with the communes and the communes were constantly at war with each other. The solution was to appoint a leader with power, or mayor but this caused individual rule, which gradually became hereditary. These hereditary oligarch families were lead by a *signore* such as the Visconti of Milan in the eleventh and twelfth centuries and the Medici of Florence in the fourteenth century. The result was that these early democratic communes segued over time into princely oligarchies.

In 1572, a form of "noble democracy" arose when the senate took over free elections in the Polish-Lithuanian Commonwealth, establishing a precedent of electing the monarch and precluding hereditary monarchy. In the sixteenth and seventeenth centuries, the Cossacks of Ukraine developed Cossack republics, which had some democratic characteristics because their leaders were elected and power resided in an assembly. The Corsican Republic established in 1755 could be considered the first true democracy because it involved female suffrage; however, it faded quickly. Previously mentioned Switzerland, which has a long history involving federalism and direct democracy originating in their district communities in the thirteenth century, established a federal constitution in 1848 whereby a referendum of fifty thousand signatures could challenge a law passed by Parliament, which then required a national vote that decided the fate of a new law by majority.

One notable exception in medieval times was cerebral French King Charles in the fourteenth century who represents a rare example of an aristocratic monarch with democratic perspectives. According to Barbara W. Tuchman's A *Distant Mirror: The Calamitous 14th Century*, he believed that the sovereign was not above the law, it was his duty to maintain the law, sanction derives from the consent of the governed and the monarch's authority ultimately is based on the people's consent. However, such lofty democratic perspectives in the Middle Ages were rare.

Throughout the Middle Ages, a critical step in the evolution of democracy were parliaments — the precursors of democracy because they had many democratic characteristics, such as assemblies, decision by voting and some independence from monarchs, especially after the Magna Carta. Parliaments arose in twelfth and fourteenth-century England and France from councils of kings where monarchs discussed affairs of state with bishops and nobles. Gradually, these councils included citizens representing wealthy towns that became known as the Third Estate. These wealthy burgher representatives' influence increased for financial reasons. The parliament of Léon in 1188 is one early example.

England holds a special place in the development of parliaments — she is often referred to as the "mother of parliaments" due to her long parliamentary tradition and Parliament's independence from the monarch. The rise of England's parliamentary authority was spurred after the signing of the Magna Carta in 1215, when the monarch's power was proscribed. It contained protections for the people from the king, such as the right of habeas corpus that prevented unlawful imprisonment and provided for the right to appeal. This was a critical foundation stone in the development of democracy because it devolved some power to the people. The first elected English Parliament was in 1265, which commenced the role of Parliament. This was another critical development for democracy because it became a forum that addressed ordinary citizens' grievances. The English parliamentary system contained some characteristics of democracy but fell short because, like most early democracies, there was no universal suffrage (officials were elected by a small percent of the population) and the monarch could call Parliament into session and dissolve it at any time.

French Parliament originated when Louis the IX acknowledged the first permanent parliament in the mid-thirteenth century. Although its early powers were restricted to legal work by jurists trained in law, in the fourteenth century, its political power expanded in relation to the king, with its new power to register the king's edicts. Similar to England, French Parliaments during the fourteenth and fifteenth centuries consisted of the nobility, clergy and rich burgher from the growing French cities. These together were known as the Three Estates.

French Parliament met as the estate's general for the first time in 1302 when summoned by French King Philip IV. They continued to be summoned frequently during the fourteenth century, during which delegates representing one of the estates often voted independent and unpopular positions in opposition to the monarch. Its influence gradually declined in the later part of the Middle Ages until it was revived for a time during the French Revolution in the late eighteenth century.

English and French parliaments were the forefront of democratic evolution in the Middle Ages, but similar parliamentary developments during the fourteenth and fifteenth centuries occurred in other parts of medieval Europe, including the Netherlands, Sicily and Bohemia.

Modern Democracy

In the history of democracy, the two modern seminal events in its evolution are the American and French Revolutions — democracy exploded into being with these. Legitimate democracy was born in the crucible of the French people casting off their aristocratic kings and American people's aspiration for independence from England's King George III. Before these events, no true democracies existed; after them, the world aspired to democracy (Alexis de Tocqueville wrote that some medieval French towns retained self-government and, until the end of the seventeenth century, they were for all intents and purposes small democratic republics). Let us analyze what happened, but first I will briefly describe the Dutch.

The Netherlands's democracy in the eighteenth century, described by historian Tuchman in *The First Salute*, could be described as an interim form, with democracy's traditional historic flaws strangely combined with a fear of tyranny. Its predictable flaws were that only the upper classes had a political voice and commoners without property could not vote. There was no universal suffrage. Unpredictably, its constitution was a many-headed hydra that created an extreme, chaotic, complex and complicated democratic system. Central leadership by the states general was subject to numerous conditions, and decisions and critical issues had to be discussed by literally thousands of people before a decision could be made. It was an ineffective and convoluted form of democracy that grew out of the Middle Ages where efficiency was sacrificed for fear of dictatorship. The French and American Revolutions signaled a break from past political systems, and modern day democracy was the result.

Even though the French Revolution (1789–1799) began thirteen years after America's Declaration of Independence and two years after the American constitutional convention, it was a critical step in evolving modern democracy. According to Tocqueville, the French King Louis XVI was engulfed by a rising tide of democracy, where the people successfully assumed authority over the ruling classes, or French aristocracy, with the Declaration of the Rights of Man in 1789. It was a revolution that would eventually lead, for the first time in history, to universal suffrage in France in March of 1848.

The French revolutionaries in 1789, however, were more interested in escaping oppression than creating a democracy. Poverty and haughty aristocrats were animating factors, but both Christopher Hibbert and Tocqueville comment that the main factor was unequal taxation. The burden of taxes had fallen on the poor peasants because the French nobility had gained innumerable exemptions from taxation. The royalists were adamant in retaining their exemption privileges and were unwilling to compromise. Unremitting anger and resentment by a suppressed lower class brought about the French Revolution.

The result was violence—and some strange politics. The immediate result was a confusing milieu of government by nobility, royalty, clergy and the common people, or Third Estate. Each had an agenda at cross-purposes that could not come to terms with the others, and the result was violence. The common people and hungry peasants (accompanied by a few brigands), spurred on by a bourgeoisie middle class intent on replacing royal authority, started killing people. The Plain and Feuillants, or the moderates, were overwhelmed by the Girondins, Jacobins and Sans Culottes, or the extreme left. Somehow, after years of bloodshed, a nascent and tenuous kind of republican democratic government evolved, which included a legislative assembly, a constitution and voting. It became increasingly chaotic due to confusion, politics and more violence. This early democratic revolution failed when Napoleon ended the chaos and became the emperor dictator.

But the French Revolution was a milestone in democracy's development because it was a seminal time when the determination of who ruled had to be decided — the king, royalty, priests or people. It was the oppressed lower classes, abetted by a few in the upper classes, who decided this critical historic contest. Through violent revolution, it brought power to the people.

Like in the French Revolution, unequal taxation was a primary cause of the thirteen colonies' rebellion against their monarchial mother country, England. Taxation without representation animated the citizens of Boston, which commenced a sequence of events that eventually lead to a new democratic American state. It was a seminal event in the history of democracy. Tuchman identified the first occurrence of democracy's birth, when the Dutch Caribbean island of St. Eustatius saluted the American ship *Andrew Doria* in 1776 — a salute that was eventually confirmed when the combined American and French forces defeated Cornwallis at Yorktown in 1781 and the independent nation of America was born. She wrote that America had notified the old world that the hour of change to a democratic age had come. For the first time, a state was created from a *tabula rasa* that borrowed from key historic thinkers, like Englishman John Locke and Frenchman Montesquieu, who were dedicated to the principles of freedom and equality.

Seventeenth-century English empiricist philosopher Locke outlined some of the central tenets of this seminal American democracy. In his famous *Two Treatises of Government*, published in 1690, he defended the doctrine of natural rights, the social contract and a conception of political authority that is both limited and conditioned on the ruler's fulfillment of his obligation to serve the public good. It was a classic formulation of the principles of political liberalism that influenced the American and French revolutions and subsequent democracies. Eighteenth-century French philosopher and satirist Montesquieu influenced the form of democracy in America. His book *The Spirit of the Laws*, published in 1750, classified governments based on policy and argued for the separation of legislative, judicial and executive powers. Both of these books profoundly influenced American Founding Fathers John Adams, Thomas Jefferson, Alexander Hamilton and James Madison, who were influential in the creation of America's founding documents, the Declaration of Independence and the Constitution.

The consequence was a new form of republican democratic country never seen before in history. Its plan was original, broad based and built on a grand scale. It changed everything — it was democracy's seminal event. It was forged in a constitutional convention in 1787 that established the form of the new democracy, which was later amended with a Bill of Rights that protected citizens' rights demanded by democracy. Its Declaration of Independence stated that men had unalienable rights to life, liberty and the pursuit of happiness, which the government was to secure and which derived its powers from the consent of the governed. In many ways, it was a convention that synthesized and congealed 2,500 years of democracy's evolution into one succinct constitutional document. Inherent in the spirit of this instrument was the theme to limit any governmental power from infringing on individuals' life, liberty, happiness and property.

The new Constitution had many of the characteristics of democracy, with assemblies, voting and majority rule, but, like most historic democracies, it lacked the critical characteristic of universal suffrage in property, gender and race.

The Founding Fathers were concerned that the many would steal from the few, so when the Constitution went into effect in 1789, it limited suffrage to property-holding and taxpaying citizens. It further did not grant suffrage to women and black slaves. Today, many feminists and minorities criticize this founding document for these flaws, but they fail to understand two things: first, ideas like democracy and universal suffrage evolve, and, given the times, the new Constitution would never have been adopted, nor would we have it today, if a nod had not been given to historic circumstances. Put another way, the feminists and critical minorities would not enjoy the freedoms they do today if this document had not been adopted. Second, and most importantly, it was the very principles of democracy contained in the Constitution — freedom and equality — that corrected these two deficiencies

It took more than half a century to eliminate the property condition (with a few minor exceptions), about eighty years to eliminate the race exception and 130 years to eliminate the gender exception. The Fifteenth Amendment in 1870 opened the polls to all people, regardless of color, with the view that no state shall abridge the right of a citizen to vote on account of race or color. The Nineteenth Amendment, passed in 1920, provided that the right to vote shall not be abridged on account of gender. Universal suffrage was attained by this fledgling democracy in 1920. More will be said about the importance of this in chapter twelve, Democracy in America.

American constitutional representative democracy has evolved to a point today where it meets many of the definitions of a true democracy. Generally, the American people ultimately hold governmental power through universal voting, and issues and elected officials are chosen by the majority. The people retain the right to oust leaders without revolution. It is not a direct democracy but rather a republican democracy, with generally sovereign assemblies, a president and an independent court system that upholds a constitution. There exists the rule of law — that courts have generally obeyed — and equal political treatment under the law, to a certain extent. Certainly, America has experienced social tension and discord, but to an extent, there exists a civil society outside of government. The Constitution that defines the framework of democracy with certain checks and balances enshrines the ideals of freedom and equality — as well as rights that protect citizens in innumerable ways from governmental oppression and from the majority — including the freedom of expression, due process, the right to petition elected officials for redress of grievances, the freedom of political expression, the freedom of speech and freedom of the press.

America's Constitution is the oldest surviving still-active constitution in the world, and the democracy that arose from this document is the longest living continuous democracy in the history of the world. It is a political system that approximates the true definition of democracy. America made democracy viable, workable, acceptable and desirable. It was the major advancement of democracy in history.

Broadly speaking, the twentieth century has witnessed an upsurge in democratic states. There was a hiatus in democracy's advancement during the mid-twentieth century for a variety of reasons, including the American Great Depression of the 1930s, which brought a general disenchantment with democracy. Also, some European states turned to alternate forms of government, including dictatorships, fascism and communism. This trend was reversed by World War II, except notably for the communist Soviet bloc, where democracy was adulterated with sham elections. However, democracy has continued to advance in other nations, and with the collapse of the Soviet Union in the late 1980s, it has experienced increasing acceptance. It has been estimated that in 2007 there were 123 democracies worldwide out of a total of 192 existing countries, which constitutes about 58 percent of the world's population. It would seem Fukuyama is right to assert that democracy is the end of history.

SECTION II

The Debate Over Democracy

Chapter Three

HISTORIC ARGUMENTS AGAINST DEMOCRACY

Historically, democracy has not been a popular political philosophy. Iconic historic figures like Plato, Georg Wilhelm Friedrich Hegel, Alexis de Tocqueville, Benjamin Disraeli, John Adams, Thomas Carlyle and many more have derided democracy for a variety of reasons. Having been born and raised in a democratic society, I found both the historic arguments against democracy sometimes strange, often vicious, occasionally true and always in earnest. Many of the objections were transparent — they were from those who had the most to lose from democracy, like rich and powerful Gouverneur Morris, who loved freedom and hated equality. Some were from ideological bents, like the aristocrat Plato, who objected because it would interfere with his communal republic lead by a philosopher king.

However, most are thoughtful perspectives that merit consideration. Hegel was concerned about democracy's chaos, Tocqueville that the new bourgeoisie ruling class would lack social responsibility, Cicero lamented that leaders would be without merit, and James Madison warned that direct democracy would bring turbulence and contention—and just about everyone agreed the poor would rob the rich.

This chapter is an effort to categorize the historic arguments against democracy, grouped into topics under which the many arguments generally fell. Earlier, the aspirational reasons for democracy, such as freedom, equality and justice, were described, but the focus here is on the historic arguments against democracy because this book is about whether it can endure. Given our experience with democracy and knowledge of its history, we are in a better position to vet the arguments against it today—unlike past authors.

The charges against democracy are grouped into three broad categories: those that are without merit, those that are true but not fatal to democracy and a few that have the potential to discredit democracy as a viable political system. These latter arguments will be expanded on at length later in this book.

Arguments Without Merit

Ten broad historic arguments against democracy without merit were discerned. They will be described in general terms and then responded to with what seems to be a reasonable retort based on historical evidence and some philosophic insight. The first argument is that democracies lack order.

The claim that democracy is chaotic rule by the mob goes back to Plato speaking through Socrates in *The Republic*. Socrates describes it as a charming form of government but full of variety and disorder. Indeed, the trial and death of Socrates could be an example of democracy's reckless and arbitrary nature. Hegel also claimed that there was a lack of rational order in democracy. Certainly, there have been disordered democracies, such as ancient Athenian democracy and, at times, and late French Revolutionary democracy. Democracies are handicapped by their inclination to cater to many ideologically driven opposing factions, and the resulting rending of these factions can end in disorder and chaos. If one coalition becomes too powerful, the democratic process can be disrupted. But this is not necessarily the case. History is full of examples of long-time stable democracies, such as in the Scandinavian countries and Switzerland. America itself has maintained a stable democracy for more than two hundred years. Indeed, one only needs to look around the globe to find many stable democratic countries.

The criticism that people cannot be ruled by an abstract political system is a curious one. Eighteenth-century conservative English politician and political philosopher Edmund Burke believed that people must be ruled by their disposition and temper — politics ought to accommodate human nature and not human reasoning. Custom and tradition are better guides when governing human affairs than disembodied reason or pure rationalism because abstractions invite imagination that has no bounds. Customs are a manifestation of wisdom because they are the accumulation of human experience, whereas new abstractions like democracy have no such history. Politics is about custom, convention, tradition, order, duty and expediency, not reason, abstraction or morality — politics is not about truth and falsity but rather good and evil. In fairness to Burke, it should be mentioned that, even though he opposed democracy, he eloquently championed the cause of the American Revolution. Other likewise thinkers were English Prime Minister Disraeli, who believed the distribution of political power is an affair of convention and not a moral or abstract right, Étienne Bonnot de Condillac who objected to philosophical abstractions, and Founding Father Thomas Jefferson, who was wary of impractical abstract metaphysical systems.

This objection to democracy particularly attacks the notion of rights because they are a characteristic of democracy. Abstract rights safeguard individual liberty against government, so it is expected that those who prefer authority from above would favor order, duty and expediency over rights. They naturally claim that power derives from convention and not any moral abstract right. But they are attacking what is precisely one of democracy's greatest attractions — individual freedom — and collaterally exposing themselves as seekers of power over others. Philosophically, it is like these detractors are espousing Edmund Husserl's phenomenology, which focuses on the pure data of consciousness uncontaminated by metaphysical theories. They prefer to emphasize and isolate the immediacy of experience in order to set it off from all abstract assumptions. Their ruse is to invoke an ontological theory cloaked in political terms in order to preserve their preferred distribution of power.

Virtually all political systems are to one degree or another abstractions. Monarchic, oligarchic, socialistic and communistic systems are all abstractions. Even ancient customs and traditions were once abstractions. The ancient aristocratic customs that favored a few and may have once been grounded in merit became convoluted abstractions. Democracy just happens to be the most recent political abstraction that prevails now. Indeed, democracy itself has become the custom and tradition of many countries, including America. History has proven the worth of rational, abstract political systems derived from thinkers like John Locke and Montesquieu. The real problem seems to arise when the abstractness of a political system strays too far from reality and become artificial — when it loses touch with reality. I will discuss this potentiality of democracy later in chapter seven, Inequality.

Some have claimed that democracy is unnecessary — things are working just fine. As an experiment, democracy is not needed because the people are already metaphysically and virtually represented or there are others that act, like fathers in a traditional household, on their behalf. The transparency of this argument makes it easy to dispatch. It would be an expected argument made by those in power, such as the nobility, to justify their position with the view they look after the people's interests. *Noblesse oblige* is an old self-serving concept turned against democracy. Indeed, the nobility in medieval France, while looking after citizens' interests, secured tax exemptions for themselves that put the tax burden on the peasants they represented, and they were unyielding in the days leading up to the French Revolution to preserve these benefits.

The criticism that democracies are unstable is more fundamental than that they are ruled by the mob. The charge goes that democracies are capricious and fickle because they are unruly. They inherently lack the kind of order necessary for any stable society to exist—anarchy is their natural consequence. Their governments are frequently elected, so power and policies constantly change both domestically and internationally. Even if a political party maintains power, vociferous, headline-grabbing protests and harsh criticism from the mass media are often enough to force sudden, unexpected political change. Democracy during the French Revolution, for example, was unstable. The *Engrales* and *sans-culottes* consisted of citizen mobs that rioted, looted and murdered people in the name of the republic and democracy—they were accountable to no one. Authority changed by whim, and leaders like Georges Danton were routinely guillotined, which resulted in unstable and unpredictable government. Further, this charge updated claims that, due to its inherent instability, democracy is not suitable for underdeveloped countries because it hinders their economic development due to its instability.

Certainly, some democracies are unstable. Early experimental nascent democracies and democracies in poor, underdeveloped countries are often unstable. But these are the exception and not the rule today. The French were endeavoring to create an egalitarian society through democracy, and to do so they literally had to eliminate a class of people who opposed it—the royalists and aristocracy. Further, many forms of government are unstable in underdeveloped countries, including kingships and communism. Given a chance to mature as a political philosophy, today we see many stable democracies worldwide. Democracy can be stable, so this criticism is flawed. One exception, which will be discussed in chapter eight, is democracy's tendency to create unstable law.

Both Tocqueville and Carlyle believed the upper class's sense of duty, their noblesse oblige, would be lost under democracy. Under democracy, the new aristocracy would no longer be based on class and heredity but rather on wealth — it would consist of the wealthy manufacturers. Because these new elites value wealth above all, they would not have a sense of social duty.

There is a little truth and a lot of falsity in this assertion. If America could be an example of a modern democracy, it is true that the manufacturer's prestige peaked in the late 1800s and early 1900s, but it has since declined. John D. Rockefeller, Andrew Carnegie and Harvey Samuel Firestone were the elites in America democracy during that time, but today their ilk are no longer the elites as they were in the past. The assertion is false to the extent that many of them were great philanthropists with a keen social conscience and sense of social duty. Carnegie built 2,509 libraries in the world between 1883 and 1929, of which 1,689 were in America. Similarly, contemporary American billionaires Bill Gates and Warren Buffet gave $28 million and $3.084 billion to charities in 2012, respectively. There are many other examples of democracy's elites sharing their wealth with society.

Poignantly, Tocqueville, who made this criticism of democracy, wrote prior to the French Revolution that the nobles had by and large abandoned their obligations to the peasants, rarely mixed with them and were preoccupied with their own interests and privileges. Indeed, it could be argued that the wealthy manufacturers of democracy do far more in providing goods and services as well as charitable work than past aristocrats. This is a criticism without merit.

Ancient Roman statesman and Stoic Seneca charged that democracies are brutal. He may have been thinking of some atrocities during Athen's golden democratic years and the tyranny of the mob. He believed democracy outdid wars and tyrants in its cruelties. It is true that during the nascent French Revolution's democracy, brutality was rampant. Murders, fights and executions were common. It is also true that democratic America dropped atomic bombs on Japan during World War II, killing many citizens. Democracy can be imperialistic and brutal.

Perhaps the reason for this is best provided by Francis Fukuyama, who wrote that democracies do not fight one another but rather totalitarian regimes. This would explain the twentieth century's brutal wars between democracies and non-democracies, as well as the relative peace during the same time between democracies. It should also be noted that democracies are remarkably tolerant of internal strife — they do not engage in mass executions or pogroms.

The truth is that far more brutality has been unleashed under past dictatorships, tyrants, despots, czars, emperors, and systems of government from oligarchies and theologies than democracies. Further, for the purposes of this chapter, brutality in and of itself does not necessarily mean the end of democracy. This also is a criticism without merit.

The criticism that ignorant voters cause poor policies and inefficiency in democracies is really two criticisms. In democracy, as the criticism goes, the ignorant voters do not understand issues, so poor policies ensue; it is these bad policies that lead to confusion, conflict and inefficiency. This criticism is true to a point. Ignorant voters do often bring poor, ambiguous policies that change with each administration. Certainly, inefficiency in government is one result, especially when roughly equal competing factions vie for the power to implement their policies. The result, as we see in America today, can be gridlock and inefficient government.

The flip side to this criticism is that many voters are informed, many ignorant do not vote, many political systems are inefficient, some democracies like America's are relatively efficient, and bad policies and inefficiency in government are not necessarily fatal. Indeed, it could be retorted that democracy's very sluggishness, which is due to the need for consensus, is one of its strengths because it prevents extremism and tyranny. Thus, this is a criticism without merit.

Supreme Court Justice Louis Brandeis once professed that "we may have democracy, or we may have wealth concentrated in the hands of a few, but we can't have both." Some have asserted that democracy is an illusion that masks elite rule. They claim that some form of oligarchy is an unbendable law of human nature due to unequal abilities and the apathy and divisions of the masses. Unlike the masses, the elites are intelligent, driven, rich, manipulative and unified. The result is that democracy only serves to shift power from one oppressive elite to another. Contemporarily in America, it is the merchants, or corporations, under democratic capitalism with their wealth that are the oppressive oligarchic elites that adulterate democracy.

Certainly, powerful oligarchies exist in democracies, as they do in all forms of political societies, and they do have tremendous influence for all the reasons mentioned. But there are many other centers of power in most democracies, including unions and political parties that have influence. Brandeis's statement asserts a false dichotomy with a straw man who is the wealthy oligarch controlling all-wealthy political donors—like George Soros and the Koch family—may influence elections, but they do not dictate them. Oligarchies exist in democracies but do not destroy their essence because there are too many other powerful competing interests. An exception to this is the tendency of democracies to concentrate governmental power, which will be discussed in chapter nine. With this proviso, this is an argument without merit.

The argument that democracies are corrupt is inflated. Certainly, some democracies experience some degree of corruption and fraudulent elections. This seems particularly true of immature democracies in developing, poor countries. It is also true that in the 1800s in democratic New York, William M. Tweed, through his Tammany Hall political machine, stole $200 million from the Brooklyn bridge project. However, it is also true that, under a free press, a characteristic of democracies, *The New York Times* and *World* newspapers exposed his corruption. Free press, coupled with the fact that democracies have frequent elections that enable the people to change leadership, makes this charge meritless.

The final criticism of democracy comes from Burke, who claimed powerful democracies breed unbridled ambition. I simply fail to see this as a serious challenge to democracy. Ambition is good, and all societies have ambitious people (like Burke); it often brings out the best in people, and it brings industry, which is good for society. So, what is the problem?

True but Not Fatal Arguments

Some historic criticisms of democracy have merit but are not serious enough to be fatal. It seems clear, for example, that democracies are not inherently brutal, which we established as an argument without merit. However, it does seem that they tend to unleash disruptive human passions, which could be a serious flaw. The difference between the following serious nonfatal criticisms and others is a matter of degree — excess is a problem in many arenas, particularly in politics. Burke believed the ideals of the French Revolution, for example, were compromised due to excess. Following are eight historic nonfatal but serious criticisms of democracy.

In *Federalist No. 10*, Madison argued that direct democracy leads to turbulence and contention. Direct democracies have been spectacles of these, resulting in the violation of personal security and infringement of property rights. Most have died in a violent struggle. They are rife with the changing falseness and temporary enthusiasms of the common people.

There may be some truth in Madison's assertions in some past direct democracies, such as in ancient Athens. There was turbulence, contention and capricious enthusiasms. The solution, as Madison argued, is representative democracy, or a republic where cool-headed rational representatives moderate the rabble that controls faction. They also had the effect of safeguarding against the tyranny of the majority. Indeed today due to Madison's influence, democracies like America's are generally constitutional representative democratic republics. Hence, the criticism, while true, appears without merit.

But Madison did not foresee the outcome of his cherished republican democracy. It turns out republican democracies also experience turbulence and contention. In advanced representative democracies, we see passionate disagreement, the diminution of property rights and a majority that dictates to an increasingly resentful minority. It appears divisiveness remains a problem.

A common criticism of democracy has been that the ignorant and illiterate lower classes will rule. In ancient Greek democracy, there was a pervasive fear that the poor, base, uneducated and irresponsible masses were both incapable of ruling and would rule in their own interests. Why, as the assertion goes, would any society allow itself to be ruled by the least capable? Would it not be better to have the smartest, most educated, most experienced and most talented people at the helm?

Certainly, the very concept of rule by the people means some ignorant rule. It also is true that democracies have an averaging effect that produces averaged legislation and mediocre leaders. But it remains the case that many in the middle and upper classes are ignorant, vote their pocket books and make poor leaders.

Experience tells us that the lower classes and the poor have greater influence in democracies, but it is not decisive. Even though they may have the majority, they often disagree on their common interests, are incapable of organizing and often do not vote or participate in civil matters. It may well be that the compulsory education in democracies such as America's is intended to solve this objection. There was no compulsory education in early America, but by 1900, thirty-four states had compulsory schooling laws, and by 1918, every state required elementary school education. However, universal education has not entirely eradicated this objection.

Because most democracies are not tyrannies by the uneducated poor, it would seem that this objection is groundless. However, it has the potential to damage democracy if the underclass's demands become excessive. Democracies are particularly vulnerable to extreme socialistic wealth redistribution schemes that result in a myriad of problems many democracies face today.

Similar to the objection that the illiterate will rule is that the majority of poor voters in a democracy will steal from the rich. This objection opens a panoply of allied criticisms for democracy. The state ought not steal, the wealthy contribute more than the poor so they should have the greater say, the vagabond poor are less frugal so the state will squander its resources, the rich will be more frugal because they have the most to lose, the rich contribute more to society, the property-less are dependent on the propertied so they lose employers and stealing others' property takes individual freedom. Further, if the majority poor vote benefits and entitlements for themselves, additional consequences could be governmental debt, inflation, loss of enterprise and, ultimately, national loss of wealth.

This was a central concern of the ancients who believed in a democracy in which the numerically preponderant poor would naturally steal from the rich. Democracy would be the political tool by which some could legally steal from others.

This fear has been the central reason for the now-obsolete property requirement to vote in historic democracies. It is also true, however, that when the rich are in power they steal from the poor and when the poor are in power they steal from the rich. Recall, for example, the rich nobility's privileged tax exemptions prior to the French Revolution that so angered the peasants. It is also true that many wealthy heirs contribute little to society.

There is a little truth in this criticism of democracy, but it's not necessarily the whole picture. Generally in democracies, the wealthy pay more in taxes but keep their wealth, and the poor take more from others in governmental entitlement programs. Most democracies function well under this system, but problems arise when the majority poor's demands become excessive. Democracy's relationship with socialism and its tendency for extreme socialism will be discussed at length later in this book.

Burke and Carlyle believed the aspiration for equality in democracy is an idea at war with nature. Equality for them is an empty ideal because nature made us unequal. Indeed, it would seem strange to handicap a fast runner in a foot race so as to give the slower runner the equal right to win. Nature is indifferent to our needs, and she bestows her benefits unequally.

They have a point but the right answer turns on the definition of equality — whether it is political or perfect. Democracy rightfully militates against historic political inequality. Aristocracies, nobilities and hereditary privilege are diminished, and the lower class's inclusion in the political process is enhanced under democracy. Democracy brings equal opportunity, equal treatment under the law and equal access to basic education. Democracy eliminates artificial inequality.

Burke and Carlyle's criticism occurs due to democracy's tendency to transform political equality into perfect equality. The demand for perfect equality usually surfaces in economic terms under democracy with disparity of wealth criticisms and wealth redistribution policies. The demand for absolute equality with others from those who are not equal has profound implications for democracy. It is an empty demand that dismisses merit, ignores nature and has the potential to commit injustice. This tendency for equality is not necessarily fatal for democracy. It only becomes a factor if political equality segues too far into perfect equality. This topic will be taken up at length in chapter eight.

The evolution of rights in democracy will also be discussed at length in chapter eight, but for this criticism, let us just say for now that the definition of a right changes in democracy due to majority vote. It is a change that trammels individual freedom. In 1842, French writer Honoré de Balzac rejected elections in a democracy because they fail to represent increasingly right-less minorities (which he believed a monarch would). The minority's historic right to be left free to act as they will is gradually limited.

There is a tendency in democracy to change the concept of a negative right, or one that protects the individual from governmental power, to a positive right, or one that confers an entitlement. Democracy does succor those who see this evolution of a right as progressive. Contemporary philosopher Raymond Wacks, in *The Philosophy of Law*, is one of those progressives that claims rights naturally evolve—an assertion that is enabled by democracy. Due to its limited development, this does not seem to be a fatal flaw for democracy unless the definition of rights changes.

The charge that democracy discourages merit was made by Friedrich Nietzsche. He wrote that democracy is Christian doctrine politicized that inculcates the virtues of pity and meekness that make citizens meek. Slave morality is championed under democracy, not heroic meritorious behavior. It is these meek and weak people in democracy that spawn subjective concepts like good and evil that enervates strength. Democracy advances mediocrity through an aesthetic ideal.

It is true that the ancient Greek ideal that the most educated, capable, experienced and morally superior citizens should rule is weakened in democracy. The majority typically has alternative, often ideologically driven reasons for voting people into power. Democracy also hobbles many of its most enterprising citizens with higher taxes and imposes innumerable mandates on successful businesses. Although immorality in leadership infects all governments to some extent, it does seem democracy has a tendency to bend moral codes for political purposes; Tweed in democratic 1800s New York could be one example.

It should also be pointed out that other forms of historic governments were not meritocracies, including aristocratic hereditary kingships. Like them, there is some truth to this criticism, but it is not necessarily fatal.

Two historians' views converge to make the next criticism of democracy. Eighteenth-century historian Edward Gibbon, in *The History of the Decline and Fall of the Roman Empire*, wrote that a reason for a society's decline is excessive enthusiasm or zeal, and Tocqueville wrote that democracy legitimizes unrestrained passions. Gibbon explained that one reason Rome failed was because tolerance gave way to dogmatic, overzealous and single-minded views that became a source of violent sectarian disputes. Tocqueville added that democracy magnifies the problem with excessive passion.

The ideals of freedom and equality in democracy may be a reason for this criticism. With greater freedom, there is less restraint on passion, and when citizens feel equal, they are more inclined to dispute than when there is a great disparity of power. Indeed, we do see passionate factional disputes in democracy leading to divisiveness.

This criticism has many manifestations that will be discussed later in this book. Excessive passion in democracies may lead to relative morality and divisiveness, two potentially fatal faults in any governmental system. However, many past societies have experienced passionate disputes and survived — the disputes themselves lead to compromises that ameliorate matters — and most societies can tolerate a degree of relative morality. This criticism is only fatal in democracy if reason falls to the passions, resulting in intolerance.

The final, somewhat neurotic non-fatal criticism of democracy deals with its influence on the individual's relation to society — it is two criticisms that are on opposite sides of the same coin. On one hand, Tocqueville wrote that democracy cuts people off from one another and destroys any sense of belonging. Democracy's freedom causes people to become each their own, privatized and selfishly devoted only to personal desires and material well-being. The flip side of the coin is the charge that democracy naturally leads to collectivism. Equality demands that each individual helps others, nobody is special and the ant colony is more important than the individual ants.

The truth is both individuality and collectivism operate successfully in democracy. Citizens both compete and cooperate. Early democracy fosters a certain self-reliant, independent-minded and freedom-loving mindset. Mature democracies naturally emphasize community due to the desire for equality — they endeavor to break down class barriers, racial barriers, oligarchic tendencies and family dynasties, and they foster a kind of help-thy-neighbor mentality. These criticisms become acute when they occur in excess. Extreme individualism and collectivism are potential problems in democracies if the former diminishes equality and the latter freedom.

Potentially Fatal Arguments

Fukuyama believed democracy was the end of human political development, but there are many powerful arguments that indicate it fails — most of which were envisioned by nineteenth-century French politician and thinker Tocqueville. Democracy's flaws are obvious; many thinking person both rationally and intuitively understands them — Tocqueville simply observed and described them. Tocqueville was trying to show his fellow Frenchmen, who had always lived under a monarchy, what life was going to be like under democracy. His seminal works were *The Old Regime and the French Revolution*, which analyzed French society before the Revolution, and *Democracy in America*, which described what he thought it would be like after the Revolution. The later book contains many cogent observations on the advantages and disadvantages of democracy. Many of the disadvantages he described are the Achilles heels of the democracy I envision. These will be described briefly here and expanded on in section three of this book.

Tocqueville was born in Paris in 1805 and died in 1859 at age fifty-three in Cannes, France from tuberculosis. He was a Frenchman and descendant of an old Norman aristocratic family. He was active in French politics from about 1830 to 1851 in many capacities. He was *conseil général*, served as a deputy of the Manche department and was elected to the Constituent Assembly of 1848. As a member, he was charged with drafting a new constitution for the Second Republic. He resisted Napoleon's coup in 1851 because he had violated the constitutional limit of terms in office. He lost the contest and returned to private life, where he began his writings on France, America and democracy. His understanding of his subject derived in large part from his extensive travels in the 1830s and early 1840s to America, England and Ireland.

Tocqueville considered himself an old friend of America even though he despised its oppressive slavery. He both praised and was skeptical of democracy. Such disparate views can only be understood with greater insight to his beliefs, which in turn explain his views on democracy. Above all, Tocqueville was an ardent and passionate supporter of liberty. He considered himself neither a revolutionary nor conservative; like Hegel, his foremost ideal was freedom. This passion explains most of his views on government, individual freedom and rights.

Predictably, Tocqueville was an ardent opponent of that which suppressed liberty — despotism and tyrannies were his enemies. He despised the 1830 French July monarchy, which temporally returned France to monarchial government, opposed church domination by supporting separation of church and state, opposed centralized government because it only excels in preventing and not doing and advocated inheritance laws because they limited the power of inherited wealth.

Tocqueville was sympathetic with democracy's ideal of equality, but he remained skeptical of it in excess. He naturally favored liberty over equality and would inveigh upon extreme forms of equality in democracy. He wrote, for example, that in the human heart there exists a depraved taste for equality that compels the weak to want to bring the strong down to their level. The pernicious consequence could only be to reduce men to preferring equality in servitude to inequality in freedom, which is perhaps one of the most telling fatal consequences of democracy.

Tocqueville lived in the heated period that spawned French and worldwide socialism. Henri de Saint-Simon, Charles Fourier, Robert Owen, Pierre-Joseph Proudhon, Louis Blanc and Karl Marx were contemporaries and ardent socialists advocating the philosophy during his time, so he was well aware of the movement and its ideas. In relation to democracy, Tocqueville opposed socialism because he saw it as a clash between classes. He presciently saw socialism as the natural consequence of democracy and, when taken to the extreme, a source of oppression and suppressor of individual freedom.

Perhaps the wisest perspective Tocqueville, like Solon, gives us is the need for balance in any governmental system, including democracy. He advocated parliamentary government that dissipates any tendency to tyranny, bicameralism that balances power within government and universal suffrage because it prevented the concentration of power. He also was critical

47

of individualism because it caused people to retreat into themselves at the expense of the common good. There must exist a proper balance between the two for democracy to survive. Of democracy's two great antagonistic ideals, Tocqueville certainly favored freedom over equality, but he understood the need for a balance between the two. One of democracy's fatal flaws is its inability to maintain this difficult balance.

There are six reasons democracy fails, most of which were discerned by Tocqueville. They are problems that arise gradually from the very nature of democratic philosophy. They emerge as democracy follows its natural cycles and only begin to do their damage in its mature stage. Ironically, some of the reasons are the very opposite of the ideals that attract people to the philosophy. Many, no doubt, will consider these reasons inaccurately described, misinterpreted or not necessarily fatal. Certainly, only time will give us the answers.

Following is a brief summary of the six flaws because each will be examined in detail in section three. The first is the loss of freedom. Tocqueville wrote that democratic societies yearn for equality and freedom, but equality comes at the expense of freedom. Freedom is gradually lost in democracies due mostly to the tyranny of the majority. Private property ownership, for example, is one sign of a free society, and democracy diminishes this right. The surprising second flaw is democracy's tendency to create an unequal society. The leveling effect of democracy is, in effect, turned against many minorities. Tocqueville, for example, correctly believed that democracy naturally enables socialism, which leads to treating a whole class of citizens unequally. He described how democracy infuses a certain contempt for those with talent and intelligence, which denies opportunity.

Tocqueville said little about injustice in democracy, the third fatal flaw, but Aristotle and famous pundit H. L. Mencken did. Mencken wrote that all government, including democracy, is in essence a conspiracy against the

48

superior man — its object is to oppress and cripple him. This is a form of injustice that Aristotle wrote about in *Politics* that causes revolutions. Injustice is particularly acute in the law in democracies. Critical legal principles, like the rule of law and equal treatment under the law, become debased as the majority votes its way with impunity. Tocqueville believed democratic governments could become despotic, the fourth fatal flaw. They would become like a protective parent, treating its citizens like a flock of timid animals in a state of perpetual childhood. Paternalistic, controlling, commanding, restraining, coddling democratic governments would naturally become highly centralized power centers. He wrote, for example, in *The Old Regime and the French Revolution*, that a mistake of the French Revolution was to create a powerful democratic government that turned its back on freedom.

Both Tocqueville and Aristotle mention the fifth flaw, which is relative morality in democracies. Tocqueville believed with the removal of restraints in democracy, the only measure would be one's own happiness, so citizens would be constantly circling for petty pleasures. He believed that democracy would suffocate traditional values. Aristotle wrote in *Nicomachean Ethics* that in some democracies, everyone has license to do as he pleases. The final flaw is divisiveness, a common problem in democratic countries, acute in early twenty-first-century America. Tocqueville believed that democratically driven equality would cause social prejudices to become bitterer because people are more equal — the closer we are in equality, the more we fight and the more we divide. Democratic Athenian majoritarianism naturally leads to anomie, balkanization and divisiveness.

Before examining these six fatal reasons, let me turn to Fukuyama's theory that democracy is the end of history.

Chapter Four

THE END OF HISTORY IS DEMOCRACY

This book was inspired by Francis Fukuyama's book *The End of History and the Last Man*, along with my personal interest in philosophy, politics, morality and justice. It was Fukuyama's thesis that democracy is the end of history that caused me to consider whether it is. I will first briefly outline his thesis and then carry on a kind of discourse with him regarding the validity of his reasons. This discourse contains the origins of my thinking about democracy, but they are sometimes irrelevant to this book's thesis, sometimes incomplete and often critically analyzing—I was brainstorming. To a large extent, it was this point-counter-point with Fukuyama's ideas that lead to my thesis on democracy.

Fukuyama's Reasons and My Refutations

Fukuyama weaves an intriguing story that begins with the assertion that there exists a universal history that ends in a liberal democracy, due in part to the advance of science, which is linear and not cyclical. Democracy is essentially the end point of man's political evolution. Fukuyama is not alone in this assertion. German philosopher Georg Wilhelm Friedrich Hegel believed in a universal history; Alexis de Tocqueville wrote that history is a logical sequence with no turning back. and democracy was inexorably and providently the manifestation of that sequence.

Relying on Hegel's dialectic, Fukuyama deduces a universal history that is driven by mankind's desire for freedom, and when humans have achieved freedom, they have reached the pinnacle of their political development. This freedom evolves on two pillars — economics and recognition. The economics pillar originates in the desire to accumulate wealth and, when coupled with scientific advancement, results in linear universal human development. Because economics alone does not explain the evolution of history, Fukuyama envisions a second pillar, which is the human thymotic drive for freedom and equality. To explain this, Fukuyama postulates an original violent struggle of recognition between masters and slaves. The masters were willing to risk their lives for recognition, and the slaves were not. The result is two classes: the masters who won and became the masters and slaves who lost. This struggle precipitates an ongoing tension between recognized masters and resentful slaves that has driven much of history. It is the resolution of the combination of these pillars, along with a reconciliation of the master and slave relationship, that culminates in the end of history or liberal democracy.

Fukuyama derived much of his thesis from Hegel who had postulated a dialectical scheme that repeatedly swung from thesis to antithesis and back again to a higher and richer synthesis. Unlike Hegel, Thomas Hobbes and John Locke's theories that postulated desire drives humans to rationally pursue survival and security in the form of wealth, Fukuyama believes that this only leaves people unsatisfied and produces a bourgeois, non-public, spirited kind of man who pursues only self-interest—a kind of rational devil who would never die for his country. It is rather the Hegelian desire for recognition, worth and dignity that explains the rise of democracy. In addition to the economic man, democracy's development must account for this need to be recognized, otherwise people could live in authoritarian capitalistic states. It is this Hegelian need for recognition that acknowledges man as a moral agent with dignity that supplants his inclinations toward pride, glory and superiority. This accounting brings humans a sense of self-respect, dignity and self-esteem that, along with the universal human aspiration for freedom, drives the historic dialectic process that culminates in liberal democracy. Indeed, two central aspirations for democracy are freedom and equality. In some respects, Fukuyama is also borrowing from German philosopher F. C. S. Schiller's view that inward freedom of the soul enables the individual to rise above physical frailties and the pressures of material conditions.

Before specifically addressing Fukuyama's reasons, permit me three general observations. First, history is full of once-popular, now-failed political systems. Pharohships, kingships, monarchies and communism are dead political philosophies today. Political systems come and go like ships in the night. Why is democracy special? Second, William of Ockham, the originator of the medieval rule of logical economy known as Ockham's razor, who states that entities are not to be multiplied beyond necessity, might say Fukuyama is making more of democracy's virtues than its vices. Could it be that Fukuyama is wrongfully assuming the existence of entities like recognition? Assuming fewer premises may result in the more simple explanation that democracy will not endure. Finally, could Fukuyama, an ostensible rational historian, really be invoking a Leibnizian theological faith? In response to the problem of evil, philosopher Gottfried Wilhelm Leibniz, in his *Theodicy*, optimistically proposed that an all-perfect God would not allow evil, which necessarily means this must be the best of all worlds. Perhaps for Fukuyama, democracy is the faith that rights all human wrongs. Voltaire rightly satirized Leibniz in *Candide*, and I prefer to retain the George Santayana view; like chastity, skepticism should not be relinquished too readily.

NO DEFINITION OF DEMOCRACY

My first objection to Fukuyama's thesis is that he fails to give a comprehensive definition of democracy. In order to build a proper thesis one must know what one is addressing. I proposed in chapter one a definition of democracy that described it as a continuum with varying definitions, conditions, characteristics and descriptions. There seems to be no one final way to define it rather only qualities that indicate it. Further, some forms of democracy are more democratic than others lying somewhere on that continuum. Certainly, a direct democracy with universal suffrage is more democratic than a representative democracy with limited suffrage. There has never been a perfect democracy. Because Fukuyama refers to democracy in a generic sense one is left wondering what he thinks democracy is and what form of democracy will prevail in the end.

THERE IS A UNIVERSAL HISTORY

Fukuyama's assumption that there exists a universal history due to science is fundamental to his thesis. To this controversial topic, it can be argued that science does not bring a universal history and history is cyclical. It seems that much of human history is driven by human nature, so the essential question is whether science can alter and/or ameliorate human nature. Absent chemical or physical alterations to individual human beings, human nature is constant through time. One only need read fifth-century BCE Greek playwright Euripides' Medea to appreciate this. Medea exhibits all of the contemporary human emotions like revenge, pride and hate, which results in her violently murdering her children. Human nature has not changed over 2,500 years — it remains constant. Science alters human's environment, which certainly affects human nature, but it does not fundamentally alter it. Further, clearly human institutions, including democracy, are ameliorating, but again human nature remains constant. It is also true that human nature can be tampered with eugenically by breeding a better kind of dog, but instincts cannot be eradicated through breeding. A placid lap poodle will still fight for its life under the right circumstances.

Historians and philosophers disagree whether history is progressive, regressive or cyclical; however, a strong argument can be made that it is cyclical. Constant human nature repeatedly brings forces that inevitably precipitate predictable counter forces that end in the same kind of circumstances. A cyclical history would mean democracy is no different than past political systems that have come and gone.

FREEDOM IS THE END OF HISTORY

It is hard to disagree with Hegel and Fukuyama that freedom is man's greatest aspiration and that it may well be that, when it is attained, the end of history has been achieved. Hegel in particular believed that the end of human history was the realization of individual freedom — human progress is human progress toward freedom — a philosophic theme that resounds throughout history. The problematic questions are how freedom is to be defined and whether democracy truly brings it.

"Freedom from external restraint" and "freedom entails responsibility" are two prevailing definitions of freedom, but a more sophisticated one proposed by Richard M. Weaver in *The Ethics of Rhetoric* is "when human's surroundings have a determinate nature in order to predict and plan for the future." Freedom moves on a set of presuppositions, and when it is tampered with, men become concerned about losing their freedom. In a democracy, it turns out that the capricious majority and non-originalist judges often tamper with these presuppositions, thereby rendering the future unpredictable. Ethically, the tendency in democracies to abrogate social contract compacts in favor of utility subtly changes the definition of freedom to a lesser form. Much will be said later about whether democracy brings freedom, so for now let us just ponder this question: does a mature democratic socialistic welfare state truly represent the highest form of human freedom? I think not.

THE END OF HISTORY IS DEMOCRACY

Fukuyama's central theme that the end of history is a free and equal liberal democracy that would contain no contradictions, thereby bringing the historic dialectic to an end, contains six debatable suppositions. It assumes that there is an end to human history, that it will be a liberal democracy, that this democracy will entail liberty and equality, that there will be no contradictions, that there is a historic dialectic and that it will end in a synthesis. For Fukuyama's thesis to be true, each one of these suppositions must be true—like the Anna Karenina principle, if one fails then the entire thesis fails. Because some of these assertions are discussed elsewhere in this book, I will focus here on his assumptions that the dialectic resolves contradictions, the dialectic results in a synthesis, and that there is an end to history.

Certainly, there exist some dialectics in history that resolve contradictions—the injustice to one in confession by torture evolved to equity for two in civil court—but this is not always the case. Contradictions exist in all democracies in all their stages, so why assume they resolve themselves? In modern democracies, the majority continues to oppress the minority, the eternal war continues unabated between rich and poor and opposing political ideologies continue to define freedom, equality and justice differently. Hegel and Fukuyama may be seeking an ontological synthesis, but the contradiction war remains within individual societies. Freedom and equality remain unbalanced, undefined and tenuous precisely because the contradiction between them has not been resolved.

One reason for this could be scarcity. Nature is indifferent to human political philosophies that scarcity makes conspicuous. It has been said that economics is the study of scarcity, and I might add that civilization the way to allocate it. Perhaps without scarcity there would be no need for contradictions. Another reason could be that democracies evolve and change with time. A resolution of contradictions may appear feasible at one point in a democracy's evolution but impossible in another. Early democracy's protection of property, for example, evolves into wealth redistribution programs that create a new set of problems, including black markets, avoidance of government and cheating that cause a new kind of undemocratic centralized government to suppress. A more sophisticated reason, supplied by Weaver, could be due to the subtle change of the very concept of a dialectic. Early positive dialectical terms and concepts that refer to something in reality as in the hard sciences give way to soft social science dialectical terms that only deal with opposites. Justice changes from an ethical concept described by Aristotle to only the opposite of injustice. The consequence is a subjective, prejudiced concept of justice that has no grounding in reality — what constitutes a slum becomes akin to defining bad weather. The user of this new dialectic subsumes facts, smuggles assumptions and indifferently passes from what is objectively true to what is subjectively moral or imaginatively true. To make matters worse, this new roaming dialectic, because it deals only with opposites, necessarily commits its user to one side or another, furthering contradiction. To say something is just only allies one with those that think likewise against the standpatters.

If a dialectic cannot resolve contradictions, how can it result in a synthesis? Both Fukuyama and Karl Marx borrowed Hegel's famous dialectic in order to prove a theory, one of which ends with democracy and the other with communism. Marx's dialectic involved a materialistic clash between bourgeoisie and proletariat classes, unlike Hegel's concept, which Marx believed would only result in the bourgeoisie capitalist class's victory. The contradiction would remain in the form of antagonistic classes. For Marx, this contradiction is only resolved and true freedom achieved when the proletariat class prevails under communism. As it turns out, communistic societies also face contradictions, such as oppression of the endowed on behalf of the less endowed, individualism opposed to collectivization, the clash with capitalism (whether in the form of unlawful black markets in the former Soviet Union or sanctioned capitalistic enterprise zones in contemporary China) and a new privileged communist elite class apart from the rest of society. Marx's political materialistic dialectic simply achieves no synthesis.

To argue that there is an end to history is brave but incredible. Fukuyama is brave for presenting a grand thesis in the face of convention and certain criticism. R. G. Collingwood, in his *The Idea of History* explained its incredulity. Collingwood was criticizing Johann Gottlieb Fichte and his claim that the present state of the world is a complete and final achievement of history. Things change in unpredictable ways, including linear science, which often hands us unexpected societal changing developments. Fukuyama is a historian viewing the past from the present, which is the only view accessible to him. Any number of past historians could have wrongly predicted their time as the end of history from the same perspective. Why is Fukuyama any different? Collingwood pointed out that a man cannot fairly evaluate matters apart from his environment, including history. Fukuyama, locked in his environment, is assuming humans are rational and responsible for everything they do; thus, history is a consequence of human will. Instead, we know humans are often irrational, act on passion and are sometimes irresponsible. This makes the future uncertain and unpredictable. Fukuyama may be smart, but he is not prescient.

HUMAN NATURE EVOLVES

Fukuyama's claim that human nature evolves is critical to his theory because without it there could be no linear universal history that would end in democracy. The alternate view discussed earlier is that human nature remains constant through time. One reason Fukuyama's claim is attractive is due to the contemporary enchantment with the word "progressive." Weaver, writing in 1950s America, described certain "God-words," or supremely revered and unassailable words, from which other positive words are derived—"progressive" is one of them. Like Fukuyama, American philosopher and educator John Dewey also claimed human nature can change due to social engineering. For Dewey, education is the solution, which explains why the word "education" today is a semi-God-word derived from "progressive."

It is from the progressive concept that Fukuyama invokes Hegel, a follower of Immanuel Kant, who famously postulated that history progresses dialectically through conflicting thesis, antithesis and finally synthesis that resolves contradictions. Hegel agreed that humans have a natural side derived from bodily needs, but, unlike his predecessors, he believed desire and circumstances like environment also form and influence human nature. Desire and circumstances are the variables that enable human freedom, and a dialectic of these factors causes human nature to evolve, perhaps progressively so.

The second part of this assertion is the implication that history is linear. This is a contentious issue among historians that will be evaluated in depth in the next chapter as it relates to democracy. It first should be observed that Fukuyama must assume history is linear, like his claim human nature evolves, for his theory to have veracity; otherwise, democracy could cycle into some other political system. The tenuousness of this assertion is made conspicuous by the reality that, before Hegel, most philosophers believed history was cyclical due to unchanging human passion. Passion is the gravity that causes the pendulum to swing back and forth. Passion made Rome great, and when it faded, the barbarians' passion overthrew it—and so goes history. Sophocles, Juvenal and François de La Rochefoucauld, in his *Maximes*, eloquently described timeless human passion.

More sophisticated explanations come from famous historians Edward Gibbon and Arnold J. Toynbee. They both believed all societies go through cycles and eventually fail. Gibbon, in *The History of the Decline and Fall of the Roman Empire*, postulated that societies decline due to enervation, luxury and soft living that gives rise to excessive zeal and despotic rulers. Toynbee, in *A Study of History*, described dominant minority oligarchs that are challenged by an external proletariat, which results in change. Poignantly, both historians agree on why societies fail—a single-mindedness that leads to disputes, internal divisions and eventually sectarian violence. In late democracies, including America today, we see all of these traits writ large—acidic disputes, uncompromising single-mindedness and division. Could sectarian violence be next?

There is an interesting contradiction in Fukuyama here. On one hand, he wants a linear history to end in democracy, but on the other he relies on a progressive philosophy that dialectically leads to democracy. But God-words like "progressive" change over time due to different societies' values, which makes them assailable. Dewey's "progressive" God-word-derivative "education," for example, is ascendant as long as "progressive" remains king. So how do you get an end of history when you rely on a progressive agenda that presupposes change? Indeed, it seems more an argument for constant change or cyclical history.

More interesting is the relationship between progressiveness, democracy and morality. Dewey, like those who champion progressiveness and, collaterally, democracy, like Fukuyama, was a positivist. Positivism is a twentieth-century philosophic movement that claimed, among many things, that morality is just a social fact — there is no timeless natural morality. This makes morality relative because society's values change. Could it be that the positivist progressives of our age like Fukuyama are really social engineers like Dewey endeavoring to artificially manipulate human nature because they want democracy to succeed? Could it be that the revered concept of equality in democracy leads to relative ethics? I believe the ascension of relative morality in democracy is one of its Achilles heels. This intriguing line of thinking will be picked up later in chapter ten on relative morality.

MASTERS AND SLAVES

Fukuyama envisioned an original violent struggle for recognition between individuals in which those willing to die became masters and those unwilling, slaves. Historian Barbara W. Tuchman, in *A Distant Mirror*, eloquently demonstrated this point in the calamitous fourteenth century. The historic result of this struggle has been overclass masters and underclass slaves. According to Fukuyama, democracy seeks to abolish these historic classes by making men masters of themselves and turning the former masters into wealth-seeking bourgeoisie last men. Apparently, the lubricant for this transformation is democracy's inclination toward tolerance.

Are this master-slave scenario and its implications spun by Fukuyama true? It would seem there are other more compelling reasons for societal stratification than just the willingness to risk life, including natural ability, luck, environment, character, effort and intelligence. Fukuyama mentions none of these. Also, does democracy truly abolish these historic classes? An argument could be mounted, for example that under majority rule in democracy, the poor masses become the former masters, and the rich minority become the former slaves. To carry this line of reasoning one step further, could it be the unendowed or less intelligent majority becomes the masters of the endowed intelligent minority? In either case, freedom does not necessarily reign for whoever is in the minority.

Does democracy turn the former aristocrat into the bourgeoisie last man? Fukuyama's use of the word bourgeoisie reveals a bias in favor of leveling democracy. It is a pejorative appellation used by socialist Marx for affluent middle-class, conventional, conservative people with a materialistic outlook on life who control the means of production and ostensibly exploit the working classes. Marx's quasi-communistic philosophy is problematic; it may well be that the very health of any society depends on this middle-class materialistic viewpoint and the oppression of this very class may result in innumerable pejorative consequences. If Ayn Rand's fictional John Galt truly quit democracy and production declined, society loses wealth. Unlike Fukuyama's vision, to be master of oneself may indeed require some to quit democracy.

Tolerance does seem to be a characteristic of democracies, but so does Stendhal's tyranny of public opinion, or what is sometimes called political correctness. Democracies have a tendency to take ideals to the extreme, whether it be anarchy for freedom or perfect equality for equality. These extremes breed single-mindedness and intolerance. The gradual blurring of the line between political and absolute equality, for example, breeds intolerance for any distinctions between citizens. Tolerance toward different religious views is also characteristic of early democracy, but when religious views challenge prevailing public opinion, intolerant disapprobation ensues. Could it be that democracies naturally become intolerant? Indeed, it would seem plausible that democracy is no different than any other political system that rejects ideas contrary to their system. In the case of democracy, it is just intolerance toward ideas that are considered undemocratic. There is no reason to believe that Fukuyama's last-man-former-master could likewise become intolerant of democracy.

HEGEL'S RECOGNITION

Hegel's concept of recognition is central to Fukuyama's thesis that democracy is the end of history. For Hegel, history is explained by humans' desire for freedom, which Fukuyama uses to claim democracy satisfies with Hegel's recognition. Democracy, as it goes, recognizes people's pride through *thymos*, or self-respect. With, assumedly, its ideals of freedom and equality, democracy acknowledges individuals' worthiness. It is this recognition that transcends humans' mere desire to satisfy their physical needs and explains patriotism, courage, generosity and public-spiritedness in a way individualistic self-centered political theories do not. Recognition, in short, satisfies the historic human need for freedom.

Fukuyama claims famous philosophers Hobbes and Locke wrongly usurped this explanation of history. Hegel and Hobbes agreed that the instinct for self-preservation is the most basic, so in an original state of nature, bloody battles for survival ensued. They disagree on the source of human happiness, though—for Hegel it is the human willingness to risk life in battle, and for Hobbes it is the fear of violent death. Hobbes, who Fukuyama considers the fountainhead of liberal democracy, got it wrong with his view that this rational pursuit of self-preservation results in a social contract in which men forgo pride and make compacts not to kill, steal or lie in order to preserve their lives. Indeed, as Fukuyama points out, Leviathan or monarchial government does not satisfy pride but rather subdues it. For Hobbes, it is the fear of death that leads to the modern liberal state. Locke continued Hobbes's point of view by agreeing that survival trumps recognition, but he transformed Hobbes monarchy into a constitutionally limited government that protected citizens' rights, including property, which had authority derived from the people. This wrongful view does not explain modern liberal democracy.

Parenthetically, I find Fukuyama's use of Hegel curious because Hegel was a statist who believed the unity of Spirit and Idea culminates in the final element of world, which is the state. For Hegel, the actualization of freedom and all organized liberty comes from the state. The state is culmination of history and is all-important. As a statist, Hegel was a collectivist and opponent of individualism. Individuals are unimportant in history and only fodder, a point that Søren Kierkegaard attacked because the individual is sacrificed to the universal and general. How does freedom derive from collectivism and an omnipotent state? Indeed, it would seem the opposite is true. This point is further muddled within a democratic state. History may well be the search to reconcile and satisfy both masters and slaves, but does a powerful, collectivized democratic state do this? It would seem that this only gives the majority a bigger club to subdue the minority and, in the process, limit their freedom. Thus, it is difficult to understand how recognition in democracy brings freedom.

These points aside, the critical contest in Fukuyama's argument is Hegel's recognition opposed to Hobbes and Locke's survival. Fukuyama endeavors to make the case that it is Hegel's desire for recognition rather than survival that drives the historic dialectic that results in liberal democracy. Which truly satisfies the historic human need for freedom that leads to modern liberal democracy — recognition or survival?

Survival trumps recognition for a variety of significant reasons. Philosophically, existence precedes concepts — one must exist in order to conceive. Kant's idealistic precepts without concepts are blind, and concepts without precepts are empty works only when a preceptor exists to assimilate precepts and concepts. Prosaically, humans will instinctively seek survival first because it is more basic than recognition. Put another way, in a state of nature, recognition means little if you are not going to survive. Imagine a primitive man faced with the choice of living or being recognized—he will want to live because without it recognition means nothing. In Fukuyama's master and slave scenario, if a master is dying from exposure, why would he care to subjugate the slave? Instinct trumps desire, and nature bats last. Indeed, Hegel, Fukuyama and Hobbes all agree that self-preservation is the more basic instinct. So what is the issue? It would seem that the point of agreement among the contestants is that survival evolving into a social contract alone is insufficient to satisfy humans' desire for freedom. Being safe and meeting one's physical needs is not enough to bring democracy; it also requires recognition to thrive and be the end of history. This may be true, but note that once survival has been achieved and freedom attained, only then does recognition afford the patriotism, courage, generosity and public-spiritedness Fukuyama describes.

Perhaps Fukuyama's error is that he confuses survival and recognition's relative importance. A more plausible explanation is that Hobbes and Locke's survival bring freedom, but recognition is that necessary added ingredient that brings liberal democracy and human happiness. Perhaps a better thesis could be that the combination of survival and recognition are what result in democracy being the end of history. It is not either or but rather together. Alternatively, if it is survival alone driving the dialectic to freedom, then humans may achieve what they historically desire without recognition, thus making democracy a woodpath.

DEMOCRACY NEED NOT SATISFY
MEGALOTHYMIA

Fukuyama's view that democracy does not need to satisfy megalothymia or the need to be better than others looks like a straw man. He assumes this is a human need, from which he explains why democracy need not satisfy it. According to Fukuyama, democracy offers innumerable alternative outlets for this assumed human drive, such as sports, mountain climbing, and auto racing (where some risk their lives), as well as rock climbing, hang gliding, skydiving, marathon running and ironman races. These outlets are sufficient to win them recognition and negate megalothymia. However, megalothymia may not be the villain, and it may not matter whether democracy need not satisfy it. Indeed, there may be bigger mortal villains for democracy that Fukuyama fails to mention, such as oppression, resentment, frustration, injustice, lack of freedom, unequal treatment and totalitarianism. Let me focus on just one for now: injustice.

Under democratic socialistic systems, most believe it is just to tax according to ability. Accordingly, the majority will invariably levy higher taxes on a few high-earning citizens. These taxes are often progressive, where higher income is taxed at a higher rate. The majority may think this is all well and good, but the high-earning minority is left with a burning resentment and anger. They feel they are being stolen from and, thus, treated unjustly. This is a deep resentment that is not placated by hang gliding — it is rather a gut anger at an unjust and unresponsive political system that was created by a majority of voters. Fukuyama may claim democracy does not admit tyranny, but to this individual, the tyranny of the majority is real. One example of this, from my book *Socialism in America*, could be Magnus Kempe.

Kempe lived in democratic socialist Sweden and is Swedish. He describes socialist Sweden as a place where individuals are taxed to death. He spent a good deal of his life studying to become an engineer and, after years of work and study, made less than an alcoholic man living on welfare who never worked a day his whole life. Kempe complains bitterly that it is impossible to save anything and that the little pleasures of living, such as going out to dinner, buying a book, or going to a movie are beyond his budget. He sees financial success in Sweden punished and businessmen who earn too much imprisoned. He describes a culture where anyone who dares to think or act independently of the politically correct socialist doctrine is questioned, while mindless emotional statements are strongly encouraged. If one refuses to join a union, he is called antisocial in front of colleagues and told his job and salary will not last long. Kempe explains that Swedish television is state-controlled and describes how satellite dishes are forbidden. The state propaganda on television was pervasive when broadcasts regularly asserted that the communists would win in Nicaragua, yet when they lost, it was never mentioned. Kempe left Sweden for another, freer country, not because he was megalothymiac but rather because he was angry, resentful, frustrated, felt oppressed and treated unjustly. Kempe is just one prototype individual created by a democracy that is not placated by sports.

Another alternative explanation to Fukuyama's claim comes from Kant's troubling view that some evil naturally exists in the human heart. Holistically, Fukuyama's theory presupposes the Greco-Roman assumption that humans progress morally and virtuously along with Christianity's view that providential wisdom works for the good despite human folly and wickedness. Kant, on the other hand, believed the irrational and immoral characteristics of pride, greed and ambition lead to evil human acts. These qualities are the source of antagonism between men, which makes peaceful society impossible. Certainly, most humans naturally have a desire to be friendly and peaceful but some also naturally want to dominate and exploit neighbors, which is

Fukuyama's megalothymia in spades. If Kant is right, then megalothymia is the inevitable spring that overthrows social systems including democracy. It may be that human nature itself drives human discontent.

Using Kempe's description of socialist democratic Sweden and Fukuyama's slave and master examples, it would appear that serious internal conflict remains in democracies aside of megalothymia. Could it be that democracy represents the succession of the former slaves to power that turn on and subjugate their former masters? Under the influence of corrupting power, could it be that former socialist slaves in Sweden are now segueing into a dictatorial tyranny of the majority perpetuating injustice on their former masters? Could it be that megalothymia is now the symptom of the former slaves?

On a broader level, could it be that what is happening is Sweden is occurring in all ostensibly stable European democratic societies, such as France and Italy? We see wealthy former masters abandoning France and religiously avoiding taxes in Italy. In these European democracies, we also see tremendous internal conflict on many levels. This causes one to ponder: is the dialectic that Fukuyama claims leads to democracy truly working? Is there a synthesis between the minds of slaves and masters that is truly evolving? Is democracy capable of achieving a balance, or does it represent a new incarnation of "might makes right"? It would appear that megalothymia is a sideshow and the end of history is further off than Fukuyama envisions.

FREEDOM AND EQUALITY ARE CONTRADICTIONS IN DEMOCRACY

Fukuyama navigates the mine-strewn field of freedom and equality in democracy with some insight. He writes that freedom and equality are the pillars of democracy but that they are not always compatible, so there remains a simmering tension between the two. If freedom reigns, inequality brings contention; if equality reigns, tyranny brings resentment. Fukuyama admits that there is no fixed point where liberty and equality come into balance or are optimized simultaneously. He admits that the very claim that people are equal is a contradiction because they are not equal. Equality does not offer the talented individual recognition for his talents. Fukuyama resolves this dilemma by saying that every society will balance the two differently and that the tension between socialistic equality and formal democratic freedom does not refute his thesis that democracy is the end of history.

Certainly, freedom and equality are the sirens for early democracy and the oppressed. People in repressive aristocratic or monarchial entrenched societies yearn for freedom and equal treatment under the law. There is a reason people of the world flocked to early American democracy. The problem is that freedom and equality are incompatible because when we are free, we are not equal and when we are equal, many are not free. Some thrive with freedom, and when this is encumbered with equality, the tension that Tocqueville described as "necessary and ineradicable" ensues. Taking either to their extreme only exacerbates this tension.

It is understandable that Fukuyama would minimize this dilemma because his thesis that democracy results in a synthesis would fail. His first explanation is simply that every society will balance the two differently. However, this only works when freedom and equality are balanced somewhat equally into a kind of free and equal political equilibrium. Unfortunately, democracy has a problem reaching this equilibrium. His second explanation is that the tension between socialistic equality and formal democratic freedom does not refute his thesis that democracy is the end of history. How can this be if the tension remains? And what if the tension grows? It would seem the fate of democracy is indeed tenuous if it must continually and precariously achieve a balance between these competing ideals.

Fukuyama simply fails to appreciate this fundamental problem with democracy. It may well be that it is structurally incapable of balancing these ideals. Indeed, rather than being the end of history it could be rather a temporary, unrealistic, idealistic and wayward political philosophy vainly in search of utopia. If Hegel is right and freedom is the essential aim of humankind, it may be that the very loss of freedom due to democracy's ideal of equality is its death knell.

DEMOCRACY RECOGNIZES RIGHTS

Fukuyama claims that one reason democracy succeeds is that it recognizes people through rights. He views rights as a thymotic force that promotes people's self-esteem. The right of freedom of religion, for example, bolsters self-worth because people can worship as they please. Similarly, the right to free speech enables citizens to voice opinions and contribute to public policy. As such, rights militate against the master-slave relationship because the former slaves now have rights and a voice in democracy.

Certainly, rights are a cornerstone of democracy and one of its greatest benefits and bulwarks against both former masters and modern tyrannical government. Rights also intuitively satisfy *thymos* because they constrain tyranny and promote freedom. However, Fukuyama fails to appreciate democracy's effect on what constitutes a right. The origins of the notion of rights was intended to promote freedom and, in particular, freedom from governmental interference. This changes as democracy ages. The right to practice one's religion freely, for example, changes as democracy evolves. In later democracies, the religious right to polygamous marriage may be denied but the sacrilegious right to marry the same sex may be approved. The ineluctable transition from negative to positive rights will be discussed at length in chapter eight, which deals with injustice.

From this perspective, it is clear that Fukuyama is right to the extent that original rights do enhance *thymos*, but could it be that, as rights change from protecting liberty to providing equality, the very slave majority in democracy becomes the new master? As Tocqueville implied, what is the difference between one king and the majority? If this is true, then the master-slave relationship is not dead but rather resurrected, there is less freedom, morality increasingly becomes relative and conflict continues. Each of these important consequences will be taken up later in this book.

COMMUNISM FAILED FOR ECONOMIC REASONS

My final exchange with Fukuyama is not so much a retort but rather a question. Fukuyama states that communism failed because it lost legitimacy—it claimed it could deliver a high standard of living, but it did not. In this he is right. The former Soviet Union professed collectivized farming was increasing crop yields, when in reality, production was declining. People knew this was a lie, and the political system lost legitimacy. Certainly, there are other reasons communism failed in the Soviet Union, but the loss of economic viability must be one of them.

My question is: why could democracy also not lose its legitimacy and fail, like communism? In many ways, section three of this book is about that question. As democracy naturally ages, could it be that it takes on characteristics that debase its legitimacy? Could freedom become oppression, equality inequality, justice injustice and morality immorality? Could citizens in democracy naturally come to prefer concentrated power over rule by the people? Individually, these changes in democracy would mar its legitimacy, but collectively, it would seem they could end it.

Conclusion

Many of the reasons Fukuyama believes democracy is the end of history derive from his view on how it originated. In contrast to Hobbes and Locke, he assumes democracy arose due to Hegel's ideas on *thymos*, recognition and freedom. Essentially, the desire for recognition explains the rise of democracy because it provides self-respect, which, in conjunction with human's aspiration for freedom, culminates in liberal democracy. Did Fukuyama get on the wrong Hegelian horse? Let me spin an alternate yarn using Hobbes and Locke's theory that derives from morality, or how we ought to live.

In many ways, the social contract moral theory explains morality, the origins of democracy and why democracy may fail. In essence, the theory is simple. In nature, without morality, we kill each other, but due to our instinct to survive, we also want to live. To live, we find it is in our interests to rationally form compacts with others where we agree not to kill each other. The results work—we find ourselves safer and freer. Unbeknownst to us, we have originated morality. In order to enforce these compacts, we created Leviathan-government, laws and police that enforce our compacts. Fukuyama argues against this Hobbesian view because he believes survival and security alone do not bring democracy. But there is more to my story.

Like Fukuyama, Jared Diamond, in *Guns, Germs and Steel*, also did not believe primitive egalitarian bands evolved into chiefdoms, and eventually states, under the social contract. His weak argument is that observation and historical evidence do not support such a dispassionate farsightedness. However, his own example of the primitive Fayu Bands in New Guinea where everyone killed each other occurred with few people. There was lots of jungle, room to roam freely and in relative safety in this state of nature. But, he also pointed out, if food production grows and the population gets denser, it becomes harder to roam freely in safety. The solution is a social contract that ushers in civilization. Even more telling is Diamond's point that those large societies require centralized authority that monopolizes the use of force in order to resolve conflicts. This is none other than the Hobbesian Leviathan that enforces the social contract, or states that naturally arise to enforce the social contract, as civilization advances.

As civilization's mixed blessings advance, we find earlier forms of government, such as emperors, kings and popes, enforcing the contract somewhat—and always in ways that are in their interests. The elite may have enforced the compact not to kill but exempted themselves from the one that proscribed stealing. One example is Tocqueville's description of seventeenth-century France prior to the democratic French Revolution where the poor paid taxes and the nobles were exempt. Early Leviathan governments forgot their role. These middle states could be characteristic of Jean-Jacques Rousseau's claim that man is born free but everywhere in chains. Ironically, the further "civilization" advanced and the social contract receded, the more humans found themselves bound.

Democracy was the natural solution. Rather than permit such intolerable, selfish and uneven enforcement of the contract, people took on the role of Leviathan themselves. Through democracy, the people took control to ensure that the compacts of life, liberty and property with the ensuing pursuit of happiness are enforced. The result in early democracies was a reaffirmation of essential ethics in the form of the social contract, sentiments of which are found in many democratic constitutions. This explanation accounts for Hegel's freedom from Rousseau's chains, Hobbes's survival and equality, with no need for Fukuyama's recognition, or *thymos*. With early democracy, people gained a political system that was ethical, fair and free.

One manifestation of this alternate explanation is rights. Locke envisioned a liberal democracy with rights that prohibit government from restricting certain individual freedoms. For Locke, rights protect rather than restricted freedom — they enlarge freedom. The right to life in democracy is, thus, the confirmation of the social compact not to kill. In this case, democracy's rights are the people's assertion of the compact in a complex society not to kill one another. Democracy is the people's way to enforce the ethical fairness found in the social contract, such as the compact not to kill. It is no accident that the concept of rights emerged about the time declining monarchies were debauching the social contract and democracy was beginning its ascent.

So how does this alternate explanation of democracy's origins square with Fukuyama's assertion that it is the end of history? It seems that democracy's future depends more on morality and what society considers fair than on recognition. If democracies have a natural evolution due to the people's will and what is moral becomes immoral, its early benefits may be forfeited. If democracy naturally embraces a utilitarian philosophy, the essential compacts of a social contract may be violated. If the concept of a right becomes so adulterated in democracy, the compacts may conflict and become worthless — the reason for them and their benefits may be lost. With these possibilities, democratic government may be just another seventeenth-century fading monarchy enforcing contracts selectively and another Soviet Union existing without legitimacy.

It may well be that Fukuyama is wrong. Hegel, *thymos* and legitimacy may not be the extra ingredient that explains democracy, there may be no dialectic at work and democracy may not be the end of history. However, much of this yarn depends on whether democracies change over time, so the next chapter is about the cycles of democracy.

Chapter Five

THE CYCLES OF
DEMOCRACY

In order to claim democracy is the end of history, Francis Fukuyama must assume history is linear and not random, history is progressive and democracy is the universal, timeless and unchanging end of that progression. This is a tall order that is akin to Gottfried Wilhelm Leibniz's claim that this is the best of all worlds because a perfect god made it.

Together, these are audacious claims past philosophers, scholars, theologians and historians have endeavored to fill in their own times but failed. They are the kind of claims Erasmus described as folly — a spree that never ends.

The Cycles of History

To answer Fukuyama's claim, this chapter will first examine whether history is linear and progressive. There are only three choices: history can be progressive, regressive or cyclical. If regressive, then history could end in a system like democracy, but then democracy would not be the best political system. If history is cyclical, then democracy would only be one stage of the historic cycle, with some other system beyond it. Therefore, Fukuyama must presuppose that history is progressive in order for democracy to be its end. The second part of this chapter will argue that democracies naturally evolve into something different. For democracy to be the end of history, it must be universal, timeless and unchanging. But how could history that is ostensibly progressing to such an end remain unchanging when one of its parts — democracy — naturally changes?

There exists a long-standing, unresolved debate about whether history is progressive, regressive or cyclical. Perhaps it could be generalized that, historically, the cyclical view prevailed, but it is being supplanted today with a more progressive view. The regressive theory has remained generally out of favor, with a few exceptions. The progressive view is that history is ameliorative and civilization is getting better. Georg Wilhelm Friedrich Hegel's dialectic ending in freedom is one example, and Karl Marx's similar dialectic where the proletariat overcomes the bourgeoisie in a communist state that withers away is another. Philosopher Henri Bergson's process philosophy embraced dynamic values, such as motion, change and evolution, that advance civilization into a novel future. Like Hegel, eighteenth-century Italian philosopher Giambattista Vico believed that history is the story of man's progressive march to freedom that entailed societies passing through stages of growth and decay. His twist on cyclical history proposed that societies advance in a circular motion that winds upward through growth and decay. There is never a return to an original starting point because every turn is higher than the one before. Vico's progressive history is edifying in that in his third stage, or our contemporary age of men, involves the emergence of democratic principles, which includes equal rights, a more inclusive society and more freedom. In keeping with his theory, however, he also wrote that this stage's decay would encounter problems of corruption, dissolution and possible reversion to primitive barbarism. Fukuyama's thesis that liberal democracy is the end of history is but one of a succession of philosopher historians' progressive views.

Regressive history theorizes that history is not ameliorative but rather in decline. Civilization is getting worse. German historian Oswald Spengler could be one of the few leading regressive historians. In his *Decline of the West*, he describes the disintegration of Western civilization due to skepticism, materialism, imperialism, megalopolises and constant conflict. Poignantly, like Vico, he believed democracy would give way to dictatorship and Caesarism. Tongue in cheek, it may well be that the true regressive historians are the wise, common-sense man who views reality from the street rather than the metaphysical theoreticians like the progressives or cyclicists.

Cyclical history, in antiquity called "eternal recurrence," states that history repeats itself. Societies naturally progress from birth, grow and decay due to forces that inevitably emerge in response to previous forces. Cyclical history is neither progressive nor regressive — it is rather repetition of the past. Human society is not necessarily getting better or worse; rather, it is just more of the same. Both Aristotle and the ancient Stoics believed in eternal recurrence. As mentioned earlier, both famous historians Edward Gibbon and Arnold J. Toynbee believed all societies go through cycles and eventually fail. Gibbon because societies decline due to enervation, luxury and soft living that give rise to despotic rulers and excessive zeal, and Toynbee due to the interaction between oligarchs and internal and external proletariats. Alexis de Tocqueville was a scribe for the doctrine of eternal recurrence when he wrote in the eighteen hundreds that after the medieval thirteenth and fourteenth centuries' European cultures were advancing to a high standard of civilization and prosperity, but at the same time their political structures were relapsing into barbarism. He wrote that strenuous endeavor, virility and pioneering virtues were passing away and institutions becoming drained of their structure. George Santayana famously wrote that those who cannot remember the past are condemned to repeat it. Few remember or even know the past and are thus condemned to repeat it, which necessarily makes history cyclical.

R. G. Collingwood had some significant things to say about cyclical history. He is a famous historian who opposed cyclical history theory but argued strenuously against linear and progressive theories. He was ambiguous on this issue. He wrote that historical progress leading to the present and the view that there are historical cycles with great ages and decadence are dogmas that show historians' ignorance. Apparently, when considering history, cyclical signifies ignorance.

However, Collingwood goes on to make four poignant points that support cyclical history. The first is that looking back gives no clues to the future. Why? Certainly, the past gives no definitive answers, but it does give strong clues. Indeed, it may be our best source of information about the future. When looking back in time, a historian can compare periods, observe certain trends and, thus, make certain claims, much the way science does. Collingwood himself wrote that historians can compare historical periods or ways of life, reconstruct people's experience for themselves and, with this knowledge, be able to ask whether any changes are progress. The point is that if we see cycles in the past, it is not unreasonable to assume we will see cycles in the future.

His second point is that historians wrongly assume they can predict the future. He charged the medieval historians with this failure because they believed history was foreordained by God. It was an ecclesiastical eschatology, or that part of theology that deals with end things like death, that told historians that there is a force that works the same way at all times. Such a view persuades historians that they can predict the future. For Collingwood, Hegel's dialectic is no different: what worked in the past will work in the future. Fukuyama falls into this illusion because he predicts that democracy is the end of history. He has not experienced the future and, thus, has no future period with which to compare to the present. Without this perspective, he cannot ask whether any change represents progress. His perspective from the present is bereft of knowledge about the future. The future is opaque, and history makes many unanticipated twists and turns that Fukuyama simply argues for or assumes.

Collingwood's third point drives to the heart of Fukuyama's thesis. It is that historians predicting any end to history, whether it is Hegel's freedom or Fukuyama's democracy, glorifies the present and denies progress. Democracy is popular today, so predicting it as the end of history means the end is not in the future but rather the present. This glorifies and idealizes the present and denies further progress is possible. This is an illusion many historians of the past have assumed about their own times.

His fourth point is that historical theories that endeavor to predict the future, whether it be Hegel's dialectic, Fukuyama's "democracy is the end of history" or cyclical theory's "ignore human will." Providence leaves nothing left for man to do. If determinism is true, then why bother trying because it is already determined? Collingwood assigns this charge again to the medieval view of history in which nations rise and fall in obedience to divine law that has little to do with the purposes of the human beings that compose them. He believed such ill-disposed theories that teach large-scale historical changes working objectively and shaping the historical process by a necessity that does not depend on the human will are wrong.

I believe history is cyclical. Certainly, there exists some progression in history — early democracy is better than monarchy, and trial by jury is better than confession by torture. However, today humans are not entirely free, communism has failed, the present is very much like the past and we see the same political corruption and wars. Even if a progressive history brings more human freedom, that freedom may not be in the form of democracy. Further, could it be that the very contentiousness found in democracy could be the origins of the dissolution and eventual barbarism that Vico presaged? More significantly, how can the limited human mind invent a political system that is good for everyone always?

To the regressive theory, I am of two minds. On one hand, it depressingly offers no hope for a better future. On the other, it does contain some truth. Indeed, the constant decay, conflict and dissolution within historic societies has been documented. Why should we expect any different outcome, even with the advent of democracy? In any case, and in opposition to Collingwood, I think a strong case can be made that history is cyclical. Cyclical history can be progressive and regressive, with societies incrementally improving and decaying, some things getting better and others worse, without an end. In many ways, cyclical history incorporates all theories, including those that are progressive and regressive, as well as Collingwood's views.

Collingwood's first point was that looking back gives no clues to the future. Alternatively, looking back may well offer some of the best clues about the future. The clues may not be definitive, but they are facts about what has happened. One of the facts we observe from the past is the continual rise and fall of societies, whether it be Greek, Roman or Ottoman. The past tells us that certain aspects of history are cyclical and many human constructs don't last. History tells us that things change. Certainly, looking to the past to predict the future may violate post hoc, ergo proptor hoc; we may wrongly assume from the past that certain consequences were caused by some prior event. However, if we observe from the past numerous similar consequences that have similar causes, we do have some grounds to connect the two. With this connection, a judgment that future similar causes may have similar consequences may be justified. It is also true that we cannot predict the future, including whether it is cyclical. It is, however a far bolder assertion that democracy is the end of history than that history is cyclical. Indeed, if we are to predict the future, the past would tell us that democracies usually fail and end in some form of dictatorship. There may be many reasons for this but I suspect one is because democracies evolve over time, which is a point Fukuyama fails to appreciate.

Collingwood's third point was that predicting an end like democracy glorifies the present and denies progress. Clearly, Fukuyama is glorifying present day popular democracy, and, with his assertion that it is the end of history, he is denying future progress as well as cyclical history. He is also evoking a circular argument where his conclusion is contained in his premises: that there is progress and democracy is the result of that progress presupposes history is progressive.

Collingwood's final point was that predicting the future ignores human will. David Hume famously made the point that reason is the slave of the passions. It may well be that history is the story of human passion, which historians wrongfully endeavor to organize rationally. There may be a universal, coherent history, as Fukuyama claims, but if it is based on passion, it may not result in the consequences Fukuyama desires. Indeed, a more likely consequence is repetition of the same — cyclical history allows for human will; there is still a lot to do, but what we do is the same as what we have always done.

Ockham's razor tells us to believe the simplest explanation — do not unnecessarily confuse things with unnecessary metaphysical speculation. In this case, the simplest explanation is that some things are getting progressively better, but human fallibility causes us to repeat the same fundamental mistakes, like war — which makes history cyclical.

The Lifecycle of Democracy

If history is cyclical, then democracy cannot be its end, as Fukuyama claims. Why is this? One reason could be that democracy is not the universal, timeless and unchanging end Fukuyama predicts but rather a political theory that naturally evolves and eventually dies. Like cyclical history, democracy goes through natural stages from beginning to end. Some characteristics are deemphasized, others emphasized and new elements added. It is just another part of the cycles of history. It just happens that democracy is popular today.

America's Founding Fathers would hardly recognize democracy in America two hundred years after its founding. It would be a very different kind of democracy from what they envisioned in 1787. They would be appalled at the size and power of centralized government, the extent of taxation and the institutionalized wealth redistribution laws. Clearly, the policies and very nature of democracy has changed in America. Historically, we see the evolution of ancient Greek democracy that ended with a Macedonian kingship, Roman republican "democracy" that ended with emperors and the bloody French Revolution democracy that ended with Napoleon. Certainly, there are many reasons for these failures of democracy, but one reason must be that it changes over time.

Some have understood this cycle of democracy. John Adams, as previously mentioned, wrote that democracy wastes, exhausts and murders itself and Friedrich Nietzsche proclaimed democracy heralds life in decline. Even educator and American Confederate General Robert E. Lee wrote in 1861 that America was doomed to run the full length of democracy. Other historic figures have not appreciated this evolution of democracy. Karl Popper, in *The Open Society and Its Enemies*, rightfully excoriated Plato's totalitarian *Republic* and championed democracy. However, he failed to appreciate that the characteristics of early democracy are in many ways similar to the characteristics of his dreaded *Republic* in late democracy. His early open democratic society includes freedom, individualism, egalitarianism and equal treatment under the law, and his closed totalitarian society has less freedom, is communal and collective and legally treats people unequally — all characteristics of late democracy. He fails to appreciate the evolution of democracy and what it naturally becomes when the people rule. Fukuyama himself, who claimed democracy is the end of history, wrote that no one regime could satisfy men completely, that democracy may not occupy a special place in history and that democracy has a tendency to give way to tyranny. There is a reason democracy cannot satisfy men completely; it is because the characteristics of democracy that appeal to many gradually erode as it ages.

Democracy evolves over time and becomes something entirely different. Let us examine some of its changing characteristics in what I term its early, mature and late stages. I use examples of American democracy often because it is well documented and has lasted over two hundred years.

FREEDOM

The overwhelming reasons for early democracy are the desires for freedom and the corresponding escape from oppression. Hegel believed all man's history was explained by his aspiration to be free. Tocqueville wrote in *The Old Regime and the French Revolution* that the urge for freedom animated the leaders of the French Revolution, and democracy was their method. George Bancroft wrote that democracy gives conscience absolute liberty. and Henry Ward Beecher said that the real democratic idea is that every one shall have liberty, without hindrance and to be what God made him. David McCullough, in *The Great Bridge*, wrote that John A. Roebling, the engineer, designer and builder of the Brooklyn Bridge, immigrated to America because there was less personal freedom and opportunity in bureaucratic Prussia. America with its democracy was where he could make the most of himself. Freedom is the primary reason for democracy and the central characteristic of early democracy. It is the principal reason people immigrated to early America; they had a greater say in government, government was more responsive and there were no despots. Democracy was freedom.

The ideal of freedom begins to erode in mature democracy. People gradually take it for granted—unaware of its fragility. They forget the sacrifices earlier generations endured to get it. The true ideal of freedom in democracy naturally succumbs to the enhanced ideal of equality and emerging desire for security. The enterprise succored by early democracy enables some to become wealthy which commences the eternal tension in society between rich and poor. The poor begin clamoring for wealth redistribution laws to meet need. The efforts to meet need rather than enhance production begin, and new kinds of political parties rise, demanding greater security for all. Such changes in democracy's mature stage causes increasing tension in society that requires the majority to superintend, hence the increasing hegemony of the majority.

In late democracy, freedom becomes security. Established wealth redistribution laws naturally create a dependent citizenry that thinks government-provided security is freedom. The real significance of the concept of freedom fades. Equality naturally emerges in democracy as the primary ideal that brings the security people demand. Indeed, Fukuyama wrote that democratic societies love equality more than freedom. Society, government and the media all come to focus on need because it satisfies the increasingly tyrannical monarchial majority. These sources commence a smothering ethic of conformity and political correctness. The result is that individual freedom succumbs in late democracy to heavy taxation, erosion of property rights and a larger more intrusive central government controlled by the majority, which increasingly acts with impunity.

EQUALITY

Tocqueville wrote in *The Old Regime and the French Revolution* that an animating reason for the French Revolution was the idea that all men are born equal — the revolutionaries wanted the abolition of class privileges, social castes and professional seniority. Feudal Europe consisted of a rigid institutionalized hierarchal class system that arbitrarily and hereditarily placed a few elite nobles, aristocracy and royalty above the mass of common people. It was an ancient system that offered no social mobility or opportunity. It was a patently unfair political system enforced by law that kept the mass of people literally enslaved. From such circumstances, revolutions are born and democracy is the beacon light solution.

For all such oppressed people of the world, early democracy offered an escape from their bondage. They were captivated with its core philosophy of equality and equal treatment under the law. Many of the historic forms of democracy, whether it be Athenian, Scandinavian, Italian, English or French, arose in part due to this human aspiration, but early American democracy, for the first time in history, embodied it. People immigrated to early democratic America because it was a place where they could be equal. This, however, was a political and social equality, not economic. Socialism had no a part of early democracy.

Early American democracy did achieve a state of proximate equality never before seen in history. It was one of democracy's greatest achievements. However, during its mature stage, equality commenced its ascendancy over freedom. The meaning of equality began changing and its new meaning drove certain divisive consequences. Equality began to be viewed as absolute rather than political and social equality. In this stage, the effort begins to create a leveling society by assuming an extremist form of equality. In mature American democracy, the passage of the Fourteenth Amendment in 1868, which concerned citizenship rights, and the Twenty-First Amendment in 1919, which granted women the right to vote, are examples. These amendments were good, but when taken to the extreme, they set laws that emerge in late democracy in motion that take away individual freedom, which is one of early democracy's great strengths.

Early democracy's ideal of freedom enabled people to succeed, usually under free market circumstances. Due to unequal abilities, some naturally succeeded more than others and got rich. In America, a new class of manufacturing elites thus began to appear, such as Henry Ford, Andrew Carnegie and John D. Rockefeller. Tocqueville and Fukuyama were right; the manufacturers become the new aristocracy in democracy. The result is disparity of wealth in early democracy and, collaterally, the beginning of socialism. Marx moved his socialist organization First International to New York in 1872, the Democratic Party took up the cause, the diminution of producers and business began and mature democracy commenced Friedrich Hayek's road to serfdom.

In late democracy, freedom becomes security. Established wealth redistribution laws naturally create a dependent citizenry that think government-provided security is freedom. The real significance of the concept of freedom fades. Equality naturally emerges in democracy as the primary ideal that brings the security people demand. Indeed, Fukuyama wrote that democratic societies love equality more than freedom. Society, government and the media all come to focus on need because it satisfies the increasingly tyrannical monarchial majority. These sources commence a smothering ethic of conformity and political correctness. The result is that individual freedom succumbs in late democracy to heavy taxation, affirmative action laws in America, erosion of property rights and a larger and more intrusive central government controlled by the majority that increasingly acts with impunity.

Under the aegis of the smothering need for equality, unequal treatment under the law emerges in late democracy. One fundamental requirement for legitimate law is equal treatment of all citizens. In order to achieve greater equality, the law begins to abandon this principle. In America, for example, affirmative action laws are promulgated that discriminate in race and gender. The Fourteenth Amendment, in this age, engenders anti-discrimination laws, and it becomes an age of "isms" — racist, sexist and ageist become pejorative terms applied to anyone who opposes absolute equality. In many late democracies, even the time-honored marriage between a man and woman comes under attack because people of the same sex are not allowed to marry. The "ism" in this case is homophobia.

The most significant emerging characteristic of late democracy occurs when equality is extended to property. It is a natural progression in democracy when equality prevails over freedom — all citizens are equally entitled to materialistic security. Thus, we see in late democracies the advent of socialism and progressive taxation, both of which treat citizens unequally under the law. Progressive taxation taxes two workers at different rates depending on how much they earn and not at the same rate. These are developments in late democracy never contemplated in early democracy. Under absolute equality, late democracy has taken matters from one extreme to the other. Tocqueville described one reason for the French Revolution was that the poor paid taxes and the privileged rich nobles were exempt; in late democracy the tables turn, and the privileged poor are exempt from taxation while the rich pay.

Democracy naturally succors socialism, which blooms in late democracy. Indeed, democracy comes to be defined as socialism. Late democratic governments establish redistribution of wealth programs that take from some and give to others. The focus in society changes from production to meeting need. Property rights necessarily become attenuated and taxes on a few soar. Democratic demagogic leaders gain power by representing the need constituency and intellectuals who push the socialistic agenda to sell books. Problematically for democracy, as Thomas Robert Malthus pointed out, the more need you feed the more you get. Democracy in this stage finds itself endlessly seeking a mirage it cannot grasp, the elimination of need, and in this Sisyphean process, it finds itself increasingly unable to succeed.

JUSTICE

Justice is another hallmark of early democracy that appeals to people. Democracy has a reputation of being just; indeed, American theologian Reinhold Niebuhr wrote that man's capacity for justice makes democracy possible, but man's inclination to injustice makes democracy necessary. Historically, democracy has offered an escape from institutionalized class, political and legal injustices.

Democracy's natural characteristics militate against injustice. They tend to resist injustice due to their cumbersome nature — they have an averaging effect that causes a kind of inertia that resists extremes. They resist oppression due to their very nature and usually have built-in limitations to centralized power. They often contain checks and balances, legislatures, constitutions and bills or rights that inhibit the concentration of power and extremist political and social philosophies. In order to do something, many people must be convinced, which is often hard to achieve. It is harder to persuade the majority of people than one king.

Compare the eighteenth-century French society described by Christopher Hibbert, in *The Days of the French Revolution*, with early democracy. Hibbert describes a society with a privileged class prior to the Revolution exempt from taxation and innumerable inequalities built into the law that resulted in a patently unjust society. Leveling early French democracy not only eliminated these historic injustices but collaterally mirrored most people's generally moderate political views. Early democracy offers oppressed people a haven from extremism and a place of justice.

Many, no doubt, will challenge this view because virtually all early democracies were to an extent unjust — they all excluded certain sects. Early American democracy, they point out, did not give slaves citizenship or women the right to vote. The response is that it was only under the aegis of democracy, with its ideals of freedom and equality, that slaves and women achieved citizenship and franchise — and with them, justice — before that they rarely had it. For them to vilify early democracy is like shooting the horse to kill the flea.

It is remarkable that democracies tend to stay, or endeavor to stay, just throughout their lifecycle. It is one of their great strengths. Even the injustices perpetuated by mature and late democracies are slight when compared to other political systems' injustices. However, injustice does creep into democracy as it ages.

Niebuhr's prophecy of justice in democracy begins a transformation in mature democracy with the emerging concept of social justice. The concept of justice begins to change, and with it many of the bulwarks against injustice built into early democracy begin to break down under majority rule. In mature American democracy, the checks and balances begin to erode, the Constitution is reinterpreted and amendments to the Constitution begin altering the intent of early democracy. Constitutions and bills of rights are hallmarks that in early democracy are intended to protect the minority and the individual liberty that comes under attack from the majority in mature democracy.

In mature democracy, positivistic law commences detaching law from morality. In American mature democracy, Oliver Wendell Holmes, Jr. declares that the law is what judges do. With this, John Locke's concept of a right begins to change, and the result is the legal diminution of freedom and injustice to some individuals.

PEACE

Early democracy tends to be peaceful, which is another of its great strengths and attractions. People faced with faction look for alternate political systems that offer the safety and security that democracy offers. Seneca's view that democracies are brutal may have been true in antiquity, but today most democratic nations are generally peaceful. However, this is a peace, as Fukuyama pointed out, between democracies. With alternate political systems, democracy can be quite brutal. One need only observe America's numerous wars with monarchists, Nazis, fascists, emperors, communists and Islamists. Internally, early democracy tends to mitigate divisive issues, achieve compromise and avoid excesses. People tend to conform to each other and the state. However, as democracy ages, internal strife increases.

In its mature stage, democracy naturally begins to experience internal strife. Due in part to the ideals of freedom and equality, issues arise that are settled politically or violently. In America's mature stage, women's right to vote and prohibition were settled politically, and the issue of slavery, violently, in the Civil War. The issues resolved early tend to be single issues that may be rendering but not fatal. As democracy ages, however, opposing issues naturally multiply that coalesce sects into polarities, which become increasingly difficult to adjudicate.

INDIVIDUALISM

A hallmark of early democracy is individualism, and in early American democracy there is no greater example than famous writer and lecturer Ralph Waldo Emerson. His essay *Self-Reliance* represented the sentiments of his time that inveighed against the collective coercive group that demands conformity and thinks they know better than individuals. He wrote that the group draws out individuals' sinews and hearts and reduces them to timorous despondent whimperers afraid of fortune, death and each other. Emerson admonished his fellow Americans to keep with perfect sweetness independence of solitude and self-reliance.

Perhaps the ethic of individualism derives from ancient philosophers, like the cynic Diogenes, whose first principle was self-sufficiency because the ability to possess within oneself all one needs brings happiness. The essence and purpose of individuality is to bring human happiness. Like Emerson and Diogenes, American Founding Father Thomas Jefferson also advocated the energetic, willful, independent, can-do, self-reliant individual.

Early democracy offers individuals freedom from smothering collectivism, totalitarian conformity and arrogant public opinion. It embodies the idea that power ultimately resides in individuals, which has the effect of empowering people. Under it, people can reach their human potentials and hone their talents unencumbered by what others think they ought to do. The epitome of early democracy is the American rugged, can-do, self-reliant individual. Indeed, Henry David Thoreau, during early American democracy, wrote (verbatim) that public opinion is a weak tyrant compared with our own private opinion — what man thinks of himself, that is what determines his fate.

It could well be that it was this individualistic philosophy of early democracy that propelled many famous people to their unique philosophies. Feminist French writer Simone de Beauvoir was a rugged individualist who championed women's rights by advising them to either find a way or make one. Individualism is an eternal desire in the human breast — to be free and unencumbered, away from collective hegemony.

In mature democracy, individualism increasingly looks like famous sociobiologist E. O. Wilson's ants. Wilson described the biological hierarchical progression of individuality from primitive jellyfish, which are perfectly collective (if one dies they all die) to ants (with a queen and some solider individuals) to humans at the pinnacle, with the greatest degree of individual freedom. Democracy reverses this trend under majority rule—most people think they know better than the individual.

In late-stage democracy, the trend is for the early democratic individualistic man to return to a jellyfish. Under the mantra of equality, the averaging majority transforms the individual in early democracy back to the collective serf of the medieval ages. The individualistic characteristic of megalothymia has not been mollified, and *thymos* has not been fulfilled, as Fukuyama claims, but rather they have been suppressed by the tyrannical majority. The majority's averaging collective excessive demands have diminished merit and enterprise, and the result is a reduced, marginalized, collectivized human jellyfish. Democracy has changed Emerson's ethic of individualistic self-reliance into collectivistic other-reliance. Conformity becomes the rule, and rugged individualism, the anathema.

One could argue that there are numerous other characteristics of democracy that change from early to late democracy, which attests to its cyclical nature. Early democracies tend to be meritocracies in which ethic fades due to democracy's emphasis on equality. The size, scope and power of the government tends to grow as intellectuals increasingly view government as the solution to all human problems. Jurisprudence changes, with a shift from natural law based on morality in early democracy to free-floating positivistic law. Along with this, the nature of rights changes, and rights' original purpose and value diminishes. Philosophically, morality gradually changes under democracy from early ethical theories that emphasize virtue, duty and contractual agreements to utility. Morality increasingly emphasizes the consequences that bring happiness to the most and, in the process, begins to impart injustice to the individual. In both early French Revolutionary and American democracies, the majority increasingly became intolerant of opposing views.

This intolerance brings a certain zeal that results in inflexibility, hostility and a resulting divisiveness. Divisiveness itself increases as democracies age. Fractionalization gradually coalesces in sects inflamed by demagogues and political parties that are endemic in late democracies. Finally, power corrupts, and when a majority maintains power over the minority in democracy for too long a period, it becomes increasingly controlling, eventually despotic and ultimately illegitimate, which in late democracy brings the very philosophy of rule by the majority into question.

Democracies naturally change over time into something they are not. They become a thing unlike the early democracy people longed for.

Conclusion

Theodore Roosevelt said a democracy must be progressive or it will cease to be a great democracy, but, like Fukuyama, he does not appreciate the lifecycle of democracy. Roosevelt believed he must improve on early democracy in order to make it great. Could it be that the "improvements" he had in mind are the vehicles that ultimately bring democracy's demise? Further, how did Roosevelt define democracy? A "grand democracy" is one of those vague and unfixed ideas described earlier by Richard M. Weaver that endeavors to define adulterated late democracy because early democracy has changed and lost its charisma. Could it be that Roosevelt's late "great democracy" is English essayist and novelist G. K. Chesterton's despotism that defines a tired democracy? Fukuyama's thesis that democracy is the end of history did not account for the Roosevelts of this world, the cycles of history or the lifecycle of democracy.

One could rightfully ask: if late democracy is so bad, why are democracies so popular today in which many historically oppressed sects, like women and minorities, enjoy unprecedented freedom and equality? Democracy is popular today, but so have been popes and kings — just because it is popular does not mean it will endure. This chapter has argued that democracy simply has not completed its natural lifecycle — we are living in democracy's heyday. The reality that women and minorities thrive under democracy is testimony to one of its greatest strengths. However, these are the strengths of early democracy, and their successes are derived from that period's ideals. As these ideals change and some fade with mature and late democracy, so could democracy's fortunes.

History is cyclical — democracy has a natural lifecycle, and it ultimately fails. Many of the reasons it fails have been alluded to earlier by historic figures and in this chapter on its lifecycle. It is now time to explain why it fails.

SECTION III

The Reasons Democracy Fails

INTRODUCTION

So far this book has examined the political concept of democracy. It was defined, its history explored, the arguments for and against it weighed, Francis Fukuyama's claim that it is the end of history evaluated and how democracy fits into historic cycles assessed. The information in these chapters coalesces a point of view, which is that democracy is just one of many flawed political systems that ultimately fail. Indeed, it is fanciful to believe any one mortal could craft a political system that satisfies all people. There are just too many variables. People differ in emotions, ideals, ability, character, beliefs and effort. When they are mixed to make a society, it results in a rainbow of structures all operating in a world of scarcity. How could democracy possibly accommodate everyone? The controversial answer is that it cannot.

But democracy defeated Nazi Germany, fascist Italy and the communist Soviet Union. Contemporarily, some claim that democracy will never replace radical Islam. Islamic religious fundamentalism will never tolerate an abstract secular non-religious political system like democracy that divorces religion from government. It will never tolerate universal suffrage that includes women or democracy's failure to recognize historic religious legal rules. This is the claim, and the violent events in the early twenty-first century between Western culture and Islamic states are examples. But democracy's ideals are too powerful to succumb to religion. Its timeless ideals of freedom, equality and justice have more appeal than religious fundamentalism. Osama bin Laden's organization Al Qaeda attacked America by flying passenger jets into the World Trade Center in New York on September 11, 2001, and America and her democratic allies responded vigorously. Now bin Laden is dead, his organization is in shambles and the Freedom Tower now stands 408 feet higher than the buildings Al Qaeda destroyed. American democracy is alive and well from external threat. The democratic West has largely subdued the Islamic Middle East. It has invaded Iraq and, with powerful Arab allies like Turkey and Saudi Arabia, literally surrounded and isolated the fundamentalist Islamic state of Iran. It seems that worldwide, democracy is doing just fine against radical Islam.

But these conflicts have been between democracy and non-democracies. Democracies are resistant to external forces, but this does not account for their internal deficiencies. To reiterate questions in the introduction of this book, could it be that democracy carries the seeds of its own destruction? Do democracies naturally fail from within? Could it be that the great irony of democracy is that the very positive characteristics that appeal to people are what bring its ultimate demise? George Bernard Shaw, for example, once wrote the truism that liberty, a cornerstone of democracy, means responsibility, but as individuals gain more freedom under democracy, many are incapable of shouldering the responsibility that entails freedom. The second half of this book is about these internal threats to democracy and why it ultimately fails from within.

100

Chapter Six

LOSS OF FREEDOM

It is indeed strange to contemplate that democracy's central attraction is one of the very reasons it does not endure. Liberty is democracy's beacon—its shining light to the world. The Statue of Liberty is the symbol of freedom in American democracy to which oppressed immigrants aspired. Eucleides, the fifth-century BCE Athenian archon, promoted democracy precisely because he believed it brought freedom. He challenged the reigning oligarchic power of his time in order to achieve this democratic ideal. Aristotle in his *Politics* wrote that the underlying principle of democracy is freedom, since only in a democracy can the citizens have a share in freedom. He believed every democracy should make liberty its aim. United States Supreme Court Chief Justice Charles Evans Hughes believed that democracy's vital breath is individual liberty.

But other historic thinkers like Alexis de Tocqueville were concerned about the interplay between democracy and freedom. He believed democracy could range from liberty to tyranny. Harvard philosopher Robert Nozick believed democracy was incompatible with libertarianism. In democracy he explained that everybody decides about everyone else, and decision makers are created for blocks of people with one vote, which results in a kind of ownership of the people, by the people and for the people. For Nozick, this is chaos, which makes the modern democratic state ant-libertarian and opposed to freedom. Democracy naturally segues into a political system that eventually takes individual freedom. Let me explain the reasons why.

It should first be mentioned that there is no perfect freedom due to the exigencies of nature; nature does not offer freedom. The concept of freedom is rather a continuum from more to less restriction of activity. At one end of the continuum is the anarchist, and the other, the collectivist. In between are thinkers like Jean Paul Sartre who believed freedom lies in the duty of self-determination and freedom of choice. For Sartre, the anarchist's attempt to deny responsibility is not freedom. Others, like anarchist Mikhail Bakunin, believe that goodness lies in freedom, which the law restricts. It is the law that makes us unfree.

To a surprising extend, Bakunin is right. Historically, humans have been subjects with no freedom. But Bakunin did not understand early democracy and its ability to deliver unprecedented human freedom. Unfortunately, the nature of this early freedom changes as democracy ages. As the ideals of democracy vie for supremacy, freedom gradually loses its true meaning and fades. True freedom entails maximum choice, responsibility and the freedom to fail — freedom can be dangerous. Aspirants for early democracy understood this equation, and those who live in late democracy do not.

Freedom and Equality

A fundamental reason democracy fails is due to the irreconcilability of freedom and equality. They are two contradictory ideals at war with each other that play out as democracy ages. Both Tocqueville and Francis Fukuyama understood the problem. Tocqueville wrote that it was both freedom and equality that animated the passions that resulted in the French Revolution. People believed they could reconcile the two with democracy; however, as the Revolution evolved, freedom lost its appeal and a dictatorship ensued. Fukuyama wrote that the principles of liberty and equality are in perpetual tension in democracy. Equality cannot be maximized without the intervention of a powerful state that limits individual liberty, and liberty cannot be expanded indefinitely without social inequality. He believed that freedom precedes equality in stable democracies but failed to appreciate how this precedence reverses as democracies age. It becomes a trade-off between the two in which the equality-preferring majority capriciously begins limiting freedom by sophistically dictating what constitutes freedom. They become the arbiters of freedom of association and discrimination, and the consequence is loss of freedom for many. My view is that freedom trumps equality.

Freedom and Security

Few would disagree that survival is a fundamental human instinct, and to achieve it, one must first escape danger and then seek a place of safety. Analogously, oppressed people in danger are naturally attracted to democracy's freedom but once this freedom is achieved, security inevitably becomes the next step. In this way, democracy's siren call of freedom inevitably flounders on the rocks of security. Freedom in early democracy becomes redefined as security in late democracy and freedom incrementally erodes.

In democracy, the battleground of this contest is property. The great French nineteenth-century thinker Frédéric Bastiat believed the social weal meant liberty and property. For him, property is liberty — the freedom to own something as you wish, unencumbered. He is right but failed to appreciate that when freedom becomes security in democracy, it begins to conflict with property. The result is the incremental loss of the right to own and use property in a democracy, which manifests in innumerable ways. The state takes it by taxation through a menagerie of laws that redistribute wealth and mandate how people or commercial enterprises spend their money and by limiting the use of property through regulations without compensation. Whatever the way, the ultimate result is the loss of some freedom due to democracy's emphasis on security.

In this battleground over property, the front line becomes money. Because people think of money as fungible with property, they come to view it as the source of freedom that becomes security in democracy. James Buchan, in *Frozen Desire*, described it as money becoming coined liberty. Money is frozen desire, and its possession increasingly satisfies desires, including freedom. Hence late democratic government's efforts to increase the availability of money by grant, direct payment, mandate, increasing its circulation by printing more currency, devaluing currency or manipulating financial institutions.

Thus arises what I call Bastiat's great ambiguity in democracy: it seeks liberty but denies it due to its diminution of property. Freedom becomes security, which diminishes some freedoms. The very concept of freedom necessarily changes wherein individual freedom gives way to a free-floating oxymoron concept of "collective freedom." Benjamin Franklin was right when he wrote that those who would give up liberty for security deserve neither.

Loss of Freedom Due to Unpredictability

Richard M. Weaver, in *The Ethics of Rhetoric*, wrote that man is free to the extent that his surroundings have a determinate nature, so he can predict and plan for the future. We create rules in order to have freedom because one is not free without rules in a state of nature. Freedom moves on a set of presuppositions, and when they are tampered with, men become concerned about losing their freedom. Indeed, many cries for liberty are really cries for unity and order, which rules embody.

Due to the capriciousness of the majority, the future in late democracies is often less determinate. The all-powerful majority constantly changes the rules of society to suit its preferences. This occurs in many venues, such as ethics, property and rights. As the consistency of rules erodes, the legality of how one ought to act today in order to be legal tomorrow increasingly becomes problematic. It is strange and counterintuitive indeed to contemplate that under this definition of freedom one may have more freedom in an autocratic, predictable society than in a democracy.

In late American democracy, two manifestations of this way of losing freedom can be seen in taxation and law. Many tax laws change every time a new political party comes to power. Citizens are left wondering what the income, capital gains tax and inheritance tax will be, which makes the future uncertain. As jurisprudence increasingly embraces positivistic law, courts begin relying less on precedent and more on a judge's view of "all things considered." This becomes particularly problematic when non-originalist judges begin reinterpreting the Constitution because the supreme law of the land becomes increasing unpredictable.

Tyranny of the Majority

The villain driving this loss of freedom is Tocqueville's tyrannical majority. It is the majority in a democracy that is the tyrant, imperiously dictating to others. What is so special about this majority? Why is it granted these dictatorial powers in democracy? Why is a collective tyrant any different than one tyrant? How does the majority make better decisions than other political leaders? What makes two out of three smarter, more capable and more authoritative than one? The answer is that the majority is not special; it is no different than any other tyrant, it makes no better decisions and two is not better than one. Many historic thinkers have voiced these opinions in their scorn of the majority.

Tocqueville, the leading critic, exclaimed that the ability of the majority to tyrannize and oppress the minority was no less than the French monarch's ability to do the same. Indeed, it was even worse, because with a king there is at least someone to blame. He explained that the moral power of the majority is founded upon the principle that the interests of the many are to be preferred to those of the few, which makes the majority's views unassailable. If the majority in a democracy, he asked, is viewed as an individual whose interests are opposed to another individual who possesses greater tyrannical power and is treated unjustly, why cannot the majority be liable to the same reproach as the individual with greater tyrannical power?

The ancient Roman Stoic philosopher Cicero was particularly critical of the majority. He pointed out the stupidity of scorning individuals but at the same time thinking they amount to something when taken as a group. He asked how anything could be more foolish than to suppose that those who individually one despises, such as illiterate mechanics, are worth anything collectively? French novelists Stendhal and Honoré de Balzac also despised the majority, Stendhal by deriding the tyranny of public opinion, and Balzac by disclaiming government by the masses is the only irresponsible form of government in which tyranny is unlimited.

Historic English thinkers were no less critical. Edmund Burke described the tyranny of the multitude is a multiplied tyranny and criticized majority rule because the minority is not in agreement with the social contract—a significant point that will be expanded upon in chapter ten on relative morality. Oscar Wilde wrote that democracy is none other than the bludgeoning of the people, by the people, for the people. Thomas Carlyle attacked democracy as an absurd social ideal and asked how truth could possibly be discovered by totting up votes. He believed government should come from those most able.

Perhaps the most able historic critic of majority rule is John Locke. His view, which was described earlier in the characteristics of late democracy, is that democracy loses legitimacy when the majority becomes a tyrant. Ultimately, the legitimacy of all governments rests on the consent of the governed, and when that government loses this consent, it becomes illegitimate. In this case it is the majority's infringement on the minority's freedom that causes the minority to declare the government illegitimate. It was Locke who inspired Thomas Jefferson to write in the American Declaration of Independence that it is the right of the people to abolish a government that abridges the right of liberty.

THE MAJORITY, EQUALITY AND SECURITY

In this chapter the contest between freedom, equality and security has been described. The significance of rule by majority is that the majority decides which of these ideals prevail. If more people are unequal and insecure in democracy, the ideals of equality and security will overarch freedom. In the case of equality, Tocqueville believed that the ideal of equality would eventually prevail in democracy under the aegis of the tyrannical majority that endangers freedom for many.

In respect to security, a central concern of those critical of democracy has been that it caters to the poor who will rob the rich. This is a fair assessment because in all advanced democracies there exists extensive wealth redistribution programs brought about by majority rule. Under the aegis of the poor majority in democracy, security becomes the ascendant ideal to which government, policies and the laws bend to accommodate. But this initiates a new historic contest, which is what constitutes freedom. Under late democracy, this question becomes whether it is equality or security, and the definition of true freedom becomes lost.

Ultimately, the issue is not so much whether this is true, but rather what happens to democracy when it happens. Many consider this alteration in the definition of freedom a great leveling strength of democracy and herald its rare historic appearance. What they fail to appreciate is the influence this new democratic philosophy has on freedom. Could it be that the majority poor becomes the tyrant under democracy? What happens to the true definition of freedom? Most importantly, could democracy lose its legitimacy with this altered concept of freedom?

THE TYRANNICAL MAJORITY AND THE RING OF GYGES

The consequence of the majority enforcing equality and security over freedom in democracy is oppression for those not in the majority, such as minorities and individuals. Burke wrote that (paraphrased) in a democracy, the majority of citizens is capable of exercising the most cruel oppressions upon the minority, and those who are subjected to wrong under multitudes are deprived of all external consolation; they seem deserted by mankind, overpowered by a conspiracy of their whole species. Wickedly and silently, oppression by the majority in democracy becomes institutionalized and, for many, normal. For the first time in history, a silent majority is able to exercise its cruel oppression with impunity under the veil of legal legitimacy.

The majority in democracy is analogous to Plato's mythical magical artifact the Ring of Gyges described in Book Two of his *Republic*. It is a ring that granted its owner the power to become invisible at will and, thus, the ability to act with impunity. With it, a person, or in this case the majority, has no fear of being caught or punished for injustices. Plato posited the ring in order to ask whether an intelligent person would be moral if they could act with impunity. Can a man remain virtuous when he can act without being discovered?

Plato's response through Socrates is true as far as it goes. He argues that the man who abuses the power of the Ring enslaves himself to his appetites, while the man who chooses not to use the Ring remains rationally in control of himself and, therefore, happy. But the majority in a democracy is different than a single man because the majority, unlike the single individual, truly has a Ring of Gyges and can act with impunity. Who in a majority is to blame? Who is accountable? Who does one accuse for bad decisions? The majority turns out to be an amorphous Wittgensteinian word used for a mysterious entity that cannot be held accountable for its actions. Unlike Plato's answer for the individual, it turns out that the majority is not the same as an individual.

Glaucon, Plato and history's eternal dupe actually gives the better explanation in this case. His essential point in response to Plato's idealistic philosophy is that morality is just social convention. He asks Plato, what if there were two such magic rings that could be put on both the just and unjust man? No man would be able to keep his hands off what he could safely take away, whether it be to steal in the market, lie with his neighbor's wife or kill enemies. With this, the just and unjust actions would be the same — it is not for the sake of justice he acts but rather what he thinks is good for him individually. All men in their hearts believe injustice is more profitable to them than justice — if they could act undetected. In anonymity, they remain irrationally happy.

Glaucon is unwittingly describing what happens to people when they vote under secret ballot in a democracy. They can act with impunity, there are no consequences to them, they vote out of necessity, they vote for what is good for them and, most importantly, they willingly vote unjustly if they think it is in their interests. These voters face no guilt, are unaccountable and it is they who are the tyrannical majority in democracy that establish oppressive policies. The profound consequence of this is the loss of freedom for many.

Consider one fictional yet probable parable that illustrates this point. A farmer is more industrious than his neighbors. He grows more crops and consequently lives a better life. The neighbors passionately believe he should not have more than them, so they form a democracy. The majority decides to tax the farmer's surplus and distribute it to everyone. The farmer is naturally incensed. The majority has treated the farmer unjustly, it has acted unilaterally and tyrannically because the farmer has no say, it has acted with impunity, the farmer has lost the freedom to keep the fruits of his labors and the majority has demonstrated Tocqueville's assertion and Glaucon's point that the blind, unchecked passions of majority classes provide no guarantee of liberty in democracy. It is not the corporations or wealthy people that Fukuyama fears will take freedom in democracy but rather the juggernaut poor majority.

Collectivism

Collectivism is a philosophic theory that emphasizes the interdependence of human beings. It stresses the priority of the group and the importance of cohesion within social groups. It is a philosophy that stresses altruism and cooperation over competition and individuality. It is a natural voluntary human instinct, particularly in families and small, closely knit communities. Literally, we would not be here without some collective instinct. Paternalistic fathers and maternalistic mothers selflessly raise us in collective environments. The problem occurs when these instinctual associations are expanded to other relationships. In particular, their significance can become corrupted when applied to large associations, such as nations. When collectivism is writ large, it becomes susceptible to totalitarianism, where it becomes mandatory rather than voluntary. Many extremist collectivist nations that embrace it also enforce it, such as totalitarian socialistic or communistic regimes.

Early democracies, with their emphasis on freedom, are less collectivistic. They often appeal to those escaping oppressive totalitarian collectivized societies who are seeking freedom and opportunity. However, as democracy advances, the ethic of collectivism naturally advances with it because the philosophies of democracy and collectivism are innately related. As the ideals of equality and security gradually supplant freedom, democracy naturally embraces collectivism and the view that we are all in it together. In democracy, rule by the people stresses the importance of the group and particularly the majority that militates against nonconformist individualistic sects or tendencies and increasingly succors the common good. It is the collective majority from which ultimate power originates, not individuals. It is only natural that democracy emphasizes the interdependence of all humans and collaterally eschews that which does not. Democracies are by their natures collectivistic. It is surprisingly counterintuitive to contemplate that, in this respect, democracy is like an authoritarian dictatorship.

Perhaps the best example of this metamorphosis in democracy comes from the famous nineteenth-century American author Ralph Waldo Emerson. Emerson was a product of early American democracy, which he extolled, but lived in its maturing stage, which he eschewed. He wrote (part verbatim and part paraphrased) about the centuries that have conspired against the sanity and authority of the soul and the coercive collective group that thinks it knows what is a man's duty better than he knows. Emerson wrote to not tell him of his obligations to put all poor men in good situations and objected to a collective society that draws out the sinew and heart of men who become timorous, despondent whimperers afraid of fortune, death, and each other. It is Emerson who wrote that it is easy in the world to live after the world's opinion but the great man is he who, in the midst of the crowd, keeps with perfect sweetness the independence of solitude. He believed society in his time was everywhere in conspiracy against the manhood of every one of its members and the virtue in most request was conformity rather than self-reliance. Emerson was objecting to the rising tide of collectivism in mature American democracy. Naturally, the legacy of Emerson as a leading American scholar and thinker extolling early democracy is fading as American democracy ages.

The point of this is that evolving collectivism in democracy takes freedom. Under collectivism the individual is subjugated to the group, the individual's goals are valued insofar as they serve the group and the result is loss of individual freedom. This exposes one of the great ironies of democracy: it promises freedom but naturally take it with its proclivity toward collectivism. It gives the illusion of independence, freedom and the ability to control ones destiny, but as it ages, the majority increasingly thwarts these aspirations under smothering collectivism. It was Friedrich Hayek who prophesied that (paraphrased) when democracy becomes dominated by a collectivist creed, it will eventually destroy itself.

Some wrongfully think collectivism represents a higher form of evolution. The view is that in crude nature, life is brutal, selfish and competitive, which collective cooperation ameliorates. With it, progressives believe we become peaceful, altruistic, cooperative and civilized. Famous Harvard professor of biology E. O. Wilson, in Sociobiology, explained why this is wishful thinking. He explained that in evolution the lowest species, such as the colonial invertebrates like coral and jellyfish, are highly interdependent and perfectly collective, with each being dependent on the other for existence. If one dies, they all die. Moving up the evolutionary ladder, social insects' behavior, such as ants, becomes less collective and more varied, and struggles occur, such as between queens and workers for the opportunity to reproduce. Higher on the evolutionary ladder in vertebrate societies, selfishness increases and acts of altruism are less frequent, group membership is not mandatory and cooperation becomes more like concession. In baboon troops, for example, life is often tense and brutal where the sick are left to die. Human beings have attained the highest form of vertebrate evolutionary society, which includes some cooperation but favors the individual at the expense of social integrity. Wilson's point is that collectivism is a recidivist characteristic.

This would seem an intuitively natural process. As humans gain consciousness of their own being and more awareness of the world around them and the limitations of nature, it gradually dawns on them that they are more than just ants in a colony. They begin to question the authority of princes, popes and kings. They desire to be free individuals unleashed from their collectivistic tether in order to be all they can be— to reach their unique individual potentials. This is precisely the attraction of early democracy that becomes adulterated in late democracy under the progressive collectivist banner.

Conclusion

Fukuyama claimed that Hegel's historic dialectic driven by mankind's desire for freedom culminates in democracy. Democracy's form of freedom is the synthesis of this historic drive and, thus, the end of history. Unfortunately, democracy does not bring the freedom Fukuyama envisions, and his dialectic thus fails. Democracy does not bring freedom because equality, security and collectivism supplant it. Indeed, the very definition of what constitutes freedom becomes adulterated in democracies. Contrariwise, it turns out that rule by an unaccountable majority that takes minorities and individual freedoms is the Achilles heel of democracy.

Chapter Seven

INEQUALITY

Equality, like freedom, is one of democracy's great attractions. It could be said that the history of humankind is one of abject political, economic and hereditary inequality. Democracy changes this equation with its ideal of general equality, equal treatment under the law and aspiration for equal opportunity. But it is an ideal that had drawn considerable criticism. Edmund Burke wrote that all men have equal rights but not equal rights to things, and one of government's purposes is to restrain the passions of citizens who unreasonably aspire to the things to which they are not entitled. John Adams viewed the radical pursuit of equality as a chimera and asserted that perfect equality shall never long exist between any two mortals. Thomas Carlyle believed the assumption of equality would not set a society aright, and under its aegis, democratic elections would only produce selfishness, ambition and partisanship. As mentioned in the

115

chapter on criticisms of democracy, both Burke and Carlyle believed equality is an idea at war with nature. Philosopher Herbert Spencer opposed equality because it involved jealousy, did not bring happiness to all and did not benefit society as a whole. Early American thinker William James wrote that democracy reduces things to twos, which implies that democracies do not necessarily bring equal ones, or unity, but rather potentially unequal twos.

There is some truth and falsity in these criticisms of equality, but two potentially fatal faults seem unassailable. Equality is an ideal that conflicts with freedom and is incompatible with nature.

Freedom and Equality Conflict

Freedom does not lead to equality; indeed, it could be said the two are opposites. True freedom brings inequality and equality limits freedom. You cannot have both because they end in different circumstances. Freedom means individuals are free to be better, to use their talents and rise and to be what they want to be, whether it is famous, rich or powerful. This is the nature of freedom. Certainly, true freedom entails limits, but this applies to one's freedom to harm another. We are free to swing our fists until they meet another's face.

Francis Fukuyama himself admitted that inequality will exist in liberal democratic societies due to equality's continuous tension with freedom, which is a tacit admission that democracy, which Fukuyama believes is the end of history, does not necessarily bring equality. Indeed, Alexis de Tocqueville described this continuous tension in democracy as necessary and ineradicable. The great irony of democracy, as Fukuyama discerned, is that freedom does not lead to equality, and one of its greatest challenges is how to reconcile the two. My assertion is that it does not.

Nature and Equality Conflict

Nature also does not offer equality, because her gifts are conditional—she gives and takes at the same time. Samuel Johnson famously wrote that (verbatim) no man can, at the same time, fill his cup from the source and from the mouth of the Nile. Samuel Johnson's points are that nature does not fulfill our desires—as we satisfy one desire, another inexorably arises—and we cannot have everything our way. His conclusion is that we should be content with the blessings nature has bestowed upon us.

The ideal of equality is like this: nature does not offer equality even though we desire it, as equality ascends, freedom recedes and there is no perfect equality, so we should be content with what nature gives us. We all know humans are not equal—some are just smarter, stronger and better looking, but nature gave us strengths and weaknesses that often compensate for the inequality nature dispensed. One may run faster, but another is smarter—each of which has unique benefits. Equality becomes problematic for democracy when it is taken to excess—when strengths and weaknesses give way to unconditional equality. With this certain inevitable counter forces emerge—the point Johnson so eloquently described. As strange as this may sound, democracy's demand for equality can only be achieved through inequality—to make everyone equal, some must be treated unequally. This point, along with its manifestations, has been the source of many historic thinkers' criticisms of democracy.

Equality and Power

Democracy endeavors to reconcile a milieu of contradictions: equality and nature, naturally unequal humans, the endowed and unendowed, as well as the eternal war between rich and poor. Early democracy's solution is to allow for strengths and weaknesses under political and social equality—everyone has a vote and nobody is socially superior to another. These solutions work initially, but as political and social equality prevail, some begin desiring to be more than equal. The reason is that humans' desire for equality occurs largely between equals and those slightly superior. Few aspire to be equal to the king, and nobody wants to be equal to the peasant. In the former case they have little chance of achieving equality, which makes the pursuit of equality in reality the pursuit of gain — one has more chance of gain from an equal than from a king. In the latter case, nobody aspires to equality because there is more to lose. Thus, as people become more equal in early democracy, the desire for equality imperceptibly transforms, as Johnson again predicted as desire that becomes competitive in its pursuit of power.

In a vastly unequal society, to use Fukuyama's terms, the masters desire power to maintain their position. Thus, we read about early American Gouverneur Morris, who loved freedom and hated equality. In the same unequal society, we read of the slaves ardently invoking the ideal of equality. As the ideal of equality ascends in democracy, the former masters pursue power to regain their former positions, and the former slaves pursue power in the form of ideologies, such as Marxist socialism, in order to attain economic equality. Ultimately, equality satisfies nobody. It never satisfies the masters or slaves; it only results in the desire for power in both cases, and the ideal of freedom, which was democracy's premier initial attraction, is completely lost in the shuffle. Like communism, democracy evolves into something completely at odds with nature due to its tendency to overemphasize equality. It turns out that Fukuyama's megalothymia that infects the former masters is contagious as democracy evolves.

Political and Perfect Equality

Political equality is one of democracy's great attractions. It is a condition in which autonomous individuals have equal rights and opportunities. In it, the state grants equal citizenship to all members who have equal authority to vote on the laws and policies of that state. It entails certain rights, such as the right to vote, contest elections and criticize the government. It allows all citizens the right to participate in the affairs of the state. Ideally, everyone is treated equally under the law.

Absolute equality is different. It is equality in all aspects, not only under the law but also socially and economically. Individuality and merit are deemphasized, and wealth redistribution policies intended to bring greater economic equality are stressed. Absolute equality brings a veritable plethora of contradictions. For example, laws based on all things equal necessarily treat citizens unequally. The subtle transition from political to absolute equality in democracy is one source of inequality in late democracy. It is a reason for democracy's failure as a political system.

The trend to absolute equality in democracy is the reason for many of its criticisms. Aristotle, in Politics, wrote that democracy's emphasis on equality leads citizens to think that all men are equal in all things. He believed that democracy arose from men's thinking that if they are equal in any respect, they are equal absolutely. He pointed out that it is this kind of desire for equality that causes revolutions. Plato, in the Republic, wrote (paraphrased) that democracy, which is a charming form of government, full of variety and disorder, dispenses a sort of equality to equals and unequals alike. Tocqueville wrote of democratic despotism championed by the French economists before the French Revolution. They advocated abolishing all hierarchies, all class distinctions, and all differences of rank—and a nation composed of individuals almost exactly alike and unconditionally equal. Finally, French philosopher Victor Cousin wrote that (verbatim) all men have an equal right to the free development of their faculties; they have an equal right to the impartial protection of the state; but it is not true, it is against all the laws of reason and equity, it is against the eternal nature of things, that the indolent man and the laborious man, the spendthrift and the economist, the imprudent and the wise, should obtain and enjoy an equal amount of goods.

It is understandable that the majority in a democracy desires absolute equality because those in it stand to gain. However, in order to adopt such a belief, one must dismiss nature, avoid reason and invest belief in an abstract utopia. This point resurrects one of the historic arguments against democracy, which is that it is an abstract political philosophy that ignores nature. In chapter three, I dismissed this as a serious threat to democracy—but on the condition that if a political system's abstractness strays too far from nature, it loses touch with reality and runs the risk of failure. Clearly, absolute equality takes democracy to that unrealistic unnatural end. Equality is an objective and not an absolute—it is used as a standard to determine how unequal we are. Humans intuitively understand this, and the most successful democracies nod to individual strengths within a framework of political equality.

The desire for absolute equality can superficially be explained by the desire for gain, survival, Fukuyama's *thymos* and perhaps even megalothymia. But these do not explain the complete disregard of reason, which leads to the conclusion that its true cause is emotional thinking and envy. The desire is not rational but rather emotional—it is, as Georg Wilhelm Friedrich Hegel pointed out, a desire that derives not from the demands of universality but rather arbitrary inclinations and opinions. Much will be said of this flaw in democracy in chapter ten on relative morality.

Envy is a touchy emotion few wish to admit experiencing. It is the human inclination to want what another has. But it is real, and democracy inflames it with its emphasis on equality. Edmund Burke wrote that envy in democracy is just the desire for some people to bring superiors down to their level. Perhaps on a deeper level, it is the slave morality Friedrich Nietzsche described that drives envy. Nietzsche, in *On the*

Genealogy of Morals, described an aesthetic ideal where the historically subjugated less able slaves express their anger and revenge against their able oppressors and punish them under the religious banner of Christianity. It is a slave morality derived from envy that glorifies weakness, emotion, religion and compassion. For Fukuyama, it is the slaves' desire for recognition that caused them to rebel in the French Revolution under the aegis of secularized Christianity, and the result has been liberal democracy. True or not, democracy inflames envy under the banner of equality.

The Consequences of Perfect Equality

The cost of perfect equality's siren is high. Because the consequences were discussed elsewhere in this book, only a few will be mentioned here as they relate to perfect equality. The first is the diminution of individuality at the altar of collectivism. There can be no individuality under perfect equality because everyone is unconditionally equal — everyone becomes ants in an ant colony. Henry David Thoreau wrote that (verbatim) there will never be a free and enlightened State until the State comes to recognize the individual as a higher and independent power, from which all its own power and authority are derived, and treats him accordingly. In many ways, the very health of any society or state depends on individuals and not the masses. Certainly, this is not an either-or issue; healthy societies are both collectivistic and individualistic. However, democracy's tendency for perfect equality sends them to the extreme end of the continuum.

Another inevitable consequence of perfect equality-induced collectivism is the loss of individual freedom. Fukuyama wrote that in the strongest and most stable democracies, freedom precedes equality. But we have seen how democracies gradually diminish freedom and enhance equality as they age. As equality comes to precede freedom in democracy and freedom is lost, then, using Fukuyama's logic, it would appear an unstable democracy begins. This point seems intuitively true for a number of reasons, the principal one being late democracy's inequitable laws. The loss of individual freedom originates with the view that, under the purview of perfect equality, it is just to treat individuals unjustly in order to right past wrongs. Laws not only become inequitable but inconsistent. Rights proliferate and conflict as late democracy ensues.

Finally, perfect equality diminishes merit and leads to divisiveness. Merit is real and ought to be recognized. The better basketball player and the harder working taxi driver ought to be rewarded. John Adams believed there exists a natural aristocracy based on personal qualities, not birth. Perfect equality levels these abilities, collaterally punishes merit and rewards those without it. On divisiveness, Tocqueville believed enforced equality increased social prejudices, which would be become bitterer in democracy. Indeed, we see in late American democracy, the incessant demand for perfect equality as a source of continuing disruption of societal cohesiveness. All of these consequences of perfect equality — collectivism, loss of freedom, inequitable and conflicting laws, loss of merit and divisiveness — will be discussed at length in chapter twelve, Democracy in America.

Political equality may not satisfy everyone, but it forms a framework within which everyone gains a certain level of equality. Some lose some freedoms and others gain some equality, which is a good Solonian compromise. Democracy's proclivity to embrace perfect equality rends this compromise and only leads to instability. There are many forms of this trend to perfect equality in democracy, but the most pernicious one is materialistically based, and it is socialism.

Socialism

Democracy is the natural host for Karl Marx's inequitist socialism. Socialism is a collectivistic political philosophy that appeals to many and punishes some. It is popular in democracies because the poor majority has the power to bring it about and enforce it. In chapter one, I defined democracy and asserted that it is not necessarily a ptochocracy, or rule by the poor. Alternatively, Marx believed there exists a struggle between the oppressed proletariat poor and oppressor bourgeoisie rich that could only be resolved by proletariat revolution that ended in socialism. It is this non-violent struggle that is played out in mature and late democracies and the result is a ptochocracy. Democracy's natural tendency to adopt socialism brings a Marxian Damocles' sword that in many ways decides her fate.

Tocqueville was alarmed at the socialistic tendencies of democracies. He presaged that the political struggle in democracy will ultimately be between the haves and the have-nots and property will be the great battlefield. For him, socialism is the worst aspect of democracy. It set one against another, glamorized violence, exalted materialism, caused governmental centralization and was incompatible with freedom.

Nineteenth-century Russian author Fyodor Dostoevsky also disliked socialism and its utopia because under it, human beings are not free to choose. He stressed personal freedom and choice — views incompatible with socialism. He wrote that humans cannot achieve freedom and happiness at the same time because freedom does not necessarily bring happiness. Thus, a utopian philosophy like socialism can only bring happiness at the expense of freedom. Philosopher and economist Friedrich Hayek wrote that when democracy becomes dominated by a collectivist creed, which socialism is, it will eventually destroy itself.

DEFINITION

Socialism is a materialistic economic political philosophy in which the state controls the means of production and distribution of wealth in such a way that each is to contribute based on ability and receive according to need. Put another way, the state will forcibly redistribute wealth based on the idea of "from each his ability and to each his need." For many, socialism is Nietzsche's slave morality incarnate—it is rule by the poor. Aristotle echoed this point when he wrote that democracy exists when those who are free and not well off, being in the majority, are in control of government. It is not the rule of all but rule by the poorest class of citizens.

It should be noted that democracy is not necessarily socialism. Democracy is a broad framework within which many economic philosophies may operate, including socialism and capitalism. Democracy is a system that describes where power and authority resides within a state, or the people, but does not prescribe how that power and authority are to be used. Socialism is a narrower philosophy with an economic agenda. It does prescribe how power and authority are to be used, which as we shall see, democracy naturally manifests.

DEMOCRACY IS THE HOST OF SOCIALISM

Many past thinkers, including socialists, believe democracy is the tool for socialism. The socialist advocates generally fall into socialism's three great phases. The first is the utopian era lead by Christianity and individuals like Henri de Saint-Simon and Charles Fourier, followed by the violent phase, lead by Marx and Vladimir Lenin. The phase we see today is its third stage of Fabian or creeping socialism, which is the effort to bring it about gradually.

Marx and Friedrich Engels presaged democracy as the tool of socialism. In their *Communist Manifesto* they wrote that (verbatim) the first step in the revolution by the working class is to raise the proletariat to the position of ruling class, to win the battles of democracy. They believed that (verbatim) the proletariat will use its political supremacy to wrest, by degrees, all capital from the bourgeoisie, to centralize all instruments of production in the hands of the state. Socialism will labor everywhere for the union and agreement of the democratic parties of all countries. Communist Lenin, in his *State and Revolution*, wrote that (verbatim) democracy is of great importance for the working class in its struggle for freedom against capitalists. But democracy is by no means a limit one may not overstep; it is only one of the stages in the course of development from feudalism to capitalism, and from capitalism to communism. Note that the great Satan himself sees democracy as just a step to be supplanted by socialism's parent communism.

The contemporary Fabian socialists, however, were the first to recognize the full significance and potential of using democracy as their tool. They knew other forms of socialism had failed and recognized the need for a viable host. Fabian English socialist leader Sidney Webb wrote they had (verbatim) learned the lesson of democracy, and know that it is through the slow and gradual turning of the popular mind to new principles that social reorganization (i.e. socialism), bit by bit, comes. He continued to prophesy (verbatim) that the inevitable outcome of democracy is the control by the people themselves, not only of their own political organization, but through the main instruments of wealth production, the gradual substitution of organized cooperation for the anarchy of the competitive struggle. He concludes that the economic side of the democratic ideal is, in fact, socialism itself. For socialist Webb (verbatim), the mainstream, which has borne European society toward socialism during the past one hundred years, is the irresistible progress of democracy.

For the Fabian socialists, democracy is a tool to be discarded when socialism is achieved. Indeed, socialist Harold Laski wrote that (paraphrased) parliamentary democracy must not be allowed to form any obstacle to the realization of socialism; rather, a socialist government must take vast powers and legislate under them by ordinance and decree and suspend the classic formulae of normal opposition.

The Fabian socialists were right: democracy is the tool for socialism. But how is this relevant to this chapter, which is about democracy and inequality? It is because socialism brings inequality, and it does so by creating two ostensibly antagonistic classes, which can be identified from its definition — the able and the needy. Right or wrong, socialism favors the needy and vilifies and perpetrates numerous transgressions against the ablest. One of these transgressions is inequality.

In many respects, history has always had the able and needy (often called the eternal war between rich and poor), but socialism takes it to a new level. Christianity favored the meek who shall inherit the earth, but this was a religion that corrected the problem with voluntary charity. Jeremy Bentham's nineteenth-century utilitarianism, or happiness for the most, also militated for those in need. But this was a voluntary moral theory. Modern American progressivism that embraces Christianity and utilitarianism naturally enforces socialism, so, thus, it could be described as a religion without a god, a moral theory that imparts injustice and a Fabian socialist creed that imparts unjust inequality.

It is only when socialism became political under the violent and Fabian socialists in democracy the coercive power of the state was engaged to bring about and enforce socialist doctrine. Socialism has rarely infected other forms of government such as oligarchies, plutocracies, theocracies or monarchies. In this respect, democracy is being used to bring about something that it is not — an evolution that was discussed in chapter five on the cycles of democracy. It is called upon to artificially correct a timeless antagonism, and, in so doing, it becomes undone itself.

There are two surprising observations that come from all of this. The first is that democracy, in its early period, is a unifying political philosophy. Many vote, and everyone ideally is equal under the law. Socialism, on the other hand, is a dividing political philosophy, pitting the able against the needy, or, as Tocqueville wrote, setting one against another.

126

The second observation is that Fukuyama may have been right that democracy is the end of history. It is not democracy that dies but rather the socialism that supplants it, as Lenin and Laski presaged and the Fabian socialists advocated. He may have been right in that early democracy without socialism is the end of history.

SOCIALISTIC DEMOCRACY TAKES PROPERTY AND FREEDOM

Late democracy, under the aegis of socialism, perpetuates inequality to some minorities and able individuals in numerous ways. Many no doubt consider this view preposterous. They would claim the poor and downtrodden have always been oppressed and treated unequally, and to claim democracy perpetuates this is mistaken. Indeed, they would claim it corrects it. They could cite the historic transgressions against the poor described by Barbara W. Tuchman in fourteenth-century France or Tocqueville's in the eighteenth century. The would rightfully cite the oppressors: the artificial classes of aristocrats, princes, nobles and kings who gained their stature by heritage and wealth by inheritance—who instituted unjust laws that perpetuated their power that maintained an unequal and oppressive society. What these critics fail to appreciate is how democracy reverses this order. Under socialism it is reversed, and the poor come to oppress the rich. The truism is true: when the rich are in power they oppress the poor and when the poor are in power they oppress the able rich. In either case, Nietzsche was right, socialism in late democracy oppresses the able under the paradigm of slave morality just as the very definition of socialistic philosophy requires.

Under socialism, the poor take the rich's property and freedom. The right to own property is one manifestation of freedom. In nature, there are no rights to own property. There are no laws, courts or police to protect property, and the result is the loss of freedom in anarchy. One can only call property their own in nature to the extent that they have the power to keep it. As Thomas Hobbes and Locke explained, governments and laws were instituted in part to protect individuals' freedom to own property — they were instituted to defend that freedom. Socialism convolutes and reverses this truth, and the consequence is a reversion to nature, where some citizens' property is not protected by government. Some lose the freedom to own property.

As we saw in the historic arguments against democracy, many past thinkers presciently pointed out that democracy segues into socialism, and the result is the usurpation and destabilization of wealth. Tocqueville warned that democracy destroys the right to property and brings on socialism with the attendant loss of freedom. English historian Alexander Fraser Tytler echoed this sentiment when he wrote that democracy is always temporary in nature; it simply cannot exist as a permanent form of government. A democracy will continue to exist up until the time that voters discover that they can vote themselves generous gifts from the public treasury. From that moment on, the majority always votes for the candidates who promise the most benefits, with the result that every democracy will finally collapse due to loose fiscal policy, which is always followed by a dictatorship. Benjamin Constant wrote that (verbatim in part) the necessary aim of those without property is to obtain some, so, if given the vote, they will encroach upon property. Adams believed that under democracy all debts would be abolished, the rich would be taxed out of their wealth and the idle would thus acquire wealth they in no way deserved. The former silent majority in early and mature democracy gradually gives way to the loud lower class poor in late democracy that commence the raid on the public treasury.

The right to own property is a litmus test of a free society — there is no private property in communist countries, and there is little freedom. Property is one of the bulwarks of freedom because with it one can hold it and use it without it being taken. Adams wrote that property must be secured for liberty to exist. Indeed, freedom requires property because without it one would exist in a state of freedom-less anarchy with all forms of ownership contested. It would return humans to the state of nature where one can only hold what he can defend. This precipitates one of democracies' great ironies — they champion freedom, but, under socialism, diminish property. This irony was elucidated by English historian Henry S. Randall who wrote that (paraphrased) under democratic government either the poor would plunder the rich and civilization would perish, or order and property would be saved by a strong military government and liberty would perish. Socialistic democracies diminish property through powerful centralized governments that diminish freedom.

Socialism meant it when it proclaimed "from each his ability," and the result is the able under socialism in democracy that are treated unequally. Kenneth Minogue, in his book Politics, wrote that democracies cater and respond to the poor. Socialism hands to the poor the reins of the state, which they understandably use in late democracy to redistribute wealth to themselves. Naturally, a host of demagogic politicians emerge to facilitate their wishes in order to gain power. Their targets include those individuals and businesses that, more often than not through ability, create wealth. These entities are taxed at higher rates and mandated to provide services, while the poor are exempt. It is the opposite of the eighteenth-century France Tocqueville described, where the nobility was exempt and the peasants taxed heavily. It rather embodies the unfair tax system described by Christopher Hibbert in The Days of the French Revolution. He cited unequal taxation as one of the causes of social unrest in France before the French Revolution, but in this case, for the poor. The exemptions for the nobility from taxes are now the exemptions of the poor. In late American socialistic democracy under its progressive tax system, 20 percent of American taxpayers pay 90 percent of federal income taxes, many poor pay no taxes and receive benefits, and businesses, which pay innumerable taxes, are accused of receiving welfare! Political equality has segued into perfect equality, economic claims have become couched in terms of social justice and Robert Reich derides the disparity of wealth. Socialism's promise is justice and security but its price is inequality and the loss of freedom for some. Democracy, which began with a clarion call for equality, ends in inequality due to socialism.

Bastiat and Proudhon

There was a famous debate in 1849¬–50 between French economist Frédéric Bastiat and anarchist cum socialist Pierre-Joseph Proudhon about socialism in democracy taking some individual's property and freedom, which results in inequality. It is a prolonged and complicated debate confounded by the language of the time, like gratuity of credit, which in contemporary terms means free or social money. There were many issues, one of which was the question of why credit or money should not be available to all.

Socialist Proudhon predictably argues that it should. For him, property is theft, and interest and rent are usury and evils that prevent this gratuity of credit. He relies principally on the economic labor theory of value, where value is based on labor alone. The laborer, in short, should be paid what the product sells for—the merchant or capitalist who owns property is entitled to nothing. In this, he espouses a now defunct economic theory of his time, which is that the only way to gain is by another's loss. Francis Bacon wrote that when one person gains, another necessarily loses, and Michel de Montaigne, in a more discouraging manner, wrote that profit to one is loss to another. This is the kind of socialistic thinking that evolved into Marx's discredited socialistic labor theory of value. This is relevant to this chapter because one of Proudhon and Marx's real assertions is that socialism brings equality. When everyone has money, they are more equal. But are they?

Bastiat points out that (verbatim) Proudhon's solution to equalize wealth is to increase paper money, but paper money is only a promise, and endeavoring to provide an inexhaustible supply of promises only debases the currency. What good is paper money to equals if it has no value? His asks what kind of economic system is best for all — one that is free or one that constrains. For him, it is a free economic system that offers an ever-rising level for all — under such a regime of liberty, it increases, universalizes and levels itself. Freedom of capital increases wealth and offers greater opportunity for equality. This is the greatest good of all. Let capital have liberty and you shall have the greatest possible total chance of equality in wellbeing, and to do away with it, you shall have equality in wretchedness. Equality is found in liberty's embrace and not the coercive utopian artifice socialism.

History tells us that Proudhon is wrong in asserting property is theft, and that money should be free and the solution is socialism. Indeed, modern economics tells us that the labor theory of value only works in a utopia where there is unlimited supply and scarce labor. But when factors other than labor become scarce, labor will not yield the same result, which is the law of diminishing returns. Additional labor, for example, on limited land will not yield a proportionate amount of value. The earlier critics of democracy were right — it is the poor who rob the rich when they can, and, in this case, it is the demand for free money.

It sounds counter-intuitive to claim that allowing free market forces to work brings more equality than extending gratuity of credit — or just giving everyone money to make them equal. But, printing social money only devalues the currency to the point where it has no value. The result is no equality, other than equality in poverty. Freedom and the economic system that flows from free markets extends credit wisely and, thus, increases prosperity and potential equality

131

for all. Certainly, it is not a perfect equality, but it is one that is real, enables freedom, does not steal others property and offers opportunity. When late democracy embraces socialism, it embraces inequality that contributes to its demise.

Under the aegis of socialism, late democracy abandons John Locke's thought that to avoid war in the state of nature and to protect private property, men enter into civil or political society. Instead, late democracies embrace Marx and cater to the poor, who vote to take others' property and return to Locke's state of war in nature. They do it through a variety of socialistic governmental programs, including redistribution of wealth tax laws, printing money, deficits and a plethora of mandates such as minimum wage and healthcare requirements for businesses. Socialism is a theft that perpetuates injustice and inequality in late democracy. Bastiat was right: the best economy for equality is a free one.

SOCIALISM SUPPLANTS DEMOCRACY

Lenin, Laski and the Fabian socialists made many wrongful predictions, but one that appears true is that socialism supplants democracy. Socialism is not a natural political philosophy; it is at war with nature so the only way to bring it about is through the coercive power of government. Government under socialism, as we see in America today necessarily grows into a many headed all powerful hydra seeking information, instituting a plethora of laws and regulations and increasingly coercively controlling all aspects of citizens lives. The walls containing government in early democracy are breached and cannot be rebuilt. Government and its bureaucracies take on a life of their own like Hal in the movie Space Odyssey that achieve the ability to insulate themselves from outside interference. The early democratic ideals of limited government and Thomas Jefferson's vision that government shall be unattractive of notice are discarded. Local autonomy, freedom and incentive vanish under the heavy boot of big socialistic government.

132

Socialism must supplant the original ideals of freedom, political equality and justice in early democracy it in order to endure. Indeed, a true democracy could conceivably undo the socialistic programs late socialistic governments promulgate. The early democratic safeguards for individual freedom, such as the Bill of Rights in the American Constitution are incompatible with socialism. Once democracy has served the socialists' purpose they will abandon it. True democracy will always be at odds with the necessities of socialism.

NIETZSCHE, CHRISTIANITY AND DEMOCRACY

In chapter four, Fukuyama's invocation of the master-slave morality and democracy's ability to abolish these historic class distinctions was criticized. Nietzsche's slave morality derives from the psychology of former slaves. It is a reactive and resentful morality obsessed with conservation and self-preservation, under which the weak and needy become good and the strong and able evil. In it, egalitarian values prevail that promote weakness and mediocrity at the expense of vitality, dynamism and excellence. Its historic roots are in slavery, and its philosophic roots are in what Nietzsche calls the aesthetic ideal, or an ideal that honors weakness, emotions and aesthetics. Its religious roots are in Christianity. Late democracy is the manifestation of this tripartite conspiracy. The slaves get the vote and become the majority, which brings about a zeitgeist that honors weakness and mediocrity that is blessed under the compassion of Christianity. Socialism is the coercive materialistic consequence in older democracies and the great loser, the ones treated unequally are the able. It is indeed a strange twist of history and bastardization of nature and instinct that democracy institutes.

Late democracies become Christianity politicized. No longer do prayers, alms or good deeds succor the needy but rather progressive taxation, mandates and reverse discrimination imbedded into law and enforced by the coercive power of the state. The aspiration to be thy brother's keeper becomes law, charity becomes the poor's right and choice becomes legal obligation. Democracy becomes a kind of enforced Christianity with the religious zeal but without the grace.

It is ironic that democracy, which originally championed freedom and equality in order to liberate the individual, becomes the tool to take freedom and institute inequality. Nietzsche, along with a host of other historic thinkers, despised socialism. It is a political philosophy that uses democracy in a way that turns it into a totalitarian tyrant.

THE VANISHING MEAN

In chapter two, ancient seventh-century BCE Athenian statesmen Solon's compromise solutions between the poor and rich and the common citizens and the oligarchs in order to avoid tyranny and violence were described. Under his constitution, each side gained and lost a little—it was a balance. However, his wise reforms appeased neither side, and neither does democracy. Democracy under the influence of perfect equality spawns socialism, which makes such compromises impossible—it takes democracy to an extreme that opposes any Solonian mean.

Democracy's early ability to achieve a mean between extremes abates as it becomes infected with socialism. It is enveloped by an ideological formula of "isms" that Carlyle so despised. Socialism takes the hopes and aspirations of people and ossifies them into formulas that replace the historic human action that leads to the dehumanization of society. Socialism guts the hopes and aspirations of early democracy and literally tears them from their roots.

Under socialism, early democracy's aspiration for freedom becomes security for some and un-freedom through loss of property for others. Any mean is lost. Equal treatment under the law in early democracy becomes unequal treatment, as two classes are created in which the able class is treated differently than the needy class. Any mean is lost. Rule by the people in early democracy becomes a ptochocracy, or rule by the poor majority, under socialism. Again, any mean is lost. The only result is the creation of a permanent, intractable and irreconcilable resentment in the able that only leads to divisiveness in late democracy. Thus, another of democracy's conditions to exist vanishes, which is a civil society outside of the law. Another mean, lost. Socialism rends democracy from its roots, destroys its fundamental ideals and erases its ability to achieve any Solonian mean.

The consequences are ruinous for democracy under socialism as a viable and fair political system. Socialism offers some short-term security gains, but due to its excesses, any mean between the benefits of free market capitalism and meeting need are erased. The productive society thrives by allowing able individuals to keep the fruits of their labors, which is lost under their increasing emphasis on redistributing property and equalizing wealth. Any thought that the inequality of wealth may actually benefit is lost in the backward, muddled and unsophisticated socialistic ideology. Everyone conveniently forgets Adam Smith's invisible hand, which derisively becomes trickle-down economics rather than bubble-up wealth. People who have earned their property ought to be able to keep it—a proposition Locke and Jefferson championed under their purview of early democracy. Any mean between the able's right to keep property and the needy's rights is lost. Utterly absent in this socialistic democratic miasma is people's individuality as democracy changes from championing the individuals and their inalienable rights to collectivism and the group, or the majority's rights—another mean down the tube.

There occurs a grand shift in democracy under the influence of socialism from production to need, and the consequences are ominous. Marx and the Fabian socialists exhorted all socialists in democracy to always emphasize need, misery and how to prevent it. This message resonates in democracy-it is a match made in heaven. All need becomes sacrosanct, and meeting it becomes the focus of late democracies under the influence of socialism. Newspapers, governmental programs, the intelligentsia and private non-profit enterprises champion this new societal slave morality zeitgeist. A day does not go by in late democracies without some public notice about need and how to meet it. The consequences in late democracy are apparent only to the non-socialists, which is that need increases. As the mantra of socialism advances in democracy, more citizens become dependent on the state. More citizens are labeled needy, there are more needy to be cared for, there occurs more demand for benefits and a culture of a dependent, captured, needy population emerges. The line between able and needy is lost as the zeitgeist becomes singularly focused on meeting need. Any consideration of a mean is lost—need becomes king.

The problem, as Thomas Robert Malthus in his *An Essay Concerning Human Population* pointed out, is that the more you feed need the more need you get. The culture of need in late democracies only brings greater need. Any thought of the cause or worthiness of need is lost as democracy focuses entirely on consequences. How to meet need supplants the question of how to prevent it. This is an important point because, as we shall discuss in chapter ten on relative morality, utilitarian philosophies fail for precisely this reason. Need becomes an insatiable bottomless pit for late democracies. The result is that late democracies gradually find themselves in an unsustainable situation, increasingly unable to meet the need they created under socialism. Under this new societal mantra, need becomes a Weaverian God-word under which important democratic ideals, like freedom, individuality and equality, lose import. The distinction between producer and consumer becomes confused and eventually lost, as a host of programs are initiated focused on increasing taxes and redistributing wealth. Need and poverty become the citadels demanding resolution from demigods who gain power by feeding need. In mature American democracy, demagogue

Franklin Roosevelt initiates the New Deal, and in early late American democracy, Lyndon B. Johnson launches the Great Society influenced in part by socialistic writers like Michael Harrington and his book *Toward a Democratic Left*. Few read Hayek's *The Road to Serfdom* or *The Constitution of Liberty*, which herald the true nature of democracy and expose the dangers of socialism's influence on it.

The truth is that the best way to alleviate need is to prevent it. It is better to stop need than feed it. Feeding need only addresses consequences and, thus, never ultimately solves the problem. Preventing need addresses its causes, which is the ultimate solution. This point will be expanded on in chapter ten on relative morality.

Socialism fails because it is an extreme political philosophy. Utopian socialism repeatedly failed under Fourier and Robert Owen; Brook Farm failed; violent socialism under Marx, Lenin and Joseph Stalin failed; and so will Fabian socialism in late democracy. Socialism is another of democracy's Achilles heels.

Conclusion

The ideal of equality is one of democracy's great strengths, but like an alcoholic, it does not know when to stop drinking the elixir. Equality must be taken in moderation because it conflicts with two greater rivals—freedom and nature. Political equality manages to finesse this conflict, but taken to an extreme, equality becomes inequality. The constant tension Tocqueville spoke of between equality and freedom becomes acute when equality ascends. Nature, as we all know, has a way of doing things her way, independent of human ideals like equality. She bends only so far and always has the last word.

Human nature being what it is, the demand for equality easily segues into the demand for power. Thus, economically and politically, what was historically done occasionally violently to the poor is done slowly and legally in democracy by the poor; it is the same destruction but by different means, different perpetrators and different victims. The origins are the same—if you have the power use it. The pursuit of an ideal utopia in which all are perfectly equal is impossible because the only way to achieve it is to treat some unequally.

The pursuits of perfect and material equality under socialism are the critical components of late democracy that undoes its ability to compromise and find any mean between competing interests. Perfect equality loses it because the mean between the endowed and unendowed fades and materialistically because socialism in democracy takes some individuals' property and freedom. Fukuyama implied that one reason democracies thrive is because freedom allows for capitalism and ultimately wealth. But as we have seen, democracies detach societies from free market capitalism and replace it with socialism. The consequences are the loss of free markets, loss of freedom, and, for some, inequality. This is not a formula that succors a thriving society and certainly one that is the end of history.

Recall that Fukuyama invoked Hobbes in order to predict that the former masters, who traditionally risked their lives in democracy, would hang up their swords and become bourgeoisie businessmen pursuing wealth. This sounds plausible as long as they are willing to do so. However, as Nietzsche's slave morality prevails in democracy and these former masters become oppressed for the reasons described, it seems entirely plausible that they may reclaim their swords and again engage in bloody battle. In many ways, this battle is being waged today, which will be described later in chapter eleven on divisiveness and twelve on democracy in America.

Chapter Eight

INJUSTICE

When Thomas Jefferson wrote life, liberty and happiness in the American Declaration of Independence, he borrowed from English philosopher John Locke, who happened to be one of the originators of the social contract ethical theory. Carl L. Becker in *The Declaration of Independence* explained how Locke was responding to Robert Filmer who asserted in his *Patriarcha* that kings are absolute, which is derived from divine right. Locke needed a contravening political philosophy, which he found in the compact theory. Jefferson had read Locke's treatises on government and incorporated the compact theory in the Declaration of Independence in order to justify revolution. Locke's also asserted that if we agree to preserve life, liberty and property, we live happier lives. Jefferson changed property to happiness, but the spirit of the union of Locke's social contract and Jefferson's nascent democratic declaration embodied these ideas, along with the notions of equality and, particularly, justice. Like American democracy, all early democracies are based on these concepts. They are the foundations for fledgling democracies, and they made America great.

This is particularly so because from historic and political perspectives, early democracies come as close to dispensing true justice as any form of government. With their constitutions protecting individual liberties and provisions for courts with the power of judicial review, early democracies are the leading edge in protecting the individual from external unjust coercion. Indeed, in early America, justice to all was one of democracy's great attractions.

Unfortunately, these fundamental ideals change as democracy evolves, a point that Francis Fukuyama failed to address, and the most significant change is the redefinition of justice. Curiously, with this change democracy gradually evolves into that which it was intended to supplant, which is tyranny, or in democracy's case, tyranny of the majority. The majority's versions of injustice take many forms in late democracy, but the principal ones are loss of freedom, socialistic utility and injustice in the law. Much of this is due to confusing ends and means for political reasons. The reasons why will be explained, but first, justice must be defined.

Justice

Justice is one of those human concepts susceptible to selfish interpretation. The one concept of justice that avoids this partisanship is found in early democracy based on the social contract. It is a non-theistic timeless and universal form of justice that exists as long as creatures like humans exist. It consists of freely formed, bilateral contractual agreements like not to kill, steal or lie that derive from our instincts to survive and reproduce, which makes justice based on our self-interest. It is a one-on-one bargain where two individuals mutually agree to restrain their desires in order to live happier lives. With this bargain both gain, both are satisfied and each walks away thinking the agreement was fair, a sentiment that originates the good faith Cicero said is the foundation of justice. It is this sense of fairness that we call justice, which makes it real, immediate, measurable and definable. This is timeless and universal justice that avoids moral relativism — it is just for everyone always.

Late democracy alters this concept of justice. Utility creeps into the concept, and what becomes important is happiness for the most. Under the mantra of making the most happy, justice becomes particular and temporal, and any eye to the universal is lost. Significantly, these laws of utility themselves often become the source of future injustices and past wrongs. As such, under the evolving definition of justice, people, and in democracy, the majority, become the arbiters of what constitutes justice. Justice becomes majoritarian fashion, and the consequence is too often injustice to individuals.

This is a significant point for the survival of democracy because, as Friedrich Hayek pointed out, man can accept injustice from nature but recoils when it is committed from another man's will. When a storm blows our roof off, we think it a tragedy, but when government overtaxes us until we can no longer stay in our home, we think it is an injustice. Humans naturally resent coercion from other humans, which is what occurs as democracy ages. This cause of divisiveness in late democracies will be discussed at length in chapter eleven.

Envy and Desert

The idea that democracy inflames envy is not new. Bertrand Russell, in The Conquest of Happiness, wrote that envy is the basis of democracy. For him, the democratic movement of the ancient Greek states was inspired by Heraclitus's assertion that in Ephesus (verbatim) there shall be none first among us. For Russell, (verbatim) the egalitarian doctrines of democracy and socialism have greatly extended the range of envy. John Adams, like Edmund Burke, wrote that (verbatim) a democracy will envy all and endeavor to pull all down, and if it gets the upper hand, it will be revengeful and cruel. H. L. Mencken, in his usual cantankerous and blunt manner, wrote that (verbatim) democracy in practice arises from the envy felt by inferior men for their superiors. The peasant craves security, the gentleman fights for liberty; since there are by definition more peasants than gentlemen, the inevitable result of universal suffrage is to make it possible for the former to persecute the latter, thus impeding human progress. Knowing that there are more peasants than gentlemen, politicians deliberately pander to the prejudices of the mob in order to wield power over those who are too principled to do the same thing.

The ascension of equality as democracy evolves engenders circumstances that are conducive for the natural human emotion of envy — an artificial, politically induced envy. If we are equal, why ought my neighbor have more? Why am I not also entitled to what my neighbor has if we are equal? These are the kinds of thoughts citizens in mature and late democracies have, which give rise to the burning feeling of envy. Compare this with natural inequality. The neighbor who can run faster because God made him faster incites admiration and awe rather than envy. There is less sense of being robbed. But in political society where humans are ostensibly equal, having less unleashes a sense of being thwarted, robbed or diminished by another human in the way Hayek described. This feeling is only naturally heightened in a democracy that values equality over other ideals, like freedom. Envy is endemic in late democracies, and the institutionalized effort to attenuate the fast runner or man with superior ability only works to debase the legitimacy of the political democratic system.

What better way to satisfy envy with impunity than to remove desert, which is what happens in late democracies.

To continue, it was Mencken who said that (verbatim) all government, in essence, is a conspiracy against the superior man: its one permanent object is to oppress him and cripple him. Mencken was talking about democracies, and he saw the consequences of democracy under the aegis of socialism more clearly than anyone when he continued to write that (paraphrased) unrestrained populism, to which direct democracy can lead, threatens one of the great intellectual possessions of modern man—personal freedom—which includes desert.

Democracy denying desert due to envy originates two of democracy's great weaknesses. The first is its increasing inability to achieve compromise. Recall Solon's efforts in ancient Greece to craft a compromise constitution between the warring rich and poor—and its eventual failure. The second is its increasing propensity to deny reward to the talented individual. When in late democracies envy incited by equality ignores merit and denies desert, it crosses the justice river, Rubicon.

Consider Heraclitus's proclamation, which was mentioned earlier, reported by Cicero in the fifth century BCE, that citizens of Ephesus should be put to death for believing (paraphrased) that no single man among them should distinguish himself above the rest; but if any such appear, let him live elsewhere amongst other men. And Cicero's own observations that (paraphrased) no value indeed can be attached to the sort of community from which the wise and good are driven away. Cicero asks why (paraphrased) those in a democracy hate the superiority of virtue. Punishing society's able is a recipe for suicide for any political system.

Envy, loss of desert, socialism, the overemphasis of equality and slave morality conspire in late democracies to cripple the superior man with unequal treatment, loss of freedom and injustice. It does this principally in three ways: through the adoption of utilitarian morality, the evolving concept of social justice and the subsequent debasement of law.

Utilitarian Morality in Democracy

Much will be said in chapter ten on democracies' tendency to adopt a utilitarian morality as they age. For now, only a brief description of utility's relationship with justice and the law will be discussed. Earlier, a definition of justice, derived from the social contract moral theory, required that justice is real, immediate, measurable and definable. Justice is between individuals, and the fair compacts humans make result in our conception of justice. It is only logical that the majority in a democracy would prefer policies that bring them fairness, justice and the resulting happiness and well-being. If the individual can achieve these, why not the many? The people rule under democracy, so why should they not have these things as well? With these circumstances, the proclivity to adopt a utilitarian moral philosophy begins in democracy.

Utilitarianism is a consequentialist moral theory that says to act in such a way that brings happiness to the most. It is consequentialist because it bases actions on consequences rather than other motivations, like duty. On the surface, it is an alluring theory, but upon closer inspection, its flaws become conspicuous. The first is that it is liable to perpetrate injustice to the individual because an aggregate of people's happiness can be deemed superior to the individuals. The classic example is the hypothetical case of a small southern town in which a white woman has been raped, ostensibly, by a black man. The town is in uproar, and its citizens' plan on killing many black people in retaliation. The utilitarian sheriff is trying to prevent any killing, so he decides it is better to arrest one innocent black man and hang him to placate the angry mob in order to save many black lives. This represents happiness for the most because more people live, yet one innocent individual dies as a sacrifice. The sheriff was basing his decision on consequences only — that more people will live — and not duty or the social contract.

Both duty and the social contract would tell him to not kill an innocent person. Hence, injustice to the individual on the alter of utilitarian "justice."

As utility permeates late democracies, it becomes the norm from which laws and policies originate that perpetrate injustices to individuals. It becomes legal to take some individuals' property if it brings happiness to many, which is a philosophic petri dish for socialism. What was once theft now becomes just. A plethora of laws are promulgated under this new morality that are intended to bring happiness to the most at the expense of individuals.

As late democratic society gradually loses its moral bearings, justice becomes expedience. It becomes more important to do what works for now than what causes injustice to individuals. Land use laws, environmental laws, gender laws, sex laws, discrimination laws, and tax laws are a few examples that contain elements of expedience rather than justice. There is a gradual ballooning of strict liability laws in late democracy that ignore intent. Unfortunately for democracy, under these trends, justice becomes subjective, laws and policies become fashion, and any concern for relative morality in law is lost. This trend is clearly seen in contemporary American late democracy with the advent of positivistic law that preaches the law is just a social fact.

Most importantly, the very concept of justice is altered. Justice, which was once considered a fair bargain, becomes capricious fashion that changes with the times whose principle objective is to bring happiness to the most. The most conspicuous example of this manifestation of democracy is the concept of social justice.

Social Justice

Justice's crucible derives from a one to one relationship where two humans are relating individually and not collectively. Influenced by the rule of the majority and utilitarian morality democracy alters this principle of justice. Justice to a group comes in competition with to an individual under late democracies. Indeed, one of the greatest challenges for late democracies is how to balance individual and group interests. With this trend the new concept of social justice arises. Granted, many use the term for political purposes in order to advance personal interests, but many come to wrongfully think social justice is justice.

Any one group has so many competing interests it is impossible to discern whether any one act against it is just or unjust. It becomes difficult to determine what injustice is ostensibly being perpetrated. It may be unjust to one of the group but not another. It may be unjust to one of the group's common interests, but those very interests vary among the individuals in the group. The ostensibly injured one is not an individual but rather an aggregate, which makes the source of injury and resulting injustice indefinable, protean and often capricious. Recall that under the social contract injustice to the individual is real, immediate, measurable and definable. Taking justice out of this one-on-one origin makes it a blank tablet without footing that anyone can write on. Under social justice a mirage of ostensible injustices arises. Justice is an abstraction that is made real only between individual people with a definable issue. Two people, for example, agreeing not to steal from each other under the social contact is a definable justice.

How can a legislature pass a just law or a court render a verdict that is just when the very concept of justice has been altered? They cannot, because under democracy, justice has become utility and subjective. Justice is what the majority decides is justice, which makes it temporal and particular. The contradiction comes with trying to declare one thing just while at the same time committing injustice. For justice to be justice, it must be just for all. Consequently, the law necessarily becomes debased by democracy as people become cynical knowing that only "might makes right." The result of this is that law segues as democracies age from natural to positive law.

Natural and Positive Law

Briefly, natural law envisioned by thinkers like Thomas Aquinas states that the law must be based on morality while modern positivistic law derived from sophists like Jeremy Bentham and John Austin states that it is not. Early democracy naturally embraces naturalistic law, which segues into positivistic law and its jurisprudential children, such as realistic law, as it ages. As an extreme of positive law, realistic law envisioned by Oliver Wendell Holmes, Jr. states that the law is simply what judges do. This important issue is a minefield that will not be fully discussed here. It is mentioned because democracy's tendency to embrace positivistic law leads to certain critical intractable problems that will be discussed shortly.

Law based on social contract morality constrains people and governments. It militates against hegemony, oligarchic power and governmental tyranny. Collaterally, it hinders mature democracy's ability to implement some of its cherished ideals, such as perfect equality. Certainly, most past political systems were detached from morality and "might makes right." But democracy became popular because it eschewed those past systems with its emphasis on freedom, equality and fairness for all. Democracy embracing positivistic law is recidivist — it is turning itself into what it intended to supplant, only this time it is by majority hegemony.

The three fatal jurisprudential flaws positivistic law causes in democracy occur in rights, equal treatment under the law and the rule of law. The latter two are particularly critical for any legal system to command respect and maintain integrity.

RIGHTS

Democracy's alteration of rights causes numerous problems for the law, including what constitutes justice. Locke, in his second of *Two Treatises of Government*, contributed numerous

147

ideas for democracy, but the idea of rights may have been his most important. His was the classic formulation of the principles of political liberalism, and his work influenced the American and French Revolutions, the Constitution of the United States of America and democracy. Jefferson borrowed the concept of rights from Locke and referred to them as inalienable, and the result was a more civilized society based on natural rights.

Philosophers like H. L. A. Hart and Francis Hutcheson, who argued in concert with Locke and Jefferson, have further delineated the nature of rights and concurred that they are negative. Negative rights prevent the government from doing certain things, like taking the right to life and liberty and the freedoms of free speech, religion and the press. All of the rights in the Constitution's Bill of Rights are negative rights. Their significance is that they establish inalienable rights that government cannot abridge. Democracy's emphasis on freedom is the natural vessel for these rights because they protect people's freedom from governmental intrusion. Historically, people have been subjects with few rights against the power of government—democracy changed this equation, which is one of the reasons it is alluring.

As democracy evolves under the influence of perfect equality, socialism and utilitarian morality, this concept of a right changes to a positive right. Positive rights are the rights to things that are often provided by the government. The right to free speech is a negative right—the government is prohibited from preventing it. The right to have the government pay for a microphone so what you have to say can be heard is positive—the government or others are obligated to provision you. This alteration in the definition of a right institutes many problems for late democracies.

The first is that positive rights succor tyranny of the majority. Twentieth-century American politician Herbert H. Lehman said that (paraphrased) the threat to democracy comes from the gradual invasion of constitutional rights with the acquiescence of an inert people though failure to discern that constitutional government cannot survive where the rights guaranteed by the Constitution are not safeguarded, even to those citizens with whose political and social views the majority may not agree. The majority controls government, and when the negative rights are attenuated that protect the individual and minority, their hegemony increases. Worse, with positive rights, any limits to what the majority desires the government to provide are reduced. The consequence is a change from protection from the government to control by the government.

Second, from these circumstances democratic governments naturally become bigger, more able to take citizens' property and more controlling. A pattern of injustice to individuals and minorities begins to emerge, abetted by the immune majority.

Finally, to complicate matters, as rights multiply, they begin to conflict. There is little friction between negative rights because they all limit the power of government. With the advent of positive rights, an individual's right to freedom is not compatible with another individual's right to security, and friction naturally ensues. Many of these contradictions remain irresolvable in late democracies. Woodrow Wilson, a progressive American politician, thought the Constitution was an impediment to progress — what he did not understand was that his concept of "progress" referred to late democracy and its multitude of problems, including injustice.

EQUAL TREATMENT UNDER THE LAW

Hugo Black wrote (paraphrased) that in democracy the most dangerous symptom is abandonment of equal justice to all — the placing of some groups in a preferred class of citizenship at the expense of other groups. True democracy must continue to war on all such beliefs. Early democracies fight such a war, and it is one of their great attractions; late democracies surrender. Both Alexis de Tocqueville and Christopher Hibbert explained that one of the animating reasons for the French Revolution and aspiration for democracy was unequal taxation. It was French law exempting the nobility from many taxes, which were then passed on to the masses, that caused a deep resentment, which exploded in violence. With certain notable exceptions, equal treatment under the law is one of early democracy's shining characteristics.

Equal treatment under the law is a fundamental requirement for any just legal system. Historically, it meant that all citizens must stand equal before the law and that justice must be blind to wealth, color, rank or privilege. Certainly, many early democracies were deficient in this high standard, but it was their aspiration — an aspiration far beyond previous political systems. As democracy evolved, it was this standard perhaps above all that demanded women and minorities be given equal rights under the law, and in mature French and American democracies, it insured they were.

Unfortunately for humankind, the same forces that animated the redefinition of rights in democracy, and in particular the advent of positive jurisprudence, also abrogate equal treatment under the law. As it turns out, in order to bring about perfect equality, equalize wealth and correct some ostensible social injustices, some must inexorably be treated unequally. The majority in modern late democracies brings about these developments, and the ironic result is a return to former antiquated political systems of coercion and "might makes right." The majority treating the minority unequally under the law in late democracy is no different than the French sovereign treating the *villiens* arbitrarily.

With the advent of unequal treatment under the law in late democracies, the concept of justice becomes debased, the law loses respect, and the legitimacy of democracy is undermined. Justice become temporal, or what the majority decides, and many citizens become cynical because they know the law does not treat them equally. Democracy loses legitimacy because it no longer represents justice to all. A minority's appeal to justice becomes an empty phrase because justice is not dispensed equally. In late American democracy, for example, women demand equal treatment but wink at affirmative action laws. Selective discrimination against minorities, the daemon of late American democracy also results in reverse-discrimination laws that bring unequal treatment policies that set precedents, and the resulting injustice becomes imbedded in the law.

This occurs because late democracies, due to their nature, abandon their original ideals. Justice becomes power, or the ability of one group to gain power over another, by means of the law. Historically, this is nothing new, but it is new to the ideals of early democracy. This trend in democracy is important because it leads to discord, which is democracy's great bane — a topic that will be expanded upon in chapter eleven on divisiveness.

THE RULE OF LAW

The rule of law means that everyone in a society is governed by written rules. Nobody is above the law. Historically, there were laws, but they were usually written by a few who were not subject to them. Tocqueville, for example, wrote of French kings before the Revolution that could change laws at will by edict. They could overhaul the legal system, change jurisdictions and alter the power of the courts at will. These kings were not subject to the law, so there was no true rule of law per se.

The rule of law is important for a variety of reasons. First, it militates against dictatorships and tyranny — despots face limitations. It establishes written rules that prevent the caprice of a dictator. All live under abstract preconceived and agreed upon rules, so no one individual has the unilateral power to alter what the law is. Second, freedom is enhanced because the laws are predictable. If individuals do not know what the law will be tomorrow, they will never know if they are obeying the law today. Hence, the loss of freedom—they are in constant fear of being a lawbreaker. Tocqueville wrote that French families under arbitrary rule felt the ground could be cut from under their feet. He wrote that nobody could be sure what law applied, which court was competent to try it and whether they were obeying the law. The rule of law is essential for any stable and fair society, and it is what early democracy embraced. Constitutions and bills of rights are the charters for early democracies that establish and enshrine the rule of law.

For all the reasons cited earlier, the rule of law becomes attenuated as democracy evolves. The demand for perfect equality, socialism, utilitarian morality and non-natural law all require changes to the charters of original democracy in order to occur. But democracy changes slowly due to built-in checks and balances created to prevent tyranny. They have a kind of inertia perpetuated by their very nature. Thus, in order to bring about change, the rule of law fades as democracy ages. Recall that socialist Harold Laski wrote that parliamentary democracy must not be allowed to obstruct socialism, so it must be brought about by decree. Laski's decree is the King of France's edict, and the rule of law is the loser.

The advocates for change' solution is to politicize the law by electing or appointing those who administer it with the ideologies that will bring about their desired changes. Positivistic law set the stage for this development in late democracies with its insistence that the law is not based on morality and is just a social fact. With this development, in order to know what the law is, one must watch what judges do. Previously, judges adjudicated based on written rules and precedent, but this changes with the advent of non-originalist judges, as they are called in late American democracy. For them what was written is less important than policy that addresses immediate problems or implements new political philosophies. These new judges alter original intents and often violate broad principles in order to achieve desired outcomes.

The consequence of this development in law is ominous. Bishop Benjamin Hoadly once wrote in *Sermon Preached Before the King* that (paraphrased) whoever has an absolute authority to interpret any written or spoken laws, it is he who is the lawgiver for all intents and purposes, and not the person who wrote or spoke them. The non-originalist judges become the lawgivers and rule by the people, which was democracy's charter, fades. With this development, democracy reverts back to the days of a sovereign who is replaced by the majority. The law becomes whatever the power of the majority decides, untethered from any morality or timeless principles of justice.

With this, democracy and it ideals become debased due to its evolving legal system and laws. The redefinition of a right, willingness to treat people unequally under the law and inclination to circumvent the rule of law diminish its legitimacy. The courts' responsibility is to determine winners and losers, and as more late democratic courts dispense injustice to an increasing cadre of resentful losers, divisiveness grows. Divisiveness in democracy will be taken up in chapter eleven.

Ends and Means

Justice, negative rights, equal treatment under the law and the rule of law are end principles. Like freedom in early democracy, all means are oriented to achieving them. With these ends, democracy, like the wise person Aristotle referred to, has the right ends. Early democracies have principled ends to which means are subordinate. Unfortunately, as democracy develops, ends and means become confused to the point that means ascend. Any means, just or unjust, become acceptable, as long as some desired end like socialism or social justice is achieved.

This occurs for two reasons. First, evolving utilitarian morality in democracy, which focuses on consequences that lead to happiness for the most, focuses on means to achieve this rather than other ends, like justice and freedom. Utility, or doing what works, becomes more important than principle, or doing what is right. Democracies become politicized. Second, many of the ends desired in late democracy like socialism and social justice cannot be achieved with the principled ends of early democracy. Perfect equality cannot be achieved when freedom and equal treatment under the law are revered ends. To achieve the new objectives, the majority must emphasize means.

The principal loser in this evolving equation is justice. Justice is an end and not a means. If justice is properly defined, then the means would not be unjust. With the proper ends, the means do not commit injustice. One example could be the demand for equality in democracy. Some believe all theories of justice require some form of equality. However, as an end in itself, equality often results in unjust means because merit must be treated unequally. Perfect equality does not offer justice; it only offers benefits to some and injustice to others. True equality as an end in the law is equal treatment under the law, a concept Aristotle himself said is the most basic form of justice.

Philosopher Peter Westen wrote that the concept of equality has become so malleable it is empty. This is what happens in late democracy. With no limits to the concept of equality, it becomes empty and increasingly loses force and content. The end under socialism becomes the equalization of wealth at all costs, whereas the just end would be to equalize wealth without stealing. The unjust end of equality at all costs would be the just end of equality without treating some unequally.

In the case of justice, the right end would be to treat all justly, which includes negative rights, equal treatment under the law and the rule of law. The vagueness of social justice would be made concrete under a social contract and not a utilitarian view of justice—there would be no injustice to individuals. In a just democratic system, the ends of life, liberty, property and happiness could not be abridged by the tyranny of the majority.

Conclusion

Such are the affects democracy has on the important ends of freedom, equality and justice — factors Fukuyama never considered. He, like Georg Wilhelm Friedrich Hegel, believed freedom in democracy was the end of history but never addressed democracy's alteration of what freedom means. He uses democracy's emphasis on equality but fails to appreciate its unnaturalness and dismisses its conflict with freedom. In justice, he claims democracy recognizes rights but never mentions its alteration of the definition of a right nor democracy's tendencies to treat citizens unequally and abandon the rule of law. He never mentions democracy's proclivity to abandon just end principles for utility end policies and the resulting injustices. Democracy is not the end of history.

Section three is about why democracies fail. I have six reasons. The first three chapters of this section gave three of them, which were the loss of freedom, inequality and injustice. The remaining three chapters describe their consequences. They are the concentration of power, relative morality and divisiveness.

Chapter Nine

CONCENTRATION OF POWER

Historically, centralized governmental power held in a few hands was the norm. Ancient Greece, the Roman Empire and most of the medieval states including France's histories are tales of centralized power controlling citizens. It is in the nature of power to preserve and enlarge itself. Alexis de Tocqueville wrote in *The Old Regime and the French Revolution* that in France, before the French Revolution, a strong central administration had gained control of all the national activities. He believed that the instinctive desire of every government is to gather all the reins of power into its own hands — it never fails to take effect. Only recently, under enlightenment thinkers like Jean-Jacque Rousseau, who worshiped individual freedom and the philosophy of democracy, have citizens begun thinking otherwise. The democratic prospect of freedom is the bane of centralized power, but this power has waxed and waned in recent times. Democracy, with its ideals of freedom and power residing in the people, is the modern day political philosophy that mitigates the historic centralization of power. Niccolò Machiavelli himself wrote that the only way to control the prince was by power from many people—which is democracy.

Dwight D. Eisenhower once said that (paraphrased) every step we take toward making the state the caretaker of our lives, by that much we move toward making the state our master. As we have seen, the freedom early democracy offers naturally segues into socialistic caretaking. A contradiction arises because people want to be both free and secure, and as democracies age, security overshadows freedom. With this, echoing what Eisenhower presaged, democratic states gradually become our masters. Historian Paul Johnson, in *Modern Times*, wrote (paraphrased) that one of the dismal lessons of the twentieth century is that once a state is allowed to expand, it is almost impossible to contract it. Democracies always expand and rarely contract.

Ancient Greek democracy ended with power concentrated under Alexander the Great, the Roman Republic ended with concentrated power amongst the emperors in the Roman Empire and the French Revolution's experiment with democracy ended with power concentrated in Napoleon. Certainly, there are many reasons for these events, but the theme is the same: power becomes concentrated in republican and democratic governments. Contemporary democracies are not immune—their causes may be different, but the consequences are the same. The statists like Georg Wilhelm Friedrich Hegel, and unwittingly Francis Fukuyama, who believe democracy brings freedom were wrong—there is no such thing as a free dictatorship.

Democracies Naturally Concentrate Power

Given their essence, it is indeed strange to assert that democracy naturally concentrates governmental power. How could it be that what they are intended to supplant they become, and the power they intended to devolve to the many becomes concentrated in a few? Concentration of power is the opposite of rule by the people, but this is what happens as democracy evolves—a point some past thinkers on democracy have presaged.

Edmund Burke compared absolute democracies and monarchies and declared them both legitimate forms of government, which makes democracy like a monarchy. Tocqueville warned of the centralization of the state under democracy and cited the French Revolution, in which, as time passed, the ideal of freedom lost its appeal, which set the stage for a one-man central authoritative government that was wider, stricter and absolute. Ralph Waldo Emerson left no doubt about his views when he said that democracy becomes a government of bullies tempered by editors.

Recall the example of democracy in medieval Italian history from chapter two. In the eleventh through thirteenth centuries, some northern Italian cities like Pisa and Milan developed democratic communes in which all males could vote. However, as these rare quasi-democracies evolved, rich and noble families gradually accumulated power, it resulted in dictatorships. Certainly, as in this case, the desire for power and money was a cause for the concentration of power, but there are other compelling reasons for this trend that emanate from the very nature of democracy. Two examples are equality and socialism.

Perfectly equal individuals within an aggregate of people and giving according to ability do not occur naturally. Indeed, one only need observe nature's natural hierarchies and survival of the fittest. Like those who desired wealth and power in medieval Italy, the expedient way to bring about their social aspirations was by suspending democracy and using coercion. It is the same today. Government is the natural choice, and in order for government to bring its desired reforms about, it must be powerful—hence the need for the concentration of power. Democratic governments are particularly susceptible to this tendency because early ones are idealistic and majorities can be hegemonic.

Ultimately, it is the majority that superintends concentrated governmental power that takes freedom and diminishes democracy. In early democracy, many eyes watched those with their hands on the fasces. But from chapter six we saw how the majority comes to control government because it is in its interest to promote centralized power—it is the source of its authority and means to implement it. The result is "might makes right" which sends many of democracy's ideals packing, like freedom and justice. In the case of socialism, the manipulation of democracies is nothing more than a throwback to the historic forms of government by kings, monarchs, despots, lords and pharaohs, who governed on might for their own benefit. And it is the majority's ability to concentrate governmental power that enables the elites' ability to bring about their economic, social and political agendas. Early democracy's ideals are thwarted, the majority rules, power becomes concentrated, elites implement their agendas and the spirit of democracy is debased.

There is nothing inherently evil with the concentration of power in democracy. Many democracies today are powerful and good places to live. The problem comes due to the concentration of power's unintended consequences. The American sociologist Robert K. Merton popularized the principle of unintended consequences, which states that there are outcomes that are not the ones foreseen and intended by purposeful action. Some consequences could be good, like the medieval hunting reserves that became parks in Europe or demilitarized zones that become natural habitats, and others, bad, such as the protection of the steel industry in the

United States from foreign competition that only increased costs to users and caused unemployment. The problem is that even though democracy's instincts may be good, its actions are full of pejorative unintended consequences. Let us consider a few of them.

Suppression of Liberty

The suppression of liberty is the most significant unintended consequence of concentration of power in late democracy. Montesquieu believed both democratic and aristocratic states are not in their own nature free—political liberty is found only in moderate governments, such as in early democracy. Tocqueville, writing from his knowledge of the French Revolution, repeatedly warned of democracy's inclination to concentrate power that suppresses liberty. He wrote that the democratic French government after the French Revolution, became stronger and more autocratic and suppressed liberty. He also wrote that the Revolution brought the view that the ideal social system was one whose aristocracy consisted exclusively of government officials. The animating passions of the Revolution were freedom and equality, but as democracy evolved, the ideal of freedom lost its appeal and the stage was set for one-man government with a central authority. He was particularly concerned with the potential for despotism in democracy. He wrote that democracies tend toward despotism due to the omnipotence of the majority, which would result in anarchy and ultimately bring about despotism. Tocqueville's despotism arising from the Revolution is the concentration of power that inexorably suppresses liberty, which democracy enables.

A poignant but oblique point on this subject comes from John Stuart Mill, who was concerned with the struggle between liberty and authority, or freedom and the concentration of power. His philosophic views militate against the latter—a society may coercively intervene to prevent one from harming another, but it has no obligation to elevate individuals' own physical or moral good. For Locke, individuals are sovereign over their own bodies and must be allowed to seek the good in their own way. Democracy's tendency to concentrate power threatens both this idea and individuality. Obedience, in Locke's view, is not an adequate end of human character.

Many intelligentsia in America today argue that elites are in control in democracy, not the masses. Thomas R. Dye and L. Harmon Zeigler made this point in The Irony of Democracy, in which they claim that the irony of democracy, which is ostensibly the government of the masses, in reality is the government of the elites. It is the elites who control government. For them, key political, economic and social decisions are made by tiny minority elites. It is hard to say whether their thesis is true — certainly some elites have tremendous influence, but it is also true that the masses voting in a democracy also have influence. The important thing, however, is to understand that it is the concentration of governmental power that enables the power of both the elites and the masses. True power from the people, local control and freedom come from decentralized power, where small autonomous groups and individuals have control over their own destinies. With no concentration of governmental power, there can be no entity the elites or majority can superintend to disseminate their political, economic and social agendas. It is of interest to note that this is an argument for states' rights, which will be discussed shortly.

There is an important lesson here for all who love democracy. This book is about why democracy fails, and this chapter argues one reason is due to its tendency to concentrate power, which takes away freedom. Early democracies, with all their deficiencies, do not have this problem. They tend to have decentralized governmental power, checks and balances and rights that protect individuals from governmental intrusion. These change under the influence of powerful, ideologically driven sects that are intent on bringing about their particular political, economic or social agendas. Their goals can only be achieved through the coercive power of government, which makes early democracy their enemy — they must discard it to achieve their objectives. Recall from chapter seven socialists Michael Harrington and Harold Laski's concerns that the democratic system hinders the advance of socialism. They prefer to suspend such impediments in order to be unfettered by democratic procedure and the parliamentary powers of democracy that impede the realization of socialism. For them, opposition, one of democracy's strengths must be suspended.

Democracy naturally concentrates power, Dye and Zeigler are right; ideological elites on both the right and left do control late democracies, and the result is the loss of liberty, which is one of the reasons democracy fails.

Unintended Consequences

The concentration of governmental power brings other unintended consequences that are harmful to democracy. One hallmark of early democracy is positive rights that protect citizens from governmental intrusion and, collaterally, from the majority and elites. As we discussed in chapter eight, rights change from negative to positive as democracy ages, which both erodes these bulwarks of freedom and collaterally hands government additional powers to be exercised under the aegis of positive rights. To make matters worse, as new rights are added to the list of rights, they begin to conflict, which the government must adjudicate by further expanding its power. Fukuyama wrote that democracies are by definition weak because they are limited by rights, but he failed to understand that under the expansion of rights and the alteration of their definition in late democracies, democratic governments' power in reality expands.

The issue of states' rights in America for many is a dead issue, but it is relevant to this chapter's topic. Sovereign states within a loose federal system enhance freedom — centralized federal power diminishes freedom. Consider the contentious issue of abortion in mature American democracy. Many Americans are for it and many against it. Under a centralized federal government, one decision made by the Supreme Court applies to all citizens. If states had the power to decide the issue, then religious Utah would be anti-abortion and liberal California pro-abortion. Then, everyone who wants to live in an anti-abortion state could move to Utah, and those who want to live in an abortion state could move to California. Voila — more freedom for people to live under the laws they choose. Centralized federal power removed this option.

Corruption has always been a problem in government, but the concentration of power accentuates it due to its unaccountability. Early democracies tend to resist corruption due to their weak governments and constraints on central power. As governmental power centralizes in later democracies, the opportunities for corruption increase. Eighteenth-century Scottish historian Alexander Fraser Tytler described the corrupt demagogues of ancient democratic Athens who gained power by causing faction and plundering the public treasury. For Tytler, demagogues and power erode early democracies' natural tendency toward virtue, which eventually becomes later democracies' corruption and decline. Centralized power provides the means for demagogues to instigate turmoil and corruption. Adolf Hitler could be one example.

Plato writing in ancient Athens seems to support Tytler's view. Plato wrote that democracy dissolves into insatiate desire that disregards everything, including constitutions. It engenders a fierce, intolerant dominant class that endeavors to redistribute property. Such circumstances breed a Protector of the People, who leads the poor against those who possess property. I call him the demagogue, and Plato calls him the tyrant. Whatever his title, he promises many things, including freeing citizens from debt and parceling out free land.

With these gestures, he pretends to be gracious, but behind the scenes he is always militating against his enemies, stirring up class warfare and purging his regime in order to retain his power. The occurrence of demagogues is a critical unintended consequence of democracy.

Perhaps the most significant unintended consequence of concentrated power is societal divisiveness. This topic will be discussed at length in chapter eleven, so it will only be touched upon here. Like Tytler, Aristotle believed the bane of Athenian democracy was demagogues who calumniated the wealthy and roused the poor against the government, thus causing opposing parties united against opposing ostensibly common dangers. For Aristotle, these demagogues create a sense of insecurity that stirred resistance and divisiveness within the populace. He believed nearly all the tyrants of old were originally demagogues, which has special meaning for democracy. History tells us democracies usually end in dictatorships, and Aristotle tells us democracies nurture them, hence the natural concentration of power and divisiveness within democracies.

Tocqueville pointed to a different source of divisiveness in French society caused by the concentration of power. Prior to the French Revolution of 1789, manufacturing in France had increased, thus causing more wealth, which enabled bigger government. As a result, the government became the largest spender and employer, which increased its debt to the point that it was often unable to pay its creditors. The result was inevitable. On one hand, some citizens got used to government handouts and fiercely opposed any suspension of benefits. On the other hand, those from whom the government had borrowed money became resentful because it did not have the money to honor its securities. Centralized power caused two irreconcilable dissident groups, and the consequence was divisiveness in French democracy.

Tytler, Plato, Aristotle and Tocqueville make significant points, but the real reason is that the concentration of power engenders divisiveness, which harms society. People are different and one rule for all will always rile some. Sure, demagogues can stir divisive passions, but at their core, people are animated when they are dictated to unfairly, taxed too heavily and denied their freedom. Concentrated power in democracies brings these about and stirs divisiveness.

In spite of R. G. Collingwood's admonitions, the concentration of power in the ancient Roman Empire offers the best example of the unintended consequences of concentrated governmental power. Democracy ignores these history lessons at its own peril. They are the growth of bureaucracies, loss of municipal responsibility, demand for security, useless and parasitic citizens, high taxes and loss of production.

Ancient Rome and the Concentration of Power

François de La Rochefoucauld wrote that little is needed to make a wise man happy, but nothing can content a fool, which is why nearly all men are miserable. I think it is important to ask whether Americans can learn from Roman history, or are we, as La Rochefoucauld says, unwise fools condemned to repeat the Roman's mistakes and live in eternal misery.

Ancient Rome demonstrates the inevitable dangers that arise when governmental power is concentrated. In Rome's case, a limited republic with some democratic characteristics was transformed into an empire, with power concentrated in an emperor and centralized bureaucracies. Rome was originally a kingship, which became a republic in 509 BCE when the Roman people threw off their last king, Tarquin the Proud. The Roman republican period was somewhat similar to democracy: there was a powerful senate with voting, majority rule, a judiciary and an executive branch with an emperor. Each had checks on the other, which kept power dispersed. Much of the Empire's administrative work was relegated to the cities, which made imperial service small and select.

In 31 BCE, Octavian, who was to become Imperial Rome's first emperor Augustus, won the battle of Actium, which transformed Rome into an imperial power that, for the Western Roman Empire, lasted five hundred years, until it fell to the barbarians. It was during this period that power was increasingly concentrated in a centralized Roman government with inevitable bureaucratization, which was overarched by an all-powerful emperor. One characteristic of democracy is checks and balances between executive, legislative and judicial branches, but in Imperial Rome, the executive branch largely controlled the legislative and judicial branches. Power became centralized in the executive branch, the bureaucracy grew and the administration of the Roman Empire centered in Rome itself.

This process of centralization accelerated as the Roman Empire aged. In 324 CE, Emperor Diocletian raised taxes and further centralized governmental power. Emperor Constantine, who rose to power in 324 CE, added to Diocletian's centralized authoritarian government with more administration and more bureaucracy. Writers on this age speak of morasses of supernumeraries relentlessly multiplying tasks of an ever-pettier nature and a culture where every phase of life became stereotyped and organized. Citizens' lives under centralized power became standardized, sober and gray.

Today, we would call a Roman Emperor a dictator, and it could be argued that dictatorships represent the ultimate concentration of governmental power. History tells us that democracies often end in dictatorships, so the consequences of the Roman experience, which will be discussed next, could be the forces that indicate democracy is not the end of history, as Fukuyama claims.

THE CONSEQUENCES

In Imperial Rome, bureaucracies grew to eventually become, according to one historian, the most elaborate and pervasive administrative bureaucracy man has ever seen. These bureaucratic structures became larger, more demanding and more complex. This was due in part to the needs of the army, but the bureaucracy became a vessel that could never be filled — the more it grew, the more it needed. The bureaucracies were formalized under Emperor Claudius around 50 CE. He assumed the collection of revenues from provinces, which was formally a local responsibility. Taxation was no longer a local issue but one decided by bureaucrats who were more interested in the central government's needs than the local community's autonomy. As the Roman Empire grew, its bureaucracies became increasingly oppressive.

Sociologist Max Weber believed individual freedom is threatened by others' agendas and a bureaucracy is nothing but government's tool to formalize policy agendas. With democracies' tendency to concentrate power, it naturally attracts those with agendas, like socialists who use the power of the state to implement their ideologies through bureaucracies. Burke wrote that a state must rule according to people's inclinations and that forcing policy only causes discord and decay. Like the Roman Empire example, democracy's bureaucratization takes freedom and sews discord.

As centralized power in Rome grew and bureaucracies expanded during the second century, local communities suffered. They gradually lost a sense of self-determination because decisions emanated from Rome and local political positions lost power and prestige. Local civil service, which had been an honored duty in republican times, became a burden to be evaded. Imperial government had to compel the gentry, who once considered service to the state an honor, to serve. Farmers, manufacturers, and tradesmen, as well as nobility, increasingly evaded civic responsibility. Collaterally, as taxing and spending powers were usurped from local municipalities, they found it easier to spend money foolishly because they expected to be saved from bankruptcy by the central government, which further eroded their sense of responsibility.

Like the ancient Roman example, Tocqueville wrote in *The Old Regime and the French Revolution* that during the eighteenth century, a mistake of the Revolution was to create a democratic powerful central government in Paris that turned its back on freedom. It was a government that robbed local provincial autonomy and community vitality. In contrast, Tocqueville wrote of one feudal French parish that escaped oppressive central power by going overseas to free America, where it was transformed into a new, vital and emancipated township in New England.

A community's welfare and robustness ultimately resides in citizens who take responsibility for their circumstances. To have responsibility requires some control, which centralized power in democracies incrementally diminishes. Perhaps one of the great ironies of democracy is that it silently emasculates its very ideal of control by the people with its proclivity to concentrate power and engender paternalistic bureaucracies that usurp local autonomy, diminish local control and rob citizen's pride in local traditions and vigor.

The concentration of power in ancient Rome brought an enormous civil service and heavy taxes. As the prosperity of the Empire declined in the late second and third centuries and the burden of taxes increased, many Roman citizens sought security through employment in the civil service. One scholar of the time wrote that these pressures caused many leaders of local communities, and members of the equestrian class in particular, to seek the security of government jobs, which was a disaster for local communities. By the fourth century, local senates, in which it had once been an honor to serve, became a kind of penal institution that leading citizens avoided.

Taxes became oppressive in late Roman history due to the centralized government's needs. They were confiscatory so citizens evaded them. In order to extract taxes, citizens were increasingly harassed by military police and a militarized bureaucracy. The result was that many Romans simply abandoned their homes, farms and businesses. Frank C. Bourne, in *The History of the Romans*, wrote that under the strains of centralized government, heavy taxes and bureaucratization, the people and state became enervated and weak and the once powerful Roman state found itself unable to resist invasions by barbarians. Fukuyama may be wrong, and democracy may be no different.

There is an interesting psychological lesson to be learned from this description of Roman centralized power and the desire for security that comes from Tocqueville. Tocqueville wrote that a man's admiration of absolute government is proportional to the contempt the feels for those around him. My interpretation of this is that as government becomes the source of security, some gain more than others from its largesse. Those who gain more revere government, and those who gain less despise it. Contempt then would only be the natural feeling, then, for those who have gained less toward those who have gained more. In the game of seeking security in life from government, there are winners and losers. These losers are a problem for the centralized government democracy engenders. Given this Roman example, it seems democracy's proclivity to centralize power does not solve the eternal war between the rich and poor.

Emperor Augustus tried to instill morality in the Romans after years of civil war, but according to Tacitus he failed. One of the reasons he failed was due to prosperity's propensity to mitigate human values. With her conquests, the Roman Empire became wealthy. Taxes from the provinces, commercial opportunities, and the usurpation of other countries' wealth allowed Rome to acquire vast riches. With this wealth, Roman luxury abounded, which attenuated many of the traditional Roman virtues. The rich Romans became decadent and less prudential, and they indulged in pleasure due to wealth. As the Empire continued to prosper this loss of Roman prudential virtues spread, and city inhabitants during the second century, according to Roman historian

Frank Bourne, became useless and parasitic. Ancient historian Polybius wrote of this trend when he observed that once incorruptible Romans were now declining moral figures. It seems the proverb is true: you cannot serve both virtue and Mammon. Prior to the concentration of governmental power, local Roman communities thrived, and citizens were empowered with a degree of control over their destinies, which resulted in a vigorous nation. Wealth changed this when it aggregated power in Rome, which spawned bureaucracies and increased taxation. Roman government emasculated cities and subjugated citizens.

The combination of continuous wars, the army and a large administration superintended by a powerful central government caused taxes to become unbearable as Rome aged. The bureaus in particular became costly as they enlarged. The central government's need for taxes became insatiable, as well as the bureau's demanding to collect them. One writer of the day complained that the government servants outnumbered the taxpayers.

Emperor Diocletian in the late third century was particularly responsible for the advent of ruinous tax policies and their consequences. As a former general, he militarized the administration by creating an imperial bureaucracy along the lines of his regimented handbook *Notitia Dignitatum* or list of officers. His relied on *curiales* to collect taxes from an increasingly over-taxed and resentful populace, and in 293 CE, he increased Roman administration with a tetrarchy and created smaller provinces to prevent any concentration of rebellious powers. This only expanded the need for an imperial bureaucracy with offices and staffs that increased enormously the weight and expense of the bureaucratic machine.

Amazingly, Diocletian would simply establish a national budget and then levy whatever tax satisfied it, irrespective of actual production. To garner these taxes, his new tax system was based on units of equal value called *jugatio* and *capitatio*. The former referred to land and the latter to labor. *Jugatio* and *capitatio* were determined in productive units, so, for example, if a farm was abandoned, the government's careful calculations would be upset. Therefore, in order to satisfy the requirements of the central government, the farmers were straightaway tied to their occupation and places of origin by the government and destined to sink into that form of serfdom. This new Diocletian tax system had the injurious effect of changing the Roman economy from free contract to one that tied citizens to an inherited trade and location. This only caused revolts, non-cooperation and abandonment. Many over-taxed peasants simply walked away from their farms or changed occupations. Some were able to seek employment as a coloni for another landlord or buy the support of a patron to protect them from powerful landlords.

One reason for the loss of enterprise was due to the development of the *Theodosian Code*, which was a collection of edicts promulgated in the fourth century that locked men of all trades and services in their place in order to secure from every subject his contribution to the coffer of the Empire. One edict, for example stated that no man shall possess property that is tax exempt.

In the later period of the Roman Empire, the government became increasingly oppressive in order to maintain the status quo. Under the strains of taxes and wars, much of the traditional Roman code of the second century broke down. Governors and procurators became ruthlessly efficient, with no concern for fairness. The result was corruption, extortion, and exploitation. One historian described the oppressive Empire in its later years as (verbatim) an economic impossibility, supported only by ruthless exploitation of the lower classes. Peasants were brutalized and taxed heavily. With ruthless efficiency and force, the tax collectors would beat peasants, put them in chains, and send them to prison if they did not pay their taxes. For many, resistance seemed futile because the armed forces lay behind the tax collector and landlord against the tenant farmers.

Centralized government and ruinous taxes were also common in fourteenth-century medieval France and England. Barbara W. Tuchman, in *A Distant Mirror*, described working class rebellions during that period precipitated by oppressive taxes. In 1378, food taxes on consumption were added to those on sales, falling most heavily on the poor, which instigated a revolt. In 1381, the English peasants' revolt lead by Wat Tyler and John Ball rebelled against oppressive taxes. In 1382, French peasant mobs revolted against high taxes and exclusionary guilds. Their targets were sheriffs, foresters, tax collectors, judges, abbots, lords, bishops, dukes and especially lawyers because they are the ones who put the peasants in prison for nonpayment of taxes. The people wanted to be free from the yoke of subsidies that only enriched nobles.

Recall that both the French and American Revolutions for democracy were precipitated in part by excessive, unfair taxation against intransigent central governmental power. In the French case it was the monarchy and nobles, and in the American case, taxation without representation came from English hegemony.

It would seem the death knell for any government, whether imperial, monarchial or democratic, rings when its most productive taxpaying citizens resist and rebel because they are overtaxed. The concentration of governmental power breeds this rebellion. Saint Denis wrote of the French revolts that a government would be better directed by the people than by their natural lords. It is not clear to me why any democratically elected concentrated government directed by the people would act any differently.

The last example of the consequences of the concentrated power in ancient Rome is the loss of production. As Roman taxes and bureaucracies increased, productivity declined. Bureaucratic control and excessive taxation became so endemic that by the fourth century agriculture declined, free enterprise was stifled and production diminished. There was a continuous reduction in the number of farmers because under governmental supervision there were fewer opportunities for profit. It is no wonder that in late Western Roman history, free enterprise, effort, incentive, and entrepreneurship were stifled.

Certainly, there were many reasons for the demise of the Roman Empire, but it seems clear the concentration of power and its unintended consequences is one. Like the Roman example, democracy naturally concentrates power, which precipitates the same problems. Those who think otherwise can only be La Rochefoucauld's unwise fool.

Democracy to Dictatorship in America

Why many past democracies have often ended in dictatorship is the story of why they fail, which is the topic of this book. How they fail, however, is another story. Ancient Athenian democracy failed in war when Sparta won the Peloponnesian War, democratic Greece failed when conquered by Alexander the Great, the Italian democracies of northern Italy in the Middle Ages failed due largely to medieval family rivalries and the French Revolution failed because things became so contentious people wanted dictator Napoleon to bring peace. Democracies fail in many ways, but how could it fail in America—histories most significant, influential and longest lasting democracy? Could democratic America spawn a Napoleon?

It seems incredible to assert that America could become a dictatorship. It is working, any internal coup seems unlikely, majority rule makes a revolution improbable, and due to its military prowess, it is doubtful an external enemy could conquer it. This is all true, but America has an executive—the president. The threat to American democracy is not external; rather, it comes from within in the form of the president of the United States. American Founding Father Thomas Jefferson was leery of executive power; he said that the tyranny of executive power will come in its turn in the more distant future. It may well be that Jefferson's distant future is dawning in America.

The checks and balances to central governmental power crafted by the makers of the Constitution have been eroding, and America now has a federal government with unforeseen and largely unchecked power. Under the right circumstances, a president could superintend this federal power and become a dictator. Parenthetically, if power were not concentrated, there would be no entity for a dictator to superintend — the concentration of power enables dictatorships. I will first describe the Constitutional powers a president could use to achieve a dictatorship and then spin a yarn.

EXECUTIVE POWERS

Phillip J. Cooper, in his book *By Order of the President: The Use and Abuse of Executive Direct Action*, described three American executive powers that derive from Article Two of the Constitution and statutory authority. They are executive orders, proclamations and national security directives. The reasons for executive powers were derived in large part from Locke, who wrote that sometimes executive prerogatives are necessary because government's lawmaking power is too slow for dispatch; it is sometimes impossible to foresee accidents and necessities that require quick action. Democracies rightfully empower the executive to act in times of crisis.

Executive orders are employed to respond to emergencies, in times of war, in foreign policy, in private disputes that affect the public, in routine business involving publicity, in debts and inter-agency issues. They are directed to governmental officials and agencies. Proclamations are general statements by the executive branch intended to advance policies. They often declare law, trigger the implementation of law and have the force of law. Unlike executive orders, they are directed to individuals outside of government.

Both executive orders and proclamations have a long history. George Washington issued the Proclamation of Neutrality, Abraham Lincoln the Emancipation Proclamation, Woodrow Wilson issued Teapot Dome executive orders, Franklin D. Roosevelt issued executive orders implementing the National Industrial Recovery Act, Harry Truman ordered the desegregation of the military, John F. Kennedy ordered a stop to housing discrimination, Lyndon B. Johnson ordered affirmative action in government contracting, Richard Nixon ordered wage and price controls and Bill Clinton blocked striker replacements. Contemporarily, in 2011, Barack Obama ordered the Justice Department to stop defending the Defense of Marriage Act and in 2014 ordered a raise in the minimum wage for federal contractors and carbon dioxide emission cuts for power plants.

National security decision directives are formal executive notifications to a governmental department requiring action. They are usually used in times of war or for defense and are usually unknown to the public and Congress because they are classified. They increasingly have had significant domestic impact in technology, narcotics and in implementing executive policy.

Abuse of Executive Powers

The potential for abuse of these executive powers in the wrong hands is enormous. They give the president the potential to write law without constitutional authority because they are unencumbered mechanisms to institute policy. The president could use them to thwart a recalcitrant Congress. Johnson, for example, unilaterally enacted the equal employment opportunity executive order, initiating affirmative action in federal contracting programs without Congress's approval. Executive powers could be used to undermine the administrative law processes that check administrative arbitrariness and abuse. They could be used, as they often have been in the past, to provide special exemptions and benefits to individuals and groups inflaming partisanship. Finally, if the president should declare an emergency and thus have the need for secrecy due to national security, he could use national security directives that make a very big end run around the public, Congress, the press, the democratic process and ultimately democracy in America.

Presidential directives are the ultimate tool for an American dictator because they control the military and are made in secret. It is a power the executive yields off the record and behind closed doors. To legitimize a president's executive orders and national security decision directives, proclamations could be made supporting them. The potential for political manipulation in this case is daunting; a proclamation could be issued supporting a national security directive that is secret. There would be no counterevidence or grounds to dispute the proclamation. In aggregate, these three powers offer the potential for an American dictator.

Certainty, many Americans may laud the reasons for executive powers because they want affirmative action and equal opportunity in housing, but the price is higher than the prize. These executive powers have the power to thwart the democratic process and bring a dictatorship that could be inimical not only to Americans' cherished desires but also their life, liberty and happiness.

The Yarn

So, let me spin a yarn on how America could become a dictatorship due in large part to democracy's proclivity to concentrate power. The year is 2076 and Americans are weary of three hundred years of democratic internal strife and contentiousness. Over the last hundred years, divisiveness has increasingly segued to hardened and intolerant sects unwilling to compromise. The upper and lower classes are fighting, minorities are marching, unions picketing, the religious militating against secularism and many resisting high taxes. The government has become paralyzed and impotent due to political gridlock and is unable to act. Behind the decaying society, ideological power politics and corruption complicate and exacerbate circumstances. America under democracy has become divisive, and widespread acts of violent insurrection and rebellion have become commonplace. The American people are ready for a change.

A young, ambitious and ideologically driven new partisan socialist president has been elected to office. He has a determined political agenda that is continually thwarted by the democratic process. His somewhat extreme policies are challenged by otherwise thinking senators, representatives and judges. He becomes frustrated and angry, seeking ways to bring about his desired policies. This new president comes to believe that it is in the American people's interest to become a dictator to solve America's problems. He is swayed because he envisions quelling the violence, instituting his policies and ostensibly giving the people what they want politically. Unwittingly, he is following socialist Laski's admonition to not let democracy frustrate his political agenda.

With the American people's support, this new president begins exerting his awesome executive powers without compunction. Because democracy has naturally concentrated power in the federal government, he has the platform to achieve his objectives, which was a development America's Founding Fathers were particularly concerned about when they crafted the Constitution.

He begins by issuing proclamations, denouncing violence and concomitantly promoting the policies he believes will solve America's problems. Like Washington who, 285 years earlier, suppressed the Whiskey Rebellion in Pennsylvania with an emergency proclamation, this new president does likewise, but now with acclaimed proclamations advancing his policies. He issues innumerable executive orders to governmental agencies in order to suppress any violence, rebellion or insurrections along with orders again implementing his desired ideological agenda. Most worrisome of all is his use of national security directives. Using local violent acts as a ruse, he declares a national emergency, and as Commander in Chief of the American military, he begins to issue national security directives to suppress all opposition. These are secret orders to America's military without appeal. The new ideologically driven American president becomes the new Napoleonic dictator of America, and democracy is suspended.

Such is my yarn. This does not seem to be too unrealistic a story: a young idealistic president doing what he thinks is right with the support of the American people in order to restore civility but collaterally suspending democracy in order to institute his cherished policies. This young president has used the concentration of power caused by democracy to undo democracy and become America's dictator.

Capitulation of the People, Congress, Press and Courts

There are four significant checks to an American executive dictator: the people, Congress, the press and the courts. Each opposes dictatorship in different ways but, in my yarn, fail. The people certainly have great power in democracy through voting, political contributions, protests and non-cooperation. However, it is not unrealistic to envision them embracing a dictatorship because they believe it can bring an end to internal strife, such as the French embracing Napoleon after the Revolution. It could also be that the majority favors the new dictator's policies and are encouraged with his new powers to enact them. In the final case, if the people did resist, the president could issue national security decision directives to the military to suppress any rebellion under the guise of restoring order.

As one of the three branches of government, Congress holds many powers that could prevent a dictatorship. They could vote laws proscribing executive powers, refuse to fund programs, impeach him or raise alarm from the pulpit. However, under majority rule, the majority of senators and representatives could also support his policies. They were, after all, elected by the people, who now also support him, and they prefer to be reelected. They could rationalize their actions by thinking that the election happened by the people for four years, and impeachment would take a majority of the House of Representatives and a two-thirds majority vote in the Senate, which are very long odds. They don't impeach him because they do not have the votes. Congress could be further nullified because they are left ignorant. The presidential directives the new dictator issues are secretive, which would leave Congress in the dark as to what is going on.

Historically, the American press vigilantly espies and exposes governmental abuses of powers. It would seem that the press would be the first to learn of a dictatorship in the making and raise the tocsin. However, it would be difficult for the press to learn what is occurring in a state of martial law where governmental orders are not made public. Like in a time of war, national security directives are secret, and, if needed, the press could be censored due to a national emergency. But these drastic measures may not be necessary because many in the press may agree with the dictator's actions. They, like the American people and Congress, may want an end to strife, and thus support the dictator. Additionally, the media in America wants readers and profits, so it publicizes news Americans want to read. If most Americans support the new dictator, it may well be that the press does, too.

The ultimate source of resistance to any dictatorship should be the courts and, in particular, the Supreme Court of the United States. If the dictator's actions violated the Constitution, the Supreme Court should be the barrier that declares those actions unconstitutional. There are three reasons the Court could fail this critical responsibility and collaterally fail to uphold democracy. The first is rather obvious:

the court has no army, as Roosevelt arrogantly pointed out. Under a dictatorship, how could the court enforce its rulings? The second reason was provided in chapter eight, whereby under positivistic jurisprudence, the Justices believe the law is just a social fact that must bend to political circumstances. For the majority of justices, upholding constitutional provisions that preserve democracy could take a backseat to ending divisiveness in America. So they yield.

The third reason is the Court's inability to uphold the Constitution under times of social stress and political pressure. There are many examples of this, but let me give one — the vitiation of the Commerce Clause. Article 1, Section 8 of the Constitution gives Congress the power to "regulate Commerce...among the several states" and the Tenth Amendment to the Constitution states that "the powers not delegated to the United States Constitution, nor prohibited by it to the States, are reserved to the States respectively, or to the people." The intention of the Founding Fathers was that the states regulate intrastate commerce and the federal government, interstate commerce. As a result, the Supreme Court regularly struck down federal laws that endeavored to regulate intrastate commerce. This came to an abrupt end with the convergence of the Great Depression, Roosevelt and the New Deal.

In the early 1930s, Roosevelt wanted to pass federal legislation to solve the Great Depression, which the history books tell us did not occur. He was continually thwarted in his efforts by the Supreme Court due to the Commerce Clause. His obstacle was The Hughes Court and the famous Four Horsemen, Justices Pierce Butler, James Clark McReynolds, George Sutherland, and Willis Van Devanter, who resolutely voted against his agenda. Roosevelt, like a dictator, fulminated publicly and threatened to pack the court. Intense political and public pressure was put on the court, which eventually capitulated. In the 1937 National Labor Relations Board v. Jones & Laughlin Steel Corporation case, the court reversed itself and ruled that the federal government could regulate intrastate commerce. In 1942, in Wickard v. Filburn, the court ruled that a dairy farmer in Ohio who grew some wheat on his farm for livestock affected interstate commerce, even though it never left the state of Ohio. Roosevelt won, the Commerce Clause in the Constitution was gutted, the Supreme Court failed its mission, the federal government garnered more power and democracy took one more step toward dissolution. So the Court yields to America's new dictator in my yarn.

It is the same perfect storm that could enable a future American Napoleon. Both American and French presidents had an agenda, there is a time of crisis and the American people support the development, just like the French did in the early 1800s. The last line of defense to prevent it, the Supreme Court, capitulates — and America has a dictatorship. America has lost its reverence for democracy, which only lives on in the hearts of a very few courageous castigated Ciceronian citizens, Congressmen, newspapermen and judges who champion democracy and oppose dictatorship.

Not a Dialectic

Fukuyama asserted that democracy is the end of history in part because it brings freedom. However, as we have seen in this chapter, democracy naturally concentrates governmental power, which suppresses liberty. Power in a society naturally increases unless it is opposed by another power. If there is no countervailing force, power concentrates, and if there is, power is diffused. Early democracy is unique because on one hand it diffuses power by giving it to the people, but on the other it takes power due to a tyrannical majority. The results are twofold. First, unlike Fukuyama's claim, there is the gradual loss of freedom. Second, minority resistance to concentrated power builds, and contentiousness and divisiveness are the result. With resistance and discord, the majority further solidifies its power, and its solution is to select a dictator that will insure the power is secure. Because democracy concentrates power, the new dictator has a powerful government available to impose policies at will. As it turns out, democracy segues into a dictatorship with the attendant loss of freedom, and history repeats itself — which is one of history's lessons about democracy. Fukuyama was wrong, and there is no dialectic, and thus no synthesis. Democracy is just more of the same historic rule by might but with more fanfare, idealism and lofty rhetoric. And once again history repeats itself, indifferent to human meddling.

Conclusion

One of the great strengths of early democracy is the lack of concentrated power. It contains competing interests that check concentrated power. As contention grows, it is at the same time mitigated, as one group is replaced by another. One interest group does not stay in power long, and the result is the healthy balance both Aristotle and Solon wrote about. It is a balance that also mitigates one of Tocqueville's concerns that the majority will tyrannize the minority in democracy.

In order to prevent one sect from gaining control, most democratic constitutions contain branches of government with checks and balances over each other and bills of rights that prevent the concentration of governmental power to infringe on citizen's freedom. Democracy's tendency to concentrate power destroys these best laid plans and the circumstances that enable a president-dictator. The great irony is that the purpose of democracy is to give power to the people, but due to its very nature, and with the support of the people, it concentrates power, which brings a dictator who takes power from the people.

Chapter Ten

RELATIVE MORALITY

Both Aristotle and Alexis de Tocqueville believed that democracies become morally relative. Certainly, all societies contain some degree of moral relativity, but democracy seems particularly susceptible. Francis Fukuyama, who believed democracy is the end of history, admitted that there exists some special relationship between the kind of society democracy engenders and a relative, utilitarian morality. He believed relativism represents a threat to democracy. It seems certain that as democracies age, they naturally embrace a utilitarian relative morality, which I have previously described as their Achilles heel. This chapter will describe why they do this and what the consequences are.

The idea that if nothing is true then everything is permitted means that if there are no universals or absolute truths then there exists nothing to limit our actions. If nothing is true then there can be no right or wrong or good or evil. Right and wrong and good and evil exist only as contrasts, so when the contrast is erased, so are the concepts. Because morality is about how we ought to live in relation to other people, it naturally codifies good and evil ways of acting and champions the good while sanctioning the bad. Morality thus naturally limits our actions — usually through some form of disapprobation. However, if nothing is true, there can be no good or bad material for non-relative morality to arise from, which means there are no limits on how we ought to act and everything is permitted. Relative morality is one consequence, and its very name is an oxymoron: if there is no right or wrong, there is no need for morality. Relative morality is another word for policy.

Positivistic philosopher Rudolf Carnap, writing in the mature stage of American democracy, was perhaps the vanguard of intellectuals denying truth. He attacked synthetic propositions and rejected metaphysics because synthetic sentences, or sentences that are based on our senses and experiences, cannot be verified empirically. He explained that an essence, absolute or truth is impossible. Pertinent to this chapter, he rejected ethics because saying killing is wrong is not a truth assertion but rather a command, and commands are neither true nor false — they are only propositions. Morality for Carnap only expresses deep feelings and emotions. Carnap represents the kind of thinking that rule by the people naturally embraces over time for a variety of reasons. Unrealistic ideals, excess, tolerance, utility and desire are just a few of them. The consequences in late democracies are that little is true, most things are permitted and morality is relative. This is our fifth reason why democracy fails.

Relative Morality Defined

The philosophic debate whether universals or absolutes exist has a long history. It could be said that the ancient sophist philosopher Protagoras initiated the debate when he claimed

186

that man is the measure of all things. Truth is what we make it. It is a relativistic claim, and in morality it means right and wrong are what they are only because we choose so. Truth depends on people and circumstances, and how we ought to act is relative depending on what people believe at any one time and place. Because times, places and circumstances vary, what is right will also vary.

It should be mentioned that there are different forms of relative morality. Descriptive moral relativism claims that only some people disagree about what constitutes morality, meta-ethical moral relativism claims nobody is morally right or wrong and normative moral relativism holds that because nobody is right or wrong, we should tolerate others' behavior even if we morally disagree with them. Because this is a book on democracy and not ethics, the common definition of moral relativism will be used: there are no universals or absolutes, people decide what is moral and there is no good or evil or right or wrong. Morality is relative.

Why This Is Important

If relative morality is true, then Germans killing Jews during World War II and present day female genital mutilation in Africa cannot be called wrong. The German people collectively believed killing Jews was good, and the majority in an African village think mutilating a woman's vagina is right. These are people making decisions at a time and place under certain societal circumstances, so, according to moral relativism, their actions are moral and others cannot call them otherwise. Their moral views are valid and there is no objective way to declare them immoral. Only individuals in a society establish morality, there are no universal standards and everything is permitted. Morality becomes mere caprice, and reality becomes opaque. Fukuyama himself wrote that without some standard of comparison, we cannot grasp reality; non-relative morality requires opposites.

Who knows what could arise in a society imbued with relative morality. Different people have different sentiments, political views, emotional make-ups and varying passions, and the result could indeed be some very pernicious moral systems. Exposing infants, pedophilia and genocide could become what the people consider moral. Certainly, it is unthinkable that any moral system would embrace such practices, but moral relativity makes it possible.

Democracy is inclined to relative morality. Like politics, it democratizes it. The majorities in democracy believe they know what is right for all, and because many democracies are ptochocracies, the solution is invariably materialistic utilitarianism. With this, morality gradually becomes detached from reality as democratic societies increasingly sacrifice the universal to the particular. Democracy debasing morality debases itself.

There are many ethical theories on how we ought to live, but the significant ones that play out in democracy are the social contract and utilitarianism. Let us briefly examine these.

The Social Contract, Utilitarianism and Relative Morality

In chapter eight on injustice, the social contract and utilitarianism ethical theories were described. The argument was made that early democracies embrace the social contract because kings and princes pursued their selfish interests rather than fulfilling their proper roles as Leviathan enforcing the compacts of the contract. The solution was for the people to take over and become Leviathan themselves in the form of democracy. However, as democracies age, they naturally embrace utilitarianism, and with this, justice becomes expedience, and the majority becomes the new evil tyrant Leviathan, no different than the earlier selfish kings and princes. In chapter six on freedom, Edmund Burke's presaged this point with his observation that majority rule is not in accordance with the social contract because the minority is not in agreement with its terms. It looks like Burke was right. Utilitarianism reigns supreme in late democracy and relative morality is the consequence. The causes of this process will be described shortly, but for now, let us examine utilitarianism in order to appreciate how it brings relative morality to democracy.

Thomas Hobbes's reasons for the social contract were simple and realistic. They were for peace, for the willingness to restrict one's liberties and for participants to perform their duties. Leviathan was to enforce these rules. These are a few timeless and universal principles that exist as long as creatures like humans exit. With them, humans gain peace, security, honesty, virtue and loyalty. This is not relative morality.

This changes as democracy ages, and appreciation for the benefits of the social contract wane. For Burke, it is the hegemonic majority in democracy that votes its tyrannical way in violation of the contract's compacts, and their natural choice is utilitarianism.

UTILITARIANISM

Like Phidias' sculpture, at a distance utilitarianism looks good, but upon closer inspection it becomes deformed. Jeremy Bentham, in his *An Introduction to the Principles of Morals and Legislation*, wrote mankind is governed by pain and pleasure; therefore, pleasure ought to be the object of all legislation. Like Epicureanism did two thousand years earlier, he failed to appreciate that pleasure is a poor master for ethics. It ignores duty and contracts and eliminates individual rights and natural law based on morality (Bentham rejected the latter two). This reminds me of Samuel Johnson, in his book *The Vanity of Human Wishes*, describing the illusion of wishful thinking: when desires distort reality, they cause false expectations. Petronius once wrote that the sky don't get no nearer wherever you are—human desire is unsatisfiable.

John Stuart Mill, another utilitarian philosopher, sophisticated Bentham's views but failed to appreciate its implications in democracy. On one hand, he advocated happiness for the most, but on the other, he championed individual liberty. In *On Liberty*, he offered a trenchant defense of individual freedom, which is the antithesis of utility. He preached that man is free as long as he does not harm his neighbor. In chapter six, it was argued that democracy takes individual freedom, which Mill did not envision in the nineteenth century.

Henry Sidgwick, an original supporter of the hedonistic utilitarian philosophy, later admitted the difficulty in reconciling ego and utilitarian duty, the need for practical reason in ethics, utility's inability to universalize ethics and utility's subjectiveness. His was a theory of value, and as his great critic Stephen Darwall pointed out, a theory of the right is prior to a theory of value.

Due in part to these deficiencies, there are five reasons utilitarianism brings relative morality. The first is the idea that morality is to bring happiness to the most. Happiness means different things to different people, so the very idea of happiness becomes splintered and relative. Also, making two happier out of three may come at one's expense, which makes the concept of equal justice irrelevant. Morality deals with our relations with other people and how we ought to live; it is more than just happiness for the most. It also entails honesty, fair dealing and keeping promises. Under the influence of utilitarianism, morality becomes subjectively democratized.

Second, in chapter eight on injustice, the point was made that in late democracies, means supersede ends—by which an unjust mean becomes acceptable. Utilitarianism is a consequentialist moral philosophy—one that considers consequences only and not causes. Thus, like ends and means, it may perpetuate injustice to one while at the same time ostensibly granting justice to the majority, which is made happier. This is utilitarian relative morality. A manifestation of this is the third reason: bringing happiness to the most invariably involves the end of eliminating need. Indeed, late democracies embrace the political philosophy that does just this—socialism. The result is that all efforts in late democracies are focused on feeding need rather than addressing its causes. It was mentioned earlier that Thomas Robert Malthus explained that the more need you feed, the more you get, and the consequence in late democracies is a bottomless pit of unsatisfiable need. With this, the cause and worthiness of need is lost. With this, relative morality is perpetuated, with the able being treated differently than the needy. An example of this given earlier is late democracies that champion equal treatment under the law but at the same time treat people unequally with progressive taxation.

The fourth and fifth reasons are straightforward. In late democracies, the majority acts largely with impunity, which ushers in "might makes right" and sends any universal morality out the door. Indeed, it is the majority that brings utilitarianism because as "the most," is stands to gain the most happiness. But in the majority's zeal to vote for its own happiness, it tramples on many others, who are made less happy. Finally, excessive passion in the form of compassion blinkers rationality. Citizens under relative morality in late democracies come to ignore causes and important just ends. Rational-less passion will be discussed shortly.

There is a reason Immanuel Kant called utilitarianism "serpent winding"—a point Fukuyama fails to appreciate, as his book's index does not mention utilitarianism's influence on democracy; an oversight that elides one of the essential reasons democracy fails. Democracy embraces utility, which brings it relative morality.

The Democratic Causes of Relative Morality

The argument in this chapter is that relative morality is endemic in democracy, which is a disease that militates against its survival. In the last section, utilitarianism was described because it is one cause of relative morality in democracies. This section will explore the democratic causes of relative morality. This section is most pertinent to this book's theme that democracy will fail because relative morality is one reason. This will be followed by a description of some consequences of relative morality in democracy.

UNREALISTIC EXPECTATIONS

Curiously, the democratic ideals of freedom and equality, when taken to excess, invariably lead to unrealistic aspirations that bend reality to ensue. The natural result is relative morality because principles must be manipulated, people treated differently and the law politicized. The result is selective application of moral laws that often leads to contradictions and dilemmas, which are common problems in late democracies.

Aristotle wrote in Nicomachean Ethics that in some democracies, everyone has license to do as he pleases. Tocqueville believed that with the removal of restraints in a democracy, the only measure would be one's own happiness — democracy's freedom makes the privatized individuals cut off from others who devolve into personal selfishness, concerned only with material well-being. Democracy idealizes freedom, and it was mentioned earlier that Giambattista Vico, in theorizing on the stages of history, wrote that freedom brings relative morality, and writer Henrik Ibsen described how personal freedom results in a permissive society.

Why do these past thinkers believe freedom brings license, selfishness and relative morality? It is because many people can't handle freedom. Freedom entails responsibility, like not dumping your waste in the stream, which sickens those downstream. Many people are irresponsible, which is just human nature. Dante, in The Divine Comedy, wrote that reason cannot cope with evil and lawless passion, and we see the consequences everywhere, writ large in late democracy, in the form of the seven deadly sins: pride, envy, anger, sloth, avarice, gluttony and lust.

Problematically, we are not all hermits, and living together in civil society requires self-control—anarchy does not bring freedom. Therefore, to truly be free, there must be some limiting factor, whether it is morality or the law, that rational people understand and to which they agree. Democracy's ideal of freedom, when taken to excess, diminishes these moral and legal restraints on freedom.

Why can't some people handle freedom? It is because as Hume explained reason is the slave of the passions. Humans are passionate beings, they are driven by feelings, desires, yearnings and aspirations which emotions democracy inflames with its ideals. When freedom is bent too far unrealistic aspirations arise, passion ensues, reason takes a holiday, nothing becomes true and everything is permitted.

The result is a weird kind of manmade fanciful democratic societal carnival with no grounding in reality. Things become what people want them to be rather than what they are, and society retreats further from actuality. Reality becomes bent, and an artificial, ungrounded man-made society emerges, detached from natural morality. The result is a zeitgeist of inconsistency, ideology, politics and relative morality. It becomes a society of some thinking they are free to dump their waste in the stream even though many downstream become sick while ardently opposing anyone upstream dumping waste so they don't get sick. This is the selective application of the principles of life and justice for all applied inconsistently; this is relative morality derived from the unrestrained majority; this is the unrestrained hegemonic majority in democracy bringing relative morality.

Parenthetically, in the ancient sense, these unreal aspirations brought on by democracy represent the loss of virtue. Virtue, in the ancient sense, was expressed as arête, or excellence. The concept evolved over time, but its immanency was character: to be the best of one's human kind, which involved the characteristics of courage, strength and will. In contemporary political terms, this could mean to courageously vote for a principle that is against one's self-interest or to be ruled by reason rather than passion or ideology. It seems that in late democracy citizens lose this virtue when they vote for corrupt politicians because the politician delivers benefits or reduces their taxes.

Like freedom, late democracy's unrealistic aspiration for equality in all respects also brings relative morality. Because much was written on equality in chapter seven, this will be brief. We know intuitively that humans are not equal—God made us unequal. Political equality and parity are good aspirations of democracy, but as an extreme, it becomes Friedrich Nietzsche's prejudice instilled by Christianity.

To bring about democracy's equality facts must be bent and reality altered which manipulation only untethers society from any solid foundation. The result is a confused malfunctioning moral compass that cannot discern right from wrong and the result is nothing becomes true. This confuses citizens because they are left adrift with no direction so they turn to the authority in democracy for answers, which happens to be the majority. But the majority has an agenda that may not be in all citizens interests. Naturally, the majority inherits the mantle of tyrant and arbiter of morality, and in this case who is equal and who is not.

The majority in democracy has no special gift to discern truth, so morality is left to the capricious and too often selfish inclinations of the citizens who happen to be part of the majority at any one time. The result is that the majority decides moral questions based on sentiment, emotion, passion, desire, envy, what is in their interests or the latest fad. Like with freedom, cause and effect, rationality and consequences are used only to support already-decided, emotionally driven decisions derived from unrealistic aspirations. As was mentioned earlier, morality becomes, as Georg Wilhelm

Friedrich Hegel pointed out, a desire that derives not from the demands of universality but rather arbitrary inclinations and opinions.

The majority's moral hegemony becomes less constrained as democracy ages. Any moral checks on the majority fade, just as the legal constraints on its power erodes, which was described in chapter eight. The majority is increasingly freed from any universal moral code or uniform principles, and the result is that it can morally do what it pleases, including treating people unequally, limiting individual freedom and subjugating some.

In order to maintain its legitimacy, the majority must increasingly resort to a variety of political legerdemains, prevarications and sleights of hand. It alters language, obliterates distinctions, obscures differences and elides natural values and principles in order to preserve the corrupt idea of equality in all respects. The justifications for morality become sophistry, and morality becomes fashion. Voila, Protagoras's man, the measure of all things, is crowned king; morality in late democracy is relative, and utilitarianism is the dénouement.

The result of this in late democracies is mass confusion and internal disagreement that is characteristic of societies in decline. Let us jump ahead and describe two situations that illustrate this point, that are found in law in mature, now entering late-stage, American democracy. In 2015, the United States Supreme Court legalized same-sex marriage. Justice Anthony Kennedy, the leader of the prevailing decision, wrote that the right to marriage is a right of everyone, including homosexuals. Chief Justice John Roberts dissented, saying that the decision raised the question of whether his reasoning could be used to legalize plural marriage. If marriage is a right for everyone, then why is it not available to polygamists, bigamists or anybody who is of age and rational to marry anyone else?

The second situation is a bakery that refused to bake a cake for a same-sex marriage on religious grounds. For this, it was vilified by the press, fined by the state and issued a gag order restraining its ability to tell its side of the story. What if a Nazi requested a celebration cake for Adolf Hitler's birthday from a Jewish bakery? The zeitgeist of the times would never tolerate the state compelling them to bake it — the majority would say it is immoral. Certainly, killing is far worse than same-sex marriage, but the principle remains, which is that in both cases morality is based on the opinion of the people. With such, morality becomes relative, and there exists no basis to declare heinous acts like mass killing — or who we have sex with — wrong universally.

These two cases illustrate the warren of conflicting and capricious laws concerning equality and freedom derived from majority rule in late democracies. It legalizes the right to same-sex marriage, but denies it to polygamists and bigamists; it protects same-sex marriage rights over religious rights; it fines the Christian bakery for not baking a cake for a same sex couple, but not the Jewish bakery for refusing to bake for a Nazi; and it allows the same sex couple to air its grievances publically while gagging the Christian bakery. Any universal moral codes that require freedom, freedom of speech, equal treatment under the law and freedom of religious expression are abridged. This is relative morality in late democracy.

The unrealistic aspirations of freedom and equality in a democracy, ruled by an emotionally driven majority with unrealistic aspirations, leads to relative morality in late democracies, where everything is permitted that the majority sanctions. The irony is the very freedom and equality democracy intended to bring are lost due to the very nature of democracy itself.

EXCESSIVE PASSIONS

In chapter three on the historic true but not fatal arguments against democracy, famous historians Edward Gibbon,

Arnold J. Toynbee and Tocqueville wrote that societies decline from excessive enthusiasm and unrestrained passion. The response was that this is a criticism of democracy without merit, unless passion is taken to an extreme that leads to relative morality and intolerance. Intolerance in democracy is discussed throughout this book and in the conclusion, so the question before us is whether democracies lead to excessive passion and relative morality.

Aristotle's ethical theory the doctrine of the mean was intended to enable human virtue and well-being. Virtue is attained by a mean between two extremes, similar to an athlete's fitness that is maintained by not too much or too little food. For example, in face of battle, the excess is rashness and the defect is cowardice, both vices, and the mean is courage. In pleasure, the extreme vices are self-indulgence and insensibility, and the mean is temperance. For Aristotle, the middle course is practiced by the wise and good man. The temperate man (verbatim) craves for the things he ought, as he ought and when he ought; this is what rational principle directs.

Plato, who was no fan of democracy, in Book Eight of the *Republic* wrote that democracies are ruled by unnecessary desires, pleasures of every variety and indulgence. No one in democracy is master of anything, and the result is anarchy, licentiousness and immodesty. For Plato, citizens become useless. Gibbon, the great authority on why societies decline, cited excessive zeal and Tocqueville believed that with the removal of restraints in democracy, the only measure would be one's own happiness, so citizens would be constantly circling for petty pleasures.

Citizens in early democracy by historic standards are free, and it is that very freedom that unleashes excessive passion. Humans are passionate beings, and democracy, with its ideal of freedom, removes restraints to that passion. With this, David Hume's famous dictum that reason is the slave of the passions finds fertile ground, and a kind of freedom emerges as democracy ages without responsibility, wherein citizens in the majority act on self-interest and passion, unencumbered by principles. Democracy unleashes human passion, which increasingly determines policy. Plato, Hume, Gibbon and Tocqueville's observations converge into a truism: democracies are ruled by desire, display excessive zeal, endeavor to satisfy pleasure and are ruled by the sentiments. With these excesses, they lose Aristotle's mean, temperateness and individual virtue.

Democratic freedom is in some ways like opening Pandora's box because it unleashes a multitude of pent-up human desires, hopes, fears and angers—it unleashes pent-up passions. Some are good, like the ideals of freedom, equality and justice. But they themselves serve as passions—motors that propel people to defend like a deity. Others are not so good, like selfishness, that is also unleashed by freedom in democracy. Citizens passionately defend and vote their selfish interests. In mature American democracy, many vote only for the demagogic candidate who brings them benefits rather than the statesman who is more concerned with society as a whole. Ideological agendas and passionate beliefs eclipse reason and common sense in late democracies.

Jonathan Swift's *Gulliver's Travels* could be a parable of late democracy. In it, the Yahoo humans and Houyhnhnm horses magically trade places. The Yahoos are devoid of rational capacity and act only on the ugly passions of lust, envy, avarice, greed and rage. They lie and make false representations. The Houyhnhnms are the opposite; they are rational, control their emotions, limit their passions, consider consequences and would never lie or make a false representation—they simply cannot understand saying the thing that is not. Swift decried moral inadequacy, lack of rationality, the inclination to act on passion and hypocrisy—he detested Yahoos. Yahoos in late democracy are like Johnson's person trying to drink from the source and mouth of the Nile—human desire is insatiable, it wants things both ways, but the only consequence is innumerable contradictions, extremes and unleashed passion. In many ways, late democratic citizens are Yahoos.

Certainly, all societies exhibit some degree of passion, but, as Gibbon and Toynbee explained, those who take it to an extreme fail. Fascism could be one example, and, remarkably, late democracy another. Passion is not inherently bad, but it is fatal to societies in excess because it leads to intolerance and divisiveness. Divisiveness will be taken up in the next chapter.

WEALTH

The cause and effect relationships between democracy, capitalism, wealth and relative morality are difficult to discern. The plethora of variables obscures coherent answers. However, there does appear to be a special relationship between democracy and wealth producing capitalism that leads to relative morality.

For Fukuyama, capitalism is part of the liberal democracy that is the end of history. His reasons are involved. Generally, the Protestant work ethic based on recognition and the desire to accumulate wealth results in capitalism, rationality, and a universal history due to science, which all conspire to create liberal democracy. As such, it would appear capitalism and the wealth it creates enables democracy. Desire and reason bring capitalism and wealth and those political systems that ignore this truism, such as communism, are doomed to fail due to lack of wealth.

But does capitalism enable democracy? Both the French and American Revolutions were animated by freedom from oppression and particularly freedom from excess taxation. They were not per se revolutions for capitalism. However, as Fukuyama wrote, capitalism requires the undermining of wealth privileges and status of the old social classes by exposing them to competition. In this scenario, capitalism and democracy could have a symbiotic relationship, with each supporting the other, like a two prong military advance, with each prong protecting its flank.

It does seem that Fukuyama is right; early democracies, with their emphasis on freedom and individuality, typically embrace free enterprise that brings wealth. But how does wealth in early democracy lead to declining morality in late democracy? Ancient historian Polybius believed formerly incorruptible Romans, most likely due to increased wealth, were declining moral figures in the late Empire. American philosopher Will Durant believed prosperity caused the decline of the Roman Empire; wealth and luxury abounded, which attenuated many of the traditional Roman virtues. Montesquieu wrote that republics come to an end by luxurious habits, and Vico asserted that spendthriftness and wasteful opulence destroyed what had been constructed in ancient societies. Wealth brings luxury that enables moral decay, but how does it cause relative morality?

It does so in two ways. The first has already been discussed: wealth brings disparity of wealth, which is an inequality democracy cannot tolerate. Its inevitable solution is socialism. To bring about socialism, citizens must be treated unequally, and the result is relative morality. The scenario is preordained: the socialist left criticizes capitalism because it makes people unequal, they eventually prevail in late ptochocratic democracy, they begin to treat the endowed differently and relative morality ensues. The second way is subtler. Wealth enables indulgence in pleasure, pleasure become supreme and infects society in the form of happiness for the most, which becomes society's creed, and, again, relative morality ineluctably ensues. The concept of an ethical social contract becomes an ancient long forgotten religion like Zoroastrianism, considered irrelevant by many for democracy's increasing problems.

Historians Tacitus and Frank C. Bourne described this relationship as a cause of the decline of the ancient Roman Empire. Tacitus described how Augustus tried to instill morality in

200

Romans but failed. He believed one reason he failed was due to prosperity's propensity to mitigate human values. Rome had become rich, which led to pleasure that ended in a permissive morality. Due to wealth, the Romans, according to Bourne, became decadent, indulged in pleasure, retreated from traditional Roman virtues and became less prudential. He described increasing greed for wealth, which caused wealth to become an end in itself, and the search for wealth through legacy hunting. To cite philosopher Durant again, he was right: wealth militates against values and (paraphrased) prosperity will lead to the decline of society. Democracy with capitalism brings wealth and luxury, which lead to the loss of the moral virtues that bring relative morality.

POSITIVE LAW

Positive law was discussed at length in chapter eight on injustice and is briefly resurrected here as an example of how democracy brings relative morality. It was demonstrated in that chapter that democracy brings positive law, which detaches the law from morality and, in particular, any universal morality. Positive law defines law as a social fact not based on morality. If law is not based on morality, then it follows that immoral acts may be permitted as long as they are social facts. Further, what is moral in one society as a social fact may be immoral in another as a social fact. Ipso facto, this is relative morality.

With the abandonment of natural law and advent of majority rule, the law becomes prey to the majority's desires, whether it is pleasure, power, wealth or prestige, all of which derive from the same motive, which is happiness. The tyrant majority rules, and its sentiments imbue society — the majority votes and brings the law into conformity with its views. As a result, law in democracy becomes the opinion of the majority and the vehicle for utilitarianism — or in this case, happiness for the majority.

The law is unique in that it often endeavors to remain rational, consistent and fair to all, but the majority's power erodes this. Principles, timeless values and natural morality are embodied in such moral theories as the social contract, and those that deal with duty and virtue are discarded as law increasingly becomes fashion. Legal precedent is increasingly disregarded if it does not conform to the majority's opinions, and tortured legal arguments ensue that sound like ancient sophist Zeno of Elea's argument that reason tells us an arrow will never hit its target.

With these circumstances, people are treated differently because there are no longer principles demanding all be treated similarly. There is no longer a universal morality that has the ability to condemn heinous immoral acts. Everything is permitted as long as the majority approves and the majority decides what is true. Democracy naturally brings positive law and utilitarianism, which engenders relative morality.

FRAGMENTATION

The charge that democracy brings disorder was discussed in chapter three on the historic arguments against democracy. Plato wrote that they bring variety, disorder, chaos, and mob rule and cater to many ideologies, and James Madison argued that direct democracy leads to turbulence and contention. Both historians Gibbon and Toynbee poignantly cited this kind of internal divisiveness as a reason societies fail, along with passionate single-mindedness, which will be discussed shortly. In that chapter, it was concluded that this argument against democracy was groundless, mainly because many stable societies, including democracies, exist with some degree of disorder and chaos. However, there is more to the story—instability and chaos in society often leads to relative morality, which is a cause of democracy's demise. How does this happen?

Democracy's emphasis on freedom enables disorder and chaos, but it also inflames the passions, which creates pockets of divergent values within society. These pockets grow and conflict which inflames social discord. In keeping with democracy's freedom, each pocket of value maintains separate moral codes, which legitimize them. But the consequence is really relative morality, because there exists no universal morality to maintain cohesion and order between the divergent pockets. Universal morality constrains and relative morality liberates, so as democracies age, less becomes true because the pockets often disagree, and more becomes permitted because the pockets want freedom. Morality, due to disorder, and like positive law in late democracy, becomes nothing more than a social fact.

So, if morality is just a social fact, who decides which moralities are true? In democracy, it is the majority. The majority holds power and decides what is right or wrong independent of any universal morality. The consequence is that people are treated differently. One of our examples of this in late democracy was same-sex marriage. Again, if marriage is a right, why must it be limited to two? This is relative morality.

Diversity

Perhaps the best example of how democracy brings fragmentation — and ultimately relative morality — can be found in the popular concept of diversity, again in mature American democracy. America's founding democratic ideals embraced a melting pot philosophy, in which citizens from diverse cultures were welcome to come and share in freedom. They did — and became Americans first and foremost. From this, an identity was created that unified citizens and created a nation. Democracy changes the melting pot norm with the demand for diversity.

Diversity emphasizes multiculturalism, ethnic and cultural diversity, and diversity of thought, religion and ideology, as well as freedom of expression. It envisions a society composed of different equal elements and the inclusion of all types of people. It is the effort to move beyond tolerance to acceptance of diverse ways and people. It wants people to feel safe and accepted. It is a sophisticated incarnation of democracy's aspirations for freedom, equality and Fukuyama's recognition, promoted mostly by minorities and feminists, but with the twist that it is for groups as well as individuals. Diversity per se is not bad because it springs from the same aspirations for individual freedom in early democracy.

But diversity is different than individual freedom in two ways. First, when multiple diverse pockets in society with different cultures, worldviews and moralities prevail, any overarching political or universal morality that shields the individual becomes problematic. It is the universals of early democracy that engendered individual freedom. Second, unlike individual freedom, which is freedom from something, like oppressive government, diversity is the effort to engage the power of the majority and government to change morality in favor of something. Specifically, it is the effort to erase disapprobation of desired beliefs and their resulting behaviors. When individuals violate moral codes, they face societal disapprobation under universal morality, but when a group under diversity has gained majority opinion in democracy, they set the moral code, and approbation is the consequence. Morality in both cases becomes relative and utterly useless.

Morality under diversity is a slogan used by pockets to gain majority power because they know society can be diverse only to the extent that the majority approves. Ironically, the tolerance and acceptance the pockets wish the majority to preach extends only to similar pocket cultures and worldviews; others are not to be tolerated or accepted.

It has been mentioned throughout this book that passionate single-mindedness is a cause of society's extinction. Recall that Gibbon believed democracy legitimizes unrestrained passion and Tocqueville thought that the removal of restraints in democracy would result in everyone seeking one's own happiness and petty pleasures. In many ways, late democracy's penchant to create pockets of diverse citizens is driven by passion fired by freedom. Passion is good, and we would not be human without it, but in late democracy, it blinkers thought. People become so passionately single-minded that they are unable to see flaws in their ideas or the advantages of alternate ideas. For example, in the mature American democracy, which pockets are to be included? Who decides which ones? What if a Nazi in democracy wanted their racist beliefs accepted under the mantra of diversity—should they be included? As previously mentioned, if same-sex marriage is to be an accepted diverse pocket, why not the polygamists? Why ought not the feminists accept the pocket of patriarchy and hierarchy they so despise? A virtual plethora of contradictions arise fueled by passion-driven relative morality that does not exist under universal morality.

Diversity ostensibly is about freedom, equality and acceptance, but it is really just a social fact that is about power, and the result is fragmentation and relative morality. Under its aegis, contradictions only multiply, and the dialectic Fukuyama thought brings democracy evaporates like smoke in a breeze. Societies can endure a degree of fragmentation and relative morality, but when they coalesce into internal passionate divisiveness, only force can arbitrate. The destructive power of divisiveness will be explored in the next chapter.

DEMAGOGUES

Certainly, all societies are infected by manipulative and unscrupulous leaders who gain power by appealing to people's emotions, instincts, biases and prejudices. Such demagogues often sow discord that rends societies. However, due to its very nature, democracy is particularly susceptible to these

kinds of leaders. Indeed, the ancient definition of a demagogue was one who represented the ordinary people.
Democracy is predominantly the rule by the ordinary people, and it is their passions demagogues solicit.

But how do democratically inspired demagogues bring
relative morality? They do it by inflaming passion, advocating unrealistic ideas, undermining true morality, causing
divisiveness and exacerbating societal problems.

There exists a complicated relationship between the
human emotions of passion, pleasure and the idea of happiness. Passion is emotion in excess that sometimes can bring
pleasure and happiness but also angst and distress. Pleasure
is a somewhat vague term that can be enhanced by passion
and lead to happiness, but in excess it causes ennui. The
indefinable state of happiness so sought by many may or
may not come by passion and pleasure. On one hand, the
ancient Greek philosopher Hegesias of Cyrene and Bentham
believed happiness is pleasure, and on the other, Boethius
believed happiness is not pleasure, and with indulgence, it
actually brought unhappiness.

This section is not about untangling these relationships
but rather how demagogues bring relative morality. They
do it partly by confusing these relationships. They promise
pleasure and happiness and inflame people's passions sophistically using whatever philosophy will do the job to gain
power. Their philosophy is usually utilitarianism, and with
its invocation, relative morality ensues. Happiness ought not
be confused with pleasure.

More broadly, when demagogues inflame passions in democracy, common sense too often takes a holiday. Issues that
could be resolved under the cold light of dispassionate reasoning too often coalesce into pockets of impassioned and
hardened ideological sects in democracy, incapable of compromise. Let us digress briefly and look at the relationship
between reason and passion.

Reason and Passion

Kant believed the only good thing in this world is good will, which is established by reason. Reason tells us to morally act in accordance with a categorical imperative, which is in such a way that it would become a universal law. It is reason and not the passions that give us this ethical proposition. Hume, in *An Enquiry Concerning the Principles of Morals*, explains why it does not. For Hume, moral judgments are matters of sentiment, and social virtues of benevolence and justice are a result of human sympathy. We approve of morals because of their utility. Justice has merit only because of its beneficial consequences. Language itself is a product of views that are in the community's interests that fixes praise or blame based on community sentiments. Hume believed reason is the servant to the passions. He wrote (verbatim) that after every circumstance, every relation is known; the understanding has no further room to operate, nor any object on which it could employ itself. The approbation or blame that then ensues cannot be the work of the judgment, but of the heart; it is not a speculative proposition or affirmation, but an active feeling or sentiment. Morality, therefore, is not based on reason but rather, emotion.

This is precisely what demagogues play on and why they flourish in democracies. Freedom in democracy unleashes people's passions, unrealistic ideals perpetuate them, diverse groups' struggle for power hardens them and the demagogues inflame them. The reason that Kant tells us reason brings goodwill fades as the demagogues kindle emotions by promising to satisfy people's desires, which are usually pleasure and happiness. Kant's emphasis on moral duty is replaced with moral theories that emphasize consequences, like utilitarianism. Utility, as we have seen, treats people differently, and the result is a subjective and relative morality.

There are other ways demagogues succor relative morality in democracies. One is that they advocate unrealistic ideas that lead to relative morality. Jean-Jacques Rousseau, in Social

Contract, famously wrote that man is born free but everywhere in chains, so all oppressed in democracy are in chains. He tells us in nature we are good, but civilization corrupts us, so those inclined to the bad believe they are bad because of society. He tells us that vice is caused by society so those with many vices naturally blame others for their failings. He writes that social organization brought the evil concept of property, which only brings inequality, so the mendicants blame their circumstances on those who have property, even if the property owners earned it. He audaciously states that human life before the formation of societies was healthy and happy with no thought to either the abject states of those in primitive societies or their ardent desire to reap the benefits of civilization.

Bentham taught that morality is happiness for the most, with no regard to the individual or consequences. He believed that individual freedom, a hallmark of democracy, in the form of rights should be dispensed with because rights interfere with his philosophy. So, should those who are not happy advocate eliminating rights? Karl Marx envisioned a bourgeoisie and repressed proletariat that can only be resolved with the advent of communism. So, all proletariats believe that their problems are caused by the small capitalist businessman merchant.

Demagogues Rousseau, Bentham and Marx are rightfully examining common failures in many societies, but in democracy their views become inflamed, unattainable, unrealistic and destructive. They imagine utopias where pleasure and happiness reside, which appeal to many people's emotions. Nowhere do they discuss responsibility, accountability, duty, obligation, industry, effort, honor or virtue. The consequence of their teachings can only be to treat individuals differently, and the result is relative morality.

Demagogues with their appeal to passion undermine universal morality based on reason. Demagogues themselves often have confused, unreasoned, passionate agendas, so how could they possibly impart a rational universal morality that must incorporate all perspectives? Indeed, their single-mindedness often brings intolerance, which leads to disbelief of alternative ideas. Tocqueville, for example, believed that the triumph of unbelief among intellectuals, or in this case demagogic intellectuals, would undermine the moral fabric of civic order. This enables a condition for any relative morality to exist. Further, with different demagogues preaching different ideas that inflame people's emotions, the natural result is increased divisiveness. It was mentioned earlier that Aristotle believed the bane of Athenian democracy was demagogues calumniating the rich, rousing the poor and creating parties. He believed that demagogues only stir resistance, create insecurity and bring divisiveness. Certainly, gasoline vapors exist to some degree in all societies, but it is the demagogues who increase and ignite them.

The Consequences of Relative Morality in Democracy

The proposition has been that democracies breed relative morality, which leads to their inevitable decline. The last section was about how democracies beget relative morality, and this section is about the consequences. Some of these consequences have been discussed elsewhere, so they will relate here only to relative morality. Some of these consequences deal with democracy treating people unequally due to the majority dictating an unjust morality, and others are consequences of relative morality.

Socialism in late democracy can only exist within a relative moral climate. The very philosophy of "from each their ability and to each their need" necessarily treats people differently. A morality that treats everyone equally would never tolerate socialistic philosophy. Socialism is not a moral theory but rather a policy driven by desire and emotion. One consequence of this emotional policy is the unremitting focus on need in late democracies. Need becomes king; how to meet it supplants how it arose, and any thought of how to prevent it is lost. The result is more unrelenting need because, as Malthus pointed out, the more need you feed the more you get. Thus, in late democracies, need becomes an unsustainable, bottomless pit. The problem of need in late democracy remains larger, unresolved and unresolvable. This occurs in part because democracy succors the morally relative ethic of utility that intends to bring happiness to the most.

Relative morality alters the essential concept of justice and in the process brings injustice in late democracies. Universal moralities like the social contract impart equal justice for all, whereas under relative morality the concept of justice becomes political and vague. Political justice in democracy is nothing more than the majority's policies in democracy — it is just to discriminate against a polygamist but not a same-sex marriage. It necessarily becomes vague in a ptochocracy because merit, ability and talent must be divorced from what constitutes justice. In nature, it is just that the faster runner wins, whereas in late democracy, nature's gift of swiftness becomes an unearned accident. John Rawls's theory of justice described earlier is a product of late democracy's concept of justice. He postulated an unreal veil of ignorance, where individuals were to be unaware of their natural talents, which he described as accidents. This kind of sophistic reasoning permeates late democracies in which the true concept of justice is lost. If the ability to run fast is an unjust accident of nature that justice must correct, then so must superior intelligence, which would mean justice would demand dumb people have the right to be brain surgeons — hopefully for the progressives in late democracy.

The advent of positive law is another consequence of relative morality in democracy. The desire to make reality conform to policy in late democracy detaches universal morality from the law. Natural law based on morality is discarded and replaced by a more accommodating kind of law

210

that is nothing more than a social fact or what judges do. The law in late democracies no longer aspires to represent some transcendent universal rules of right and wrong but rather succumbs to being the servant foot soldier for majority opinion.

Morally relative law creates a labyrinth of problems and contradictions in late democracy, many of which have been previously described. One example is unequal treatment under the law where, in mature American democracy, anti-discrimination laws protect classes of people but discriminate against other classes and some individuals. The natural consequence is inconsistency and caprice, which debases one of law's great gifts, which is precedent. One example of this was given earlier about when Franklin D. Roosevelt pressured the Supreme Court to alter the intent of the Commerce Clause in the Constitution. Under relative morality, it does not matter what laws have been written but only what the majority and their resulting policies demand. Relative morality debases the law.

One of relative morality's most pernicious consequences involves the loss of human dignity that was alluded to by Fukuyama, Kant, Hegel, Ralph Waldo Emerson, James Fenimore Cooper and Nietzsche. Kant and Hegel, for example believed that humans had superior dignity, and American novelist Cooper wrote that (paraphrased) the tendency in democracies is to mediocrity. This is ironic because Fukuyama believed it was *thymos*, or self-respect, that enables democracy to be the end of history.

Human dignity means self-respect, self-esteem and pride—it means humans *are* special in some way. Humans are special because they have a brain that is unlike other animals'. Their brain conceives and creates vehicles that can go one hundred miles per hour, things that can fly in the air and receptacles of data containing fathomless information. The other animals cannot do this. Perhaps not ontologically, but certainly temporally, humans *are* special.

Relative morality in late democracy attacks this special-ness by devaluing both human and individual dignity. If everything is relative, then nothing is special because nothing is true. Under relative morality, worse and better fade, and the engine for that change is the capricious opinion of the majority. In mature American democracy, this is sometimes called political correctness.

Nature made humans with varying degrees of abilities. In order to achieve perfect equality, late democracy must erase these abilities and reinvent human nature. Hence Fukuyama's point that relativists claim that human beings constitute nothing distinctive against non-humans. Further, the relativists claim that individual dignity is not special because some groups are more important than the individual. The concept of a universal humanity with specific human dignity is dismissed by collectivist relativists, who assert that certain group identities are more important than individual humans. Hence, Fukuyama's point that democracy has a tendency to grant equal recognition to unequal people. This is relativism in spades.

In order for the relativists to achieve equality, they necessarily must reinvent the concept of what constitutes human nature. To this end, they claim humans are only a product of their environment and not nature, which gives them a tabula rasa on which they can write their own scheme of human nature. This is one reason so much emphasis is placed on education in late democracies—schools in many ways become the institutions that indoctrinate youth with who they are and what they are to be.

With this relativist agenda, myriad problems arise, including that humans are no different than non-humans, humans are not special, no one individual is special and, as Fukuyama puts it, we are just rational slime. This debases human dignity. Compare this view with the ancient Greek's ideal of *arête*, in which strength, courage, ability and talent are considered virtues. It embodied the ideas that humans

212

can be great and individuals can be the best they can be. This is a view of human nature that mirrors nature and enhances human dignity.

In their contest with nature, the relativists find themselves, as Fukuyama pointed out, unable to provide a cohesive and comprehensive definition of human nature and explain why some humans are superior to others. With their ideologically driven view of human nature, strength becomes weakness, ability becomes a vice, revenge becomes self-destruction and anger becomes destroying the vessel. They cannot explain human and individual strengths and uniqueness. Nothing is true because everything is relative.

One result is that late (ostensibly advanced and civilized) democracy becomes almost surreal where nothing is real. Citizens find it increasingly difficult to navigate the artificial corridors of normalcy created by the relativists. To aide them, psychiatrists, psychologists and counselors are needed to help them deny their natural instincts and remain sane. One favorite paladin of these professions draws from the ancient philosophy of Stoicism, which taught that the world is a consequence of our judgment of impressions, or in modern language, the world is as we make it. All of our problems arise from us. Because relativists cannot explain reality from without, it must alter internal thought to accommodate their unreality.

Other problems include truncated human beings, loss of individual strength and mediocrity. As Emerson so eloquently wrote, under the boot of the collective coercive group's demand for conformity, the individual is reduced to timorous despondent whimperers afraid of fortune, death and each other. In late democratic socialist France, the young become truncated, idle café loungers, and productive and overtaxed actor Gérard Depardieu leaves the country. There is less vigor, valor, virtue and *arête*; only compliance remains. The truth is that it was individuals who conceived of the cars, planes and computers mentioned earlier and not the collective group—individuals bring vigor and innovation, not committees. Late democratic relative collectivism saps individual strength and takes people's dignity.

Relative morality leads to mediocrity because it denies excellence. Fukuyama's *thymos* in democracy has its merits, but in the end, it makes everyone equal and denies talent. Everybody is the same with no acknowledgment of ability. Fukuyama was right to point out that true morality requires distinctions between better and worse but these terms become pointless when humans are defined through the lens of the relativists and not nature. With the relativists' effort to remake human nature, they lose its essence, so excellence becomes a mirage that always recedes when approached. Humans under relative morality lose, as Fukuyama pointed out, any true direct experience of value. If aristocratic society is defined as one based on ability, Nietzsche was right—human excellence is only possible in aristocratic societies and if not, they are mediocre.

Fukuyama's last man with no chest is the product of this mediocre society spawned by relative morality. Fukuyama describes him as a man who is preoccupied with personal health and safety, avoids exertion, focuses on self-preservation, is jaded by history, has no horizon, is content to sit at home, has no beliefs and, thus, has no chest. He satisfies need through economic activity and returns to being an animal, or a Lockean satisfied pig. He no longer fights for freedom but rather surrenders it to security, a topic that was examined in chapter six on the loss of freedom. He has physical security and material plenty, but he is dissatisfied with himself. He is a man who lives in mediocrity.

Two final consequences of relative morality in democracy are the loss of tolerance and divisiveness. Tolerance in democracy was discussed earlier in the arguments against democracy and in chapter eight on injustice. Considered historically, tolerance is indeed a chief virtue of early democracy. Fukuyama was right to claim democracy brings the kind of tolerance Voltaire espoused, which was that one may disapprove of what another says but will defend to the death their right to say it. What Fukuyama failed to appreciate is how tolerance ebbs and the sphere of tolerance decreases as democracy ages. In late democracies, there is tolerance for pro-democratic conflicting views, such as views on equality, but increasing intolerance toward non-democratic views. It becomes the contest described earlier between freedom and equality, and in democracy, freedom eventually loses.

So how does relative morality in democracy bring this intolerance about? There are three reasons. First, the majority becomes increasingly intolerant of ethical views that contravene their cherished utility. Duty, virtue and compacts do not necessarily bring happiness for the most. Second, freedom in democracy enables the kind of excessive zeal described by historian Gibbon that leads to intolerance. In the chapter on the historic arguments against democracy, this charge was dismissed unless it became excessive. In late democracy, under relative morality, it does become excessive, intolerance is the result and, as Gibbon presaged, it is fatal to any political system.

The third reason is that the utilitarian morality spawned by democracy flourishes in a relativistic environment where nothing is universally true. If nothing is true, not only is everything permitted, but there remains no universal right or wrong to adjudicate what is to be tolerated. With the loss of any universal moral compass, only passion, sentiment, prejudice and bias remain to decide what is to be tolerated. The consequence is excessive capricious intolerance.

The final consequence of relative morality in democracy is divisiveness. Divisiveness is the last of the six reasons democracy fails, and because it is the topic of the next chapter, this discussion will be brief. How democracy brings relative morality, utilitarianism and fragmentation have been described earlier. The result is a kind of hedonistic moral ennui characteristic of late democracies. It could be a state similar to ancient Greece after the conquests of Alexander the Great and the destruction of the polis. Some sought to deny the resulting moral atomization through Stoic denial and control of judgments, and others remained indifferent through Skepticism. Many, however, turned to philosophies that enhanced pleasure, such as Hedonism and Epicureanism, which in modern terms are similar to utility. Whatever the morality, it was man, or the majority, in democracy, who determined which prevailed, which was not universal morality.

With the ascension of man, imagined consequentialist relativistic utility life for citizens becomes confusing, uncertain and vague. Because the new morality is relativistic, with an end that favors happiness for the most, some citizens naturally are treated differently. Living in such a moral climate becomes akin to playing a rigged game. Under universal morality, there are clear rules known in advance, which results in winners prevailing based on natural qualities. Under relative morality, the rules are constantly being changed as the game progresses to insure a predetermined artificial outcome—the winners are those who the rules favor, irrespective of natural qualities. Living in relative morality in late democracy is like this, and the losers who were hobbled and handicapped seethe with resentment because the game is not fair. It was mentioned earlier that man accepts injustice from nature but bridles when it is dispensed by other men.

Citizens are not treated the same under relative morality, which only results in an increasing number of underground platoons of passive resistance poised for active rebellion in late democracies. As democracy progresses under these circumstances, different cultures arise, deepening fissures emerge and balkanization begins. Relative morality brings divisiveness because it does not bring justice to all.

Two examples of these consequences of relative morality are found in sex and violence, which will be discussed next.

216

SEX

In order to ground ourselves in truth, a brief, sophomoric review of sex's purpose is in order. Asexual organisms reproduce themselves without mates because offspring arise from a single organism. If humans were asexual, there would be no need for a morality dealing with sexuality, because there would be no other partner to regard — we would just reproduce spontaneously, and that would be that. But humans are not asexual, and their offspring arise from the fusion of gametes from two — thus, the occurrence of morality. Further, asexual organisms are primitive, and their offspring thrive due more to nature than nurture, whereas sexual organisms are more advanced, with offspring that require more nurture. In the case of humans, it takes many years to raise and socialize children in order for them to successfully navigate the complexities of civilization.

Human morals dealing with sex are intended to regulate the process of the non-asexual, procuring and civilizing children in a way to enhance their success and survivability. Put another way, the principle purpose of human sexual morality is for children. A panoply of sexual mores arise from this simple premise, which includes the appellations of father and mother, each carrying certain obligations, the institution of marriage, monogamy, abstinence and the concept of a family. Uncivilized sexually reproducing Rhesus monkeys have no such mores, concepts or morality. The resulting biological human family in civilized societies thus involves a paired male and female, usually with the father provider and mother nurturer, procreating, supporting and raising children.

William Manchester, in *Goodbye, Darkness*, writing in mature American democracy about families in early American democracy, said that (paraphrased) parents adored their children, mothers were beloved, fathers were obeyed, marriage was a sacrament, divorce was disgraceful, pregnancy meant expulsion from school or dismissal from a job, boys who impregnated girls had to marry them, couples did not keep house until married and there was no wedding until the girl's father approved. Certainly, the evolved rules governing sex and children are not perfect, but they have existed for thousands of years and generally work when adhered to.

So, the purpose and function of sexual morals is for children and procreation of the human species. Now, consider what happens with the advent of utilitarianism in late democracy. The function of sexuality changes from children and procreation to pleasure. Sexual mores bend to offer pleasure to the most, which causes the true function of sexuality and reason for sexual mores to become obfuscated, attenuated and often abandoned. Sex for pleasure alone has no ontological biologic function; morality becomes the Playboy philosophy: pursuit of pleasure.

This is a strange issue to discuss because it is so salacious and base. However, in order to fully understand unrestrained homosexual and lesbian sexual practices so detached from sexual morals purpose legitimized in late American democracy, a description is necessary. Male homosexuality involves one male putting his penis in another male's anus, which is an organ not designed for an erect penis but rather excretion. Female homosexuality involves one woman stimulating another woman's clitoris and fondling her vagina, which, along with the uterus are organs with bigger purposes. There are bisexuals, or one of one gender doing what has been described with both genders, and transvestites, who change genders and do what was described with their former gender. If pleasure is the moral objective, then why is pederasty excluded? In ancient times, homosexuality and sex with children was common. The ancient Spartans institutionalized male homosexuality and catamites, or young boys raised for the purpose of sex with older men. In ancient Rome, girls were often married to older men and impregnated if possible when very young. In late democracy, the Playboy pursuit of sexual pleasure has no moral bounds, and the function of

218

human sexuality becomes lost in an unnatural maze of exotic exchange of fluids and stimulations under the aegis of utilitarian happiness for the most.

Certainly, licentious sex has always been a part of human history. Ancient Greece had Bacchanals, Rome orgies and catamites; Persia had harems, and Paris, brothels. But these pale in comparison to sexual excess in mature American democracy with its homosexuality, lesbianism, bisexualism, transgenderism, legalized prostitution, strip clubs, internet pornography, promiscuity, youthful and pre-marital sex, free condoms, same-sex marriage, naked bike rides, unionized sex workers, internet sites that cater to cheating spouses and the ubiquitous use of sex in advertising and movies. Only in this environment could the LGBTQ, or lesbian, gay, bisexual, transgender and queer movement, thrive. Sexual passion prevails, the function of sex is lost; its only purpose becomes the satisfaction of pleasure, and any morality that deals with sexual matters disappears.

One of human's relatives, the Rhesus monkey, has a sex life that could be described as expedient. When the female is in estrus, every male copulates with her, females not in estrus are left alone, and the males always have a new female eager to copulate. It is an orgy of sex based on pleasure that produces many Rhesus monkeys. It seems sex in America is returning to its primitive Rhesus monkey roots.

Is humans' ontological purpose to be sexually satisfied creatures? Is their purpose pleasure alone? It seems that they are more than this. Sexual licentiousness does not represent human advancement but rather a degradation to a relative sexual morality where everything is permitted, when passions are indulged, when desire reigns supreme, when selfish hedonism emerges from antiquity, when pleasure becomes the standard for happiness and when sex becomes a free for all devolving into debauchery, depravity, dissolution and dissipation. Any universal morality has been lost, and the result is decadence. Decadence is a word that means the process of decline or decay in society, especially in regard to morals.

Over millennia, humans have created moral circumstances that optimize care for children. This becomes lost in a sea of sensuality. Moralities that pair males and females with described roles that are intended to succor children fall away. A man asking a woman's parents for the right to marry, for example, becomes risible. Under utility, the function of sex becomes pleasure, and any connection between pleasure and duty is lost as consequences become divorced from causes under a consequentialist moral philosophy. The result is moral ambiguity, confusion, hypocrisy and immorality.

Non-relative morality regulating human sexual behavior arose for a reason, which was children and their welfare. It is a kind of morality based on reason that necessarily and universally controls and proscribes certain human sexual behaviors. Rhesus monkeys have no such ability to create morality, so when we lose ours, we return to being them. It is the perfect alignment of freedom, rule by the majority and subsequent utility that causes late democratic societies to lose their sexual moral compasses. They abandon other regarding moralities, like the social contract and Kantism, that deal with obligations, which collaterally affect children and their welfare.

The consequences of this moral degradation are devastating to families and children in mature democracy. Fukuyama wrote that American families have been breaking down for the last couple of generations, which coincides with America's mature democratic state. The institution of marriage with a man and woman procreating and raising children is the building block of any society. When it is weakened so is the society. Relative morality is inimical to the integrity of this biological family unit. It attenuates sexual mores, which makes genders less likely to mate and more likely to wander once married. Husbands and wives increasingly cheat because there are no moral consequences. It becomes easy to marry,

220

and easy to divorce because nobody is at fault. It generates a virtual smorgasbord of alternate forms of parenting, with homosexual same-sex parents, bisexual parents and transgender parents, in which children don't know who their real parents are. Eventually, these alternate forms of marriage begin to compete with heterosexual marriages for financial resources and children.

Children without biological parents are lost in a virtual sea of relative morality in mature democracy with the disintegration of the family. They lose their natural parents, their extended family, their heritage and, often, their financial support. The solution is to return to a universal sexual morality that controls sexual passion—a solution relative morality cannot abide. Utility's solution is to throw money at the problem in the form of state welfare and hope the problem abates. But its solutions fail, and one result is the increasing need for socialism, described in chapter seven. With this, people are treated unequally, which in this case includes traditional biological families whose parents are already shouldering the financial responsibility of raising children and are made to pay for those who cannot.

It was mentioned earlier in unrealistic aspirations that under relative morality, principles must be manipulated, which necessarily leads to contradictions. Here are two that relate to sexuality. Contemporary mature American relative morality sanctions same-sex marriage but not polygamy and bigamy. To legitimize same-sex marriage, it appeals to the principle that everyone has the right to marry, but it denies this very principle to those that want to marry more than one spouse. It applies the principle selectively and not universally based on majority whim. Second, having illegitimate children without wedlock is acceptable, but a bigamist having multiple children in wedlock is not. In both cases, the children are by traditional definition illegitimate, but society treats the unmarried woman and man with a child differently than the married man with multiple wives with children.

Again, the legitimacy of children is extended to one but not the other. Indeed, if one had to choose, it would seem the latter case should be the more acceptable because at least a line of financial responsibility would be established from a father who the children would be more likely to know.

Human sexuality walks a thin line between nature and civilization. On one hand, humans are animals with an instinct to reproduce, so sex is natural. On the other, civilization necessarily proscribes the sexual appetite for a variety of reasons, one of which is to promote families and the welfare of children. It is a mean, and as we have seen, as democracy ages, it finds it increasingly difficult to maintain means. This is particularly acute with sexuality in late democracies under the sway of utility. Sexuality becomes more indulgent and animal-like retreating to a more primitive state, and the result is decay due to relative morality.

VIOLENCE

A similar process occurs in violence. Like sex, civilization moderates humans' violent nature for safety, which abates as relative morality in society ascends. It was described earlier how democracies embrace the naturalistic social contract in which individuals agree to limit their freedom. This limitation includes the freedom to kill another, which is a violent act. Under the aegis of relative morality where nothing is true this changes, and violence becomes increasingly permitted. Certainly, all societies experience violence, but late democracies are particularly susceptible in part due to their emphasis on freedom, which frees passion. Like the mean in sex, democracies are increasingly incapable of finding that mean between civilization and the potentially violent human animal — nature.

It was mentioned earlier that early democracies tend to be peaceful but become prone to internal discord and violence as they age. The later stages of the fledgling democratic

French Revolution could be one example, and America in mature democracy could be another. America is a violent society with murders, gangs, drive-by shootings and occasional massacres. Democratic freedoms in the form of rights, such as the rights to free speech, free press and to bear arms, are double-edged swords. On one hand, they enhance individual freedom, but on the other, they release and arm human passions, which often ends in violence.

There are many manifestations of these enhanced freedoms in democracy, one of which is immoral art. Some claim that art is special and cannot be immoral, but examples seem to prove otherwise. One could be the Columbine High School massacre of twelve students and one teacher and the wounding of twenty-three others on April 20, 1999. Eric Harris and Dylan Klebold were young, impressionable high school students who unleashed a barrage of bullets that caused carnage in a middle class neighborhood high school. How could this happen in ostensibly peaceful democracy?

According to reports on this horrific massacre, both Harris and Klebold were obsessed with the video game *Doom*, which depicts graphic violence. Harris, who was reportedly the ringleader, created WADs (blog sites where *Doom* aficionados share information), for this game and a large mod (a *Doom* game) named Tier. He called this his life's work. Experts debated what influence this video game had on Harris and Klebold's actions and concluded they were psychopaths, or people who recognize others only as means to satisfy their desires. Psychopaths feel no guilt and do not grasp what they feel or comprehend emotions like love, hate and fear.

Susan L. Feagin in *The Pleasures of Tragedy* analyzed these psychopathic personalities in more detail with her direct responses, or a response to the quality and content of work in art and meta responses, or the response to the direct response. She explained that the important meta response is a higher order response where people intellectually observe how they feel about their direct response, such as to a piece

223

of art. Direct responses draw only on our feelings. Our meta responses are critical because with them we feel satisfaction when we respond negatively to human pain. She explained that meta responses make moral action possible; they are the source of sympathy for others. It appears Harris and Klebold lacked meta responses, which enabled this horrific tragedy. So, what has this got to do with democracy?

Because late democracy brings unrealistic ideals like perfect equality and contradictory ideals like equality and freedom, it must necessarily bend moral reality to justify its ends. This opens the door for relative morality in which nothing is universally true. When nothing is true, everything is permitted, including violence. This is precisely what happened to Harris and Klebold; they lived in a free permissive mature democratic society without meta responses immersed in an unreal world, out of touch with reality. Under relative morality, they lacked meta responses, or a conscience. Universal morality creates meta responses because its uniform and stringent rules check injurious direct responses and engender meta responses. This takes us back to an earlier theme, which is that late democracies increasingly fail to find proper means, which in this case was civilization's failure to moderate Harris and Klebold's violent behavior.

In their artificial violent world there were no actual consequences due to relative morality. It was a game, and when it was over, they just turned off the computer and did something else. In their world, there was no real human suffering to observe, so they never developed a sense of sympathy for others. For them, people were only a means to entertainment. Because they had never experienced the suffering of others, they lacked any sympathetic emotion toward others, and thus felt no guilt in taking their lives. They were troubled young men so immersed in a contrived world that they failed to gain experience with people in the real world. In the real world, they would have observed and felt what really happens when someone is harmed. From this experience, they would have developed empathy for others, which in turn would have given rise to an inner moral sense that inflicting suffering is wrong.

Late democracy brings relative morality, immoral art and violence. Its characteristics engender an environment that allows video games like *Doom*, which enable certain potentially violent personalities like Harris and Klebold's. For some, it is a world bereft of meta responses, sympathy for others, conscience and any universal morality. This inclines late democracy to violence.

Fukuyama and Relative Morality

Fukuyama claimed that democracy is the end of history due to dialectic, but a political dialectic cannot occur in a society based on moral relativity. From such a "moral" society Fukuyama himself admits that there are no solid footings, no privileged perspectives and no truth. In chapter four it was demonstrated that his dialectic depends on a universal history to succeed, but how can this be in a democracy imbued with a relative morality that has no ultimate truths? Any thesis and antithesis must assert a truth to be valid, and their resolution in a synthesis is supposed to embody truth, like Fukuyama's assertion about democracy. If the truths of the premises are constantly changing under relative morality, they cannot necessarily be truths. Significantly, how does one get a true synthesis with premises that are not true?

Indeed, late democracy under the influence of relative morality brings a kind of unreality detached from truth. With its emphasis on utility, equality and positive law, any distinction, as Fukuyama pointed out, between better or worse and good and bad becomes obfuscated. With this, opposites disappear. How can there exist true opposites when nothing is true or false? For something to be true, something else must be false. To understand darkness, one must know light. In late democracy there are no strong or weak, good or evil, or virtue and vice, because the capricious majority under the influence of inclination, passion and emotion often capriciously changes its mind. Fukuyama himself wrote that his vaunted *thymos*, or self-respect, must be related in some degree to accomplishment, which is the opposite of failure. Norms in society become relative, which offers no foundation on which to build an ontological dialectic.

Fukuyama also claimed that democracy ends in freedom. His original struggle between masters and slaves is supposed to resolve into freedom, equality and *thymos* for all. However, late democracies bring loss of freedom, inequality and a slave morality. Fukuyama himself wrote that relativism in democracy does not lead to liberation of the great or strong but rather, the mediocre. Further, true freedom requires predictability. A prerequisite of liberty is to know that what you do today will be true and legal tomorrow. Relative morality under the influence of the majority does not offer predictability — it only offers political correctness. Fukuyama's democratic dialectic fails under the aegis of relative morality.

Conclusion

Relative morality discredits democracy in many ways, some of which have been described in this chapter. It is analogous to the debate between foundationalism and coherentism in epistemology: Is knowledge based on foundational truths? Or is it just how knowledge coheres? In the case of democracy, removing any true premises is like removing the foundation of a house that supports it and expecting it to remain standing. Certainly, truth is hard to discern, but any political system that avoids the question eventually fails. Democracy's abandonment of certain moral truths derived from the social contract and embracement of utility described in chapter four is one example.

In some ways, the decay, confusion and discord found in late American democracy is like the later stages of ancient

Greece. Alexander the Great's conquests in the late fourth century BCE atomized the traditional Greek polis, and the result was a potpourri of competing moral theories offering, among other things, happiness. Along with the declining Platonist and Aristotelian schools, Stoicism, Epicureanism and Skepticism competed for adherents. Greek citizens then, like Americans today in late mature democracy, lost their bearings and were seeking answers. Like then, relative morality today offers no answers. It only offers confusion and discord, which results in divisiveness. Divisiveness is the last of six reasons democracy fails, and it will be taken up next

Chapter Eleven

DIVISIVENESS

Divisiveness is the last reason democracy fails. The first five reasons, or loss of freedom, inequality, injustice, concentration of power and relative morality are the causes that lead to the ultimate consequence, which is divisiveness in late democracy. Divisiveness is what ultimately undoes democracy — it is the guillotine that separates the people body from its government head. Divisiveness violates one of the conditions for democracy to exist. In chapter one on the definition of democracy, one of its conditions was civil society outside of government. Democracy cannot exist long in anarchy or violent civil strife. Early democracies are generally civil, but as they age, fractures appear and widen. They find it increasingly difficult to find any Solonian mean.

Past Thinkers and Fukuyama on Divisiveness

Thomas Hobbes believed monarchy was superior to democracy because there was less contention in governmental decision-making and, thus, less factionalism. As mentioned earlier, Edward Gibbon believed that one reason societies fail was due to excessive zeal, which is an emotional state that naturally leads to contention and divisiveness. Arnold J. Toynbee believed that societies decline when an external proletariat challenges the oligarch, which is another circumstance that naturally leads to divisiveness. Significantly, both historians agreed that societies fail due to a single-mindedness that leads to internal divisions, disputes and eventually sectarian violence.

James Madison argued in *Federalist No. 10* for a republic instead of pure democracy because it would ease factionalization, which is a tacit admission that democracy is divisive. He wrote that (paraphrased) a pure democracy cannot cure the mischief of faction. In the chapter on inequality, it was mentioned that William James believed democracy is not a unifying political philosophy because it reduces things to twos, a condition that breeds contention and ultimately divisiveness.

Francis Fukuyama himself admitted that democracy can only resolve differences to a point. He wrote that it fails when diversity passes a certain limit, which is significant because a central effort in mature American democracy is to bring diversity. Certainly, there has always been contention, factionalization and divisiveness in democracies, and they have survived. But most of these divisive issues have been single disagreements, whether it be the democrats against the oligarchs in ancient Greece, the citizens against the aristocracy in eighteenth-century France or slavery, prohibition and women's rights in American democracy. Late democracy evolves into a multitude of irreconcilable worldviews that collide, and the result is divisiveness.

Failure of Past Democracies

History is replete with the failure of democracy due to divisiveness. In ancient Greece, the peacemaker Solon was unable to reconcile the division between democrats and oligarchs, and later Pericles superintended a state that vacillated between democracy and oligarchy due to constant divisiveness. If the republican period of ancient Rome in the sixth through first centuries BCE could be called a democratic republic, it failed when Emperor Augustus ascended due to civil strife. Recall how the democratically minded cities of northern Italy in the eleventh through thirteenth centuries failed due to strife when oligarchic families feuded with communes. Perhaps the best example could be the French Revolution, in which fledgling democracy ended in Napoleon's dictatorship due to internal strife, divisiveness and violence. Indeed, we see divisiveness writ large today in mature American democracy, with acidic disputes between two cultures at war with another, and the resulting legislative gridlock.

Democracy brings divisiveness, which is its Achilles heel. It brings it about for eight reasons.

The Reasons Democracy Brings Divisiveness

LOSS OF PROPERTY

The ascendancy of socialism in democracy discussed in chapter eight initiates a number of contentious issues. One of them is government taking a disproportionate amount of some citizens' property, which diminishes their freedom. The result is a permanently angry and resentful citizenry, as well as festering irresolvable issues in late democracy. This is the source of much of the divisiveness found in democracy.

John Locke in *Two Treatises of Government* believed that any government that takes people's property is at war with the people who then have no obligation to obey that government.

He wrote:

> *Whenever the Legislators endeavor to take away, and destroy the Property of the People,* or to reduce them to Slavery under Arbitrary Power, they put themselves into a state of War with the People, who are thereupon absolved from any farther Obedience, and are left to the common Refuge, which God hath provided for all Men, against Force and Violence. Whensoever therefore the *Legislative* shall transgress this fundamental Rule of Society; and either by Ambition, Fear, Folly or Corruption, endeavor to grasp themselves, *or put into the hands of any other an Absolute Power* over the Lives, Liberties, and Estates of the People; By this breach of Trust *they forfeit the Power,* the People had put into their hands, for quite contrary ends, and it devolves to the People, who have a Right to resume their original Liberty.

A similar sentiment was echoed by Thomas Jefferson in the Declaration of Independence. It seems democracy was born under the assumption that government that takes citizens' property deserves to be opposed and abolished. It seems that democracy itself offers a legitimate resolution to those whose property it takes, which is resistance. This is a source of divisiveness.

Earlier, Madison's promotion of a republic in *The Federalist Papers* in order to avoid democratic faction, turbulence and contention that attenuates the right to property was discussed. Unlike socialism, Madison believed one of the primary purposes of government was to protect citizens' unequal faculties in acquiring property. He was concerned that in democracies, the predominate party will unjustly diminish this right. He believed that this is why democracies had short lives. With this historic insight, it should come as no surprise that contention and divisiveness are a natural result of socialism in late democracies. When productive citizens' property is taken, they ardently resist, and society divides.

Disparity of Wealth

If a government followed Madison's advice and protected citizens' property, one consequence can be a disparity of wealth. Some consider this a divisive issue. Robert Reich, who was America's Secretary of Labor under Bill Clinton, demonized the disparity of wealth in his book *Aftershock: the Next Economy and America's Future*. This is a sentiment that derives from democracy's inclination to perfect equality that defies historic analysis. Virtually all past and present societies have disparity of wealth and remain peaceful. Why it becomes contentious generally depends on whether the wealthy earned their wealth. Thinking people accept rewarding talent and effort because it was earned. Most agree that Bill Gates is entitled to his wealth because he created Microsoft and the taxi driver in New York should keep his higher income because he works sixty hours a week, compared to another's forty. Thinking people acknowledge that disparity of wealth is mostly due to unequal human ability and accept that. In this form, the disparity of wealth is not a divisive issue.

The problem comes with hereditary rights and inheritance. This is a topic beyond the scope of this book and will only be mentioned here as it relates to democracy. Historically, wealth was perpetuated through generations under law, which caused a vast disparity of wealth. Medieval estates and lands were passed from generation to generation, irrespective of ability or talent. Contemporarily, much wealth is also passed to new undeserving generations. People do resent undeserved inherited wealth that allows heirs to live lives of luxury without talent or effort. Andrew Carnegie, in his *Gospel of Wealth*, addressed this very issue and concluded that any man who passes on excessive wealth to future generations is immoral.

The problem is that as democracy ages it blurs the line between earned and inherited wealth. It no longer matters where wealth originated, only that a disparity exists. With its emphasis on equality any disparity becomes an issue that demagogues like Reich dramatize beyond truth. The disparity of wealth is an issue late democracy wrongly enlarges to the point of divisiveness.

UNEQUAL TREATMENT UNDER THE LAW

There are many forms of injustice perpetrated in late democracies. Perhaps the worst is unequal treatment under the law, and the best example could be inequitable taxation. Socialism in democracy instigates a "tax the rich" mentality that affects most productive citizens, and the result is resentment and ultimately divisiveness. Individuals who are targeted by their government to carry the burden of taxation usually respond with bursts of furious indignation and sometimes rebellion.

Consider the French peasant rebellion in 1358, called the Jacquerie. The French nobility, merchant elite and clergy, or privileged classes, had forced the peasantry to pay ever-increasing taxes, such as the hated taille, while they themselves held exemptions. The burden of taxes fell on one sect of the population, and the result was the peasant rebellion. Tocqueville wrote that unequal taxation was the central cause of the French Revolution. The result was a permanent estrangement between those who benefit and those who suffer. The two classes' estrangement stiffened over time to the point that they could agree on little. The tax burden grew, the estrangement widened, a great divisiveness was caused and the French Revolution was the result. The French peasants' anger for being treated unequally under the law and targeted for higher taxation was justified and righteous.

234

Fast-forward to the year 2000 in mature American democracy in which a new group has been singled out to be treated unequally under the law in taxation. Now, 25 percent of American earners pay 84 percent—and 1 percent pays 37 percent—of all federal income taxes, while many Americans pay no taxes at all. It is medieval France in reverse, with a powerful centralized federal government and an exempt citizenship with an insatiable appetite for benefits that singles out a few to pay. It has become Friedrich Nietzsche's aesthetic ideal writ large in a mature ptochocracy. The poor now are the privileged majority class, exempt from taxation and able to pass the burden of taxes on to others.

Like the French medieval peasant, the Americans who earned their income also feel anger for being treated unequally under the law and targeted for higher taxation. Their anger is also justified and righteous. Both the French peasant and American earner were treated unequally, both were targeted for higher taxes by a class that was largely exempt and both felt indignation. Unequal treatment under the law, particularly in taxation, is a major source of divisiveness in late democracies. Indeed, in mature American democracy, observe the 2009 Tea Party rebellion and the gridlock in Congress, where two classes agree on little.

EQUALITY BRINGS CONTENTION

Given the discussions on equality in this book, it should come as no surprise that equality in democracy causes divisiveness. This is ironic; democracy became popular because it embraced an equality that was supposed to end hierarchal societies' chronic divisiveness. In chapter seven, it was described how political equality changes to perfect equality, or equality in all respects, as democracies age. The reason was that as people become more equal they become bolder, forceful and contentious due to jealousy and envy. In the end, nobody is satisfied.

In all respects, the aspiration to unrealistic equality unleashes a barrage of divisive issues. The demand for equality segues into the quest for power, the tyrannical majority increasingly superintends who is equal and who is not, individual freedom succumbs to collective demands, merit is diminished and socialism ascends. With these developments, political positions become hardened, and compromise becomes increasingly difficult to achieve. The result is intractable divisiveness in late democratic societies.

CONCENTRATION OF POWER
AND IMPERIOUS POLICIES

Alexis de Tocqueville wrote that there are periods in a nation's life when men differ from each other so profoundly that the notion of "the same law for all" seems preposterous. This truism is magnified by democracy, as it gradually splinters into a multitude of competing views. This fragmentation is exacerbated by the majority that increasingly imposes its particular view. The result is a majority view opposed to a multitude of excluded minority views, and the consequence is contention. It may be easier to blame a king than a majority, as Tocqueville wrote but the unjust authority of the majority is resented more. This contention become injurious when, a centralized powerful government enforces the majorities "politically correct" view on all, and the result is divisiveness. Recall Friedrich Hayek's comment that it is easier for people to bear the wrongs done by God than by other men, or in this case, the majority that controls the government.

The list of historic powerful centralized governments that imposed single-minded imperious polices on all is a long one, and the consequences of their policies have been pernicious. In ancient Greece, it could be the oligarchs imposing their view on the people, resulting in continuous internecine conflict. In ancient Rome, it could be the emperor imposing his views on taxation. Recall how the Roman Empire's centralized administration imposed heavy and unjust taxes on a few citizens, like farmers, that resulted in various revolts such as in Gaul and Spain, and non-cooperation. Many peasant farmers simply walked away from their livelihoods and tax obligations or changed occupations. In eighteenth-century France, it was class stratification that lead to inordinate taxation on the poor, which lead to the French Revolution. The American Revolution began largely in response to imperious tax laws, such as on tea, imposed by England. Fast-forward two hundred years, and the now powerful centralized American federal government is doing what England did earlier. It is an imperious government that imposes single policies on a multitude of different views. Abortion, taxation, healthcare, same-sex marriage, religion and the very size of government are deeply divisive issues that only increase in magnitude when government dictates "same for all" policies.

One of democracy's early strengths is to accommodate a multitude of views. Democracy's proclivities to produce multiple views and centralized government promulgating laws that force one solution for all is a deadly mix, and the consequence is divisiveness.

RELATIVE MORALITY

The simple explanation for relative morality causing divisiveness is that when everything is permitted, the hegemony of the majority is unleashed in democracy, which results in the many minorities' resentments. When the United States Supreme Court decides that abortion is legal throughout mature democratic America, it does so at the behest of majority opinion, and the result is a permanent intractable estrangement in society between those for and against abortion. This is divisiveness.

But the answer is more complicated. Relative morality causes divisiveness in two ways, both of which have been discussed in this book but not brought together to explain this phenomenon. The first derives from chapter one, which describes two conditions required for democracy to exist. The first was the rule of law, and the second, adherence to written law. If an individual, such as a dictator or judge, can arbitrarily change the law, then that person becomes the lawgiver, and not those who promulgate it. In democracy, this means the people who vote and enact laws are not the lawgivers because their laws can be readily overturned. In late democracy, the majority is that someone else. With no restraints, such as a Constitution or universal morality, the majority does as it pleases and, in the process, violates two of the conditions for democracy to exist.

The second way derives from chapter ten on relative morality. Relative morality's very definition is that morality is a social fact not grounded in any universal morality. This is a blank check for the majority that unleashes, legitimizes and enables it to enforce its opinion on all. In the case of our pervious example, this means if the majority wants abortion legal, it will be legal. Certainly, one could ask what is the difference between historic kings, aristocracies and oligarchies that also imposed their will on others? There are two responses. The first is that democracies intent to bring freedom ultimately fails, and the second is that under freedom in democracy there far are more moral powerful "pockets" that resist the majority's dominance. For these two reasons, under the sway of relative morality the tyranny of the majority in democracy brings divisiveness.

Fukuyama argued that democracy is the end of history in part because it offered individuals recognition and satisfied the human thymotic drive for equality and ultimately freedom. Moral relativity working through these two ways thwarts those aspirations, which makes democracy a woodpath.

238

DIVERSITY AND LOSS OF
THE MELTING POT ETHIC

The fragmentation diversity brings, discussed in chapter ten, inevitably leads to divisiveness. Diversity was defined as multiculturalism, diversity of thought, freedom of expression, inclusion of all people and tolerance for diverse ways and people. On the surface this sounds good, but upon closer inspection, it is another statue by an ideologically driven Phidias. Diversity is a pseudonym for equality in all respects and social justice, which are two of late democracy's reasons for failure. On a deeper level, diversity is about eliminating opposites in order to reorder reality, which is a process that necessarily makes nothing ontologically true. The result is that under diversity everything is tolerated and permitted. The truth is diversity leads to divisiveness.

Fukuyama wrote that democracy fails when a society's diversity passes a certain limit. He believed a successful democracy depended on the existence of a political community that agrees on certain basic shared values and institutions. Paul Johnson, in *Modern Times*, had a more trenchant view based on history. He wrote that all European nations up to 1919 had, due to goading by the academics, stressed the linguistic and cultural differences between peoples at the expense of traditional ties and continuing economic interest that urged them to live together. Ultimately, for them, this argument for self-determination resulted in a nightmare of racial animosity and thirty years of European war. For him, it enabled the pursuit of racial advantage. Every reform the philosophy created caused more problems than it solved. In the end, diversity is an idealistic pseudonym for tribalism, or a reversion to a primitive state where individual tribes with no overarching morality, ideals or authority exist in a state of perpetual warfare. Early democracy's embracement of Voltaire's famous quote—"I may not agree with what you say, but I will defend to the death your right to say it" — fades, and society becomes contentious as competing sects vie for power, which increasingly results in discord and divisiveness.

Richard M. Weaver, in *The Ethics of Rhetoric*, discussed earlier in this book, shed some light on this issue. He wrote that we can infer information about a civilization from its debates and controversies. Do they come from outpost positions or rather within the citadel itself? If they come from an outpost position, much has been assumed in the form of settled conclusions, and the foundations of society are not threatened. However, diversity emphasizes outpost positions, which assail and diminish the citadel. This generates disagreement in the citadel that involves fundamental norms that place the survival of society at stake. The citadel increasingly struggles with what is critical and what is extraneous, and as a result is assailed with destructive doubts and disagreements over the most fundamental subjects. Citizens are left puzzled over who they are and what has meaning. The former pillars of the citadel's ordered demarcations that gave us order and thus freedom are toppled.

A similar viewpoint was advanced by legal philosopher Hans Kelsen who postulated that *grundnorms*, or common basic beliefs, in certain overriding, transcendent fundamental norms establish the order and rules, which are the basis of a legal system. The idea is that for any theory to exist there must be a point of origin on which all can agree. It is this original consensus that lends the theory and law legitimacy. Like the law, democracy also requires a point of origin and *grundnorms* to exist and be legitimate. If they are lost, then so is the theory and political system. Certainly, there have always been divergent norms in democracies, but under diversity, their differences are multiplied, and disagreement surfaces over fundamental matters.

Some could claim that diversity is a *grundnorm*, or fundamental norm. However, this would result in a contradiction that would nullify the assertion. If there are to be diverse norms, how can there be one overriding norm? The proposition of diversity itself, which is to diversify, demands that there exist numerous norms; this makes one overriding *grundnorm* impossible.

There is an ironic consequence of this. On one hand, as a result of this process, according to Weaver, people become free-floating experimenters because they have lost faith in fundamental connecting propositions. He wrote that when a society's fundamental cultural propositions are under attack, citizens begin thinking for themselves, so things become reversed; where they once thought in propositions, like "freedom is a good," they now require evidence, like "show me whether I am free." With this development, propositions like "freedom is good" fades, and the substructure of society with it. On the other hand, one characteristic of democracy's freedom is free-thinking individuals. This is one of democracy's great attractions and strengths. So, what is the answer? It seems Fukuyama was right when he wrote that when diversity passes a certain limit, democracy fails. With the ascension of diversity in late democracy, *grundnorms* are lost, and with them, societies' cohesion.

Diversity in democracy initiates the emergence of multiple cultures with different worldviews. It becomes a culture defined by its opposites, in which everyone is fighting over some issue. The consequence is increasing conflict, bitterness and irresolvable viewpoints. This leads to divisiveness, which is one of democracy's Achilles heels. Diversity in democracy will be explored in more detail in the next chapter as it relates to contemporary America.

REBELLION OF FORMER MASTERS AND NON-COOPERATION

Recall that Fukuyama envisioned an original violent struggle between masters who were willing to die and slaves who were not, which resulted in a historic class struggle that democracy resolves. He claimed democracy transforms the master into a satisfied bourgeoisie last man imbued with a newfound sense of democratic tolerance. Is this true? Are the former masters placated, or do they rebel?

Imagine their circumstances in late democracy. They are the kind of productive, restless, ambitious and active people who are now expected to be satisfied with a secure mundane merchant middle class life. But this is not the entire story. In late democracy, it has been argued that the former slaves have become the masters—the poor masses become the tyrant majority. It is the realization of Nietzsche's slave morality. These former masters find themselves one of many minorities whose freedoms have been suppressed by the majority. They find themselves slaves of their former slaves. But they are unlike the other minorities because they have both intrinsic and historic pride, which Fukuyama calls megalothymia, that is not easily placated.

So what would be the natural inclination of these former masters facing slavery and the loss of freedom under the banner of evolving democratic institutions like socialism? It seems plausible that they could reclaim their sword and again engage in bloody battle. The tolerance, characteristic of early democracy and so necessary for its survival, has faded for the reasons discussed earlier. Democracy's tendency to take ideals to their extreme breeds a single-mindedness that rejects contrary ideas. In keeping with the very spirit of late democracy the former masters also develop a passionate single-minded intolerant view, but in this instance against democracy, and rebel.

It is injustice that causes people to rebel. It was injustice that caused the ancient Roman farmers to rebel, in eighteenth-century France, the peasants, and in America, the Bostonians. Contemporarily, it occurs underground in Sweden, where apartments are secured on the black market; in Cuba, where food is obtained directly from the farmer and not the government stores; in Italy, where the avoidance of taxation is

242

common; and in the former Soviet Union, where it was estimated that half the economy was off the books.

Some rebel violently, and others through non-cooperation. It seems entirely plausible that the former masters could simply stop cooperating with the institutions of late democracy—they just quit. It could be a scenario like that sketched by philosopher Ayn Rand in *Atlas Shrugged*. John Galt, a former producer, simply stopped working, endeavoring to excel, achieve or advance. The consequences of former masters quitting the game manifest themselves in innumerable ways including loss of production, loss of incentive and declining wealth and abundance—but the most significant is divisiveness.

DEMAGOGUE POLITICIANS
EXACERBATE DIVISIVENESS

The role of demagogues in democracy was described earlier, so this section will deal only with their cause of divisiveness. Aristotle was right when he wrote in Politics that democracies usually enter revolutionary times because the demagogic intemperance of its leaders. Few would disagree that democracies are factious political systems. The reasons for this have been described throughout this book. Faction becomes acute in late democracies for many reasons but the principal ones are power-seeking demagogues. These agitators come in many forms, whether it is individuals on the fringes, leading citizens or, as Aristotle pointed out, those who hold the reigns of governmental power.

In any contentious political environment, power is readily attained by advocating a cause rather than by looking for common solutions. Contentiousness is a breeding ground for demagogues who seek power by pandering to the masses by advocating an issue they know is popular. History is rich with such examples. Tocqueville wrote that before the French Revolution administrative authorities blamed each other for the sufferings of the laboring classes. A king of France blamed the arrogance of parliament and the greed of the rich for the people's misfortunes, and Louis XIV inflamed the poor by deriding landed estates, which pandered to the people's view that their superiors were responsible for their evils. This, according to Tocqueville, inculcated revolutionary ideas in the poor that set the stage for socialism in France. It also caused divisiveness in society that succored the French Revolution. Christopher Hibbert, in *The Days of the French Revolution*, described the inflammatory pamphlets produced by middle class doctors and lawyers deriding the French aristocratic system and the individuals, like fiery former aristocrat Honoré Gabriel Riqueti, Count of Mirabeau and Georges Danton, who lead it. In the American Revolution, leading citizens like Samuel Adams and pamphleteer Thomas Paine advocated separation from England. It is significant that in early American democracy, political parties advocating issues were less significant than those found in mature American democracy. Many leaders, like George Washington, were statesmen who eschewed political parties.

The point of all this is that as democracies age, contention increases, and factions become less tolerant, which makes compromise more difficult. These circumstances make for fewer statesmen looking for unifying common ground and more demagogues seeking to gain power by inflaming issues. The result is divisiveness in late democracy.

Why Divisiveness Ends Democracy

Divisiveness ultimately causes democracy to fail. At the beginning of this chapter Stendhal's explanation why the French Revolution failed was iterated. After the Revolution, late–eighteenth-century France was in turmoil. Its new democracy was consumed with strife, divisiveness and violence. There were plots, beheadings, trials, intrigue, corruption and fractionalization. As a result, as Stendhal explained, the

French people decided a dictatorship that could bring peace and security was better than democracy. The people chose dictator Napoleon, who did put an end to both reactionary and revolutionary efforts, brought peace, put an end to crime and restored order. Divisiveness brought about the end of democracy because the people themselves decided there was a better alternative.

An imaginary scenario for America's future, and perhaps the future of democracy, was spun in chapter nine on the concentration of power. It could well be that the kind of divisiveness that occurred in eighteenth-century France could be the same divisiveness that causes Americans to acquiesce to a president who aspires to dictatorship. Again, it would be the people choosing an alternative political system to democracy. This scenario's broader implication is that Fukuyama's dialectic, which determines democracy is the end of human history, fails.

Fukuyama and Divisiveness Reprise

Recall Fukuyama's dialectic with two pillars, which brings Hegelian freedom, that manifests in the end of history, which is democracy. The first pillar was economic and scientific advancement, and the second was recognition and the thymotic drive for freedom and equality. In the second pillar, Fukuyama described how democracy resolves the age-old master and slave struggle. The unfortunate answer is that democracy does not resolve this struggle, and divisiveness in democracy is the evidence. Indeed, as democracies age, cooperation and tolerance fade, and divisiveness increases for all the reasons given in the book and chapter. A few examples are loss of freedom, inequality, injustice, the consequences of the concentration of power and relative morality, as well as loss of property and unequal treatment under law. One consequence mentioned earlier also includes the non-cooperation of rebellious former masters.

Fukuyama could retort with two objections: give one example of a late democracy in the world today that is failing, and it takes time to resolve the master and slave relationship for democratic thymotic freedom to prevail. Indeed, where is the evidence of decay? Democracies begin by fits and starts, evolve, and some fail—but they eventually become a democracy. Why is the dialectic wrong?

The first response is that the weaknesses of political systems take time to emerge. America, the world's longest living democracy, is only two hundred years old. Past systems like pharohships and kingships endured for centuries before fading. Democracy has not been around long enough to endure the test of time. The response to his second retort is that increasing divisiveness in democracy is evidence of not only its decay but also its inability to resolve the tension between masters and slaves. The conformity between people that Fukuyama wrote liberal democracy requires for success and stability dies away. One of the very conditions of democracy, which is a civil society outside of government, also dies.

The result is predictable: chaos, contention and divisiveness increase as democracy ages, democratic citizens begin yearning for peace and safety and eventually they choose another political system that offers it. It is the people who eschew Georg Wilhelm Friedrich Hegel's vaunted freedom and Fukuyama's *thymos* and chose something else like dictatorship. Fukuyama's dialectic fails, and democracy is not the end of history.

Conclusion

It is ironic that many of the problems that lead to divisiveness in democracy described in this book arise from the very definition of democracy. Part of that definition is rule by the people, so the people naturally come to believe that they have some control over their lives and freedom. They come to think power resides in the people, citizens and themselves. But who exactly are "the people"? The term is so vague and subjective that it can have many different meanings. Certainly, all citizens in a democracy do not have the ability to rule, so what the term really means is rule by some people and not a dictator.

But who are these "some people"? In democracy it is the majority. It is the majority that has the power, and not necessarily the people. Laws, policies and leaders are ultimately chosen by the majority. In spite of what some think, it is not the government, big business, billionaires, unions or corporations that decide matters. All they can do is endeavor to persuade the majority to vote a certain way. In the end, power in democracy resides in the majority, and to them everyone else is subservient.

So what does this have to do with divisiveness? Democracy holds the ideal of rule by the people, but in reality, under majority rule, a cruel illusion is perpetrated. Citizens naturally come to think that they have power, when in reality, it is the majority that has the power, many people have little power and on single issues the minority has no power. Thus, many live in a duality where they believe they have something when they do not. The result is tremendous frustration, disillusion and subsequent anger. They end up fighting harder for something they believe they should have; something they believe democracy promised to deliver but did not.

The predictable results are vast disenfranchised minorities and individuals who become contentious, protest, sometimes become violent and occasionally cause rebellions. It is a problem that only becomes more acute as democracy ages. It is this unrestrained contentiousness indigenous to late democracies that leads to divisiveness and democracy's ultimate failure.

SECTION IV

Democracy in America

Chapter Twelve

DEMOCRACY IN AMERICA

This book has surveyed democracy, and this chapter will examine its dénouement in America. Its definition and history, historic arguments for and against it and its cycles were explored. In light of these, Francis Fukuyama's thesis that democracy is the end of history was examined. If Fukuyama is right, then democracy in America would appear to be the highest and final form of human political development. Democratic America would be the end of the line and should last forever. However, six reasons why democracy is not the end of history were also examined. The loss of freedom, inequality, injustice, the concentration of power, relative morality and divisiveness are problems for democracy. No one reason alone is sufficient to cause its failure, but taken in aggregate, they are fatal. Each of these problems does not abate; rather, they have advanced in America and become more chronic. So, let us now examine American culture in the early twenty-first century entering her late democratic stage. This chapter will endeavor to demonstrate why democracy will fail in America.

The assertion that democracy will fail in America is not a rogue one. Democracy has not only historically failed, but Plato, Cicero, Thomas Carlyle, Friedrich Nietzsche, François Guizot, John Winthrop, Leo Tolstoy and H. L. Mencken, along with some American Founding Fathers like John Adams and Elbridge Gerry also thought it would. Alexis de Tocqueville believed that democracy was the wave of the future but at the same time presciently described its weaknesses. Tocqueville did not have the fortune to see how these weaknesses played out in late American democracy. The democracy he witnessed and America's Founding Fathers envisioned became something vastly different over its short two hundred years. Democracy, it turns out, is just one more human-created fallible political system that is popular now but will inevitably run its course and perish in due time. Its initial appeals of freedom, equality and justice have changed.

The historic arguments against democracy without merit described in chapter three do seem irrelevant to contemporary American democracy. America is ordered, its democracy is abstract, there is no mob rule, its society is generally stable, most citizens feel a sense of duty, its society is not brutal, its government is generally efficient, it is not entirely oligarchic and it has limited corruption. Also, many of the poor do vote, but its economic system is intact, and there is relative political equality, most rights are negative, merit can rise, passion is generally in check and many still enjoy a degree of individualism. Unfortunately, the few fatal historic arguments against democracy are also being played out. There is some loss of freedom, society is becoming unequal for some, injustice is increasingly being dispensed, governmental power is increasingly dictatorial, relative morality is pervasive and divisiveness is on the rise.

252

The Cycle of Democracy in America

The general cycle of democracy was described in chapter five, and many of the characteristics of that cycle can be seen in America today. This section will briefly describe some contemporary non-fatal manifestations of those characteristics and only allude to a few fatal ones, which will be described later in this chapter. Certainly, many of these observations are overgeneralizations with numerous counter examples. Irrespective of these failings, the trends they signify in American democracy are unmistakable. As before, the characteristics are broken down into early, mature and late American periods.

EARLY

Prior to becoming a nation, America's roots were clearly democratically inclined. Jamestown, the Virginia House of Burgesses (which was the forerunner to the Virginia General Assembly) and the Puritan, Baptist and Quaker pilgrims all organized themselves on democratic principles. Indeed, America's birth certificates, the Declaration of Independence and the Constitution, embodied many democratic ideals.

From America's inception in the late 1700s to the mid-1800s before the Civil War, American democracy emphasized freedom, equality, justice, peace and individuality. This is the period when Tocqueville visited America (1831) and the one Walt Whitman celebrated. With two egregious exceptions, freedom reigned supreme. The Declaration of Independence cited it four times, with phrases like "free people" and "free states." It was only natural that immigrants fleeing totalitarian regimes valued freedom above all. It was political freedom. Because they were escaping societies of casts, they also understandably valued social equality. It was the kind of equality defined by the Constitution as "equal station" and "created equal." Significantly, the Constitution does not mention equality itself, but it does mention justice. Justice

253

was a motivating reason for early democracy, and it meant freedom from arbitrary coercion. This also was only natural for a people who had been ruled by the caprice of a king. The founding documents refer to the King of England obstructing justice and being deaf to the voice of justice, as well as the need for justice to form a more perfect and tranquil union. This sentiment was imbued in the Constitution's Bill of Rights, which were all negative. Justice meant not only fairness but also to not be treated unjustly by arbitrary power. In many respects, justice meant to be left alone. This would also explain their adherence to the rule of law in early American democracy. Immigrants had tasted arbitrary power and thus preferred fair laws based on morality that limited government's power. With this ethic, judges generally adhered to written law and precedent.

With the desire to limit governmental power, new citizens also naturally favored checks and balances between the branches of government, a Bill of Rights amendments to the Constitution (which is a characteristic of early democracies) and a federal government that could not tax income. They wanted a central government that was small and unattractive of notice, to use Thomas Jefferson's words. In hindsight, even Chief Justice John Marshall's establishment of judicial review, enhancing judicial power, was a manifestation of this zeitgeist because it limited the legislative and executive branches powers, which diffused power.

It is also understandable that the early citizens of democratic America valued peace. Many had lived in perpetually warring European nations for which they were the fodder. Once the War for Independence was won and the War of 1812 finished, most wars were less catastrophic. Generally, they involved subduing Native Americans and securing trading rights. Compared to many eras, early democracy was relatively peaceful. Individuality was prized and celebrated in the form of the rugged individual. Ralph Waldo Emerson in particular championed this ethic in early American democracy in his essay *Self-Reliance*. It was a time of individual energy, independence, enthusiasm and success. It eschewed conformity, consistency and living in others' opinions.

The immigrants were also poor, so they sought sources of wealth in commerce and manufacturing. They desired a higher standard of living free from want. So, early democracy naturally embraced capitalism, entrepreneurship and business. They worked hard, established a meritocracy and were generally rewarded for their efforts. There was no thought of socialism and robbing Paul to pay Peter. It was a simpler society imbued with a universal social contract morality where all were treated fairly and equally. To maintain these new principles of society, the idea of a melting pot naturally arose that would abolish old-world prejudices and make newly assimilated American citizens imbued with this new zeitgeist. People did assimilate, and an American culture formed.

Certainly, like most societies, early democracy America had divisive issues. The Jeffersonians and Federalists fought over the role of government, the patriots and loyalists jockeyed over English loyalty and tradition and the contentious issues of women and minorities' citizenship rights persisted. However these were single evolving issues that were not fatal to early democracy. The spirit of the times was more for cohesion than division.

MATURE

America's mature democratic stage was from the mid-1800s to the 1960s. Early democracy's emphasis on capitalism created unimagined wealth, which caused a disparity of wealth, envy and concomitantly the demand for security. Citizens' demand for limits on business resulted in the Sherman Antitrust Act of 1890, the Sixteenth Amendment to the Constitution in 1913 that allowed for a federal income tax, which quickly became progressive, and the Wagner Act of 1935. The process of reigning in capitalism and redistributing the wealth it created began, and there was a virtual explosion of wealth redistribution laws. The 1930s' New Deal initiated innumerable governmental programs, such as Social Security, that were the harbingers of the future. In the 1960s, Lyndon B. Johnson's Great Society brought a host of security programs like Medicare and Medicaid that set the stage for universal socialized medicine in the early twenty-first century. Unheard of socialism took root, as the socialist First International moved to New York in 1872, the Socialist Labor Party of America was founded in 1877, The Socialist Party of America began in 1898 and America began to see socialist candidates for president, like Robert M. La Follette, Sr. in 1924 and Norman Thomas in 1936. The Democratic Party becomes the political tool for this new demand for security, which it advances under the appellation of progressivism. Silently, with these developments, the definition of freedom changed to security, and the loss of freedom, inequality and injustice were the unintended consequences.

Under the ideal of early democracy's equality, many good seeds are planted in mature democracy that gradually become mutated deformations under the aegis of late democracy's equality in all respects. The Fourteenth Amendment in 1868 endeavored to abolish race inequality but morphed into the Civil Rights Act of 1964 and the creation of protected classes, then privileged sects and finally affirmative action or reverse discrimination in late democracy. The previously mentioned Wagner Act of 1935 intended to bring about equality between employer and employee by protecting unions but could do only by, as Senator Robert F. Wagner said, tying one hand of business behind its back. This is a comment that speaks volumes about mature democracy's view on equality. Rightfully, women and minorities gradually gained a degree of equality, but others, including white males and businesspeople, were increasingly treated unequally. The good seeds of negative rights began to change in mature American democracy to the unrecognizable mutated positive rights in late mature

256

democracy. The demand for universal primary education was good, and America by and large achieved it by 1918. By the 1950s, however, higher education increasingly became viewed as a right, so the federal government initiated student loans. Equal in all respects in late democracy naturally produced socialist Democrat Senator Bernie Sanders demands that all higher education be free. The seeds of positive rights were planted in mature American democracy, and the demands for free healthcare, housing, education and welfare are the consequences in late democracy.

In order to bring equality at all costs, America in its mature stage had to adopt positive law. In order to offer the positive rights equality demanded, citizens had to be treated unequally. Progressive taxation began in the early twentieth century, which treats taxpayers unequally, innumerable business taxes were promulgated and both citizens and stockholders are now taxed differently than other taxpayers. Federal mandates on businesses and municipalities also began. The goal might be handicapped access, but rather than tax all of the citizens who gain from this mandate, a few are forced to pay. One benefit that serves a few and should be paid for by all is foisted on a few who do not directly benefit. The rule of law came under attack with Franklin D. Roosevelt's court packing scheme in 1937, the Supreme Court did an about-face on the Constitution's Commerce Clause and ignored the First Amendment's right to free speech with its decision to support the McCain-Feingold Act. The law has increasingly become just a social fact in America.

The concentration of power manifest in the federal government began in America's mature stage. A plethora of federal laws were initiated covering all aspects of citizen's lives, much like in ancient Rome. One solution for all national laws began to emanate from bureaucratic Washington, covering education, environment, health, commerce, agriculture, wildlife, housing and law enforcement. As a result, Americans' lives are becoming increasingly micromanaged.

It is the beginning of the age where government is thought to be the source of all solutions. Presidents including Woodrow Wilson, Roosevelt, Harry Truman, John F. Kennedy and Johnson issued a slew of executive orders during this period circumventing the democratic process. With this, the concept of checks and balances within central power began to erode and Americans became less concerned with arbitrary power. With acceptance of centralized power and security replacing freedom, the era of the rugged individual died. Conformity began its ascent in the form of political correctness. The ideal of community ascends, and the collective view that we are all in it together and interdependent gradually becomes the new zeitgeist.

Relative morality based on nothing being true and everything permitted explodes onto the landscape in the 1950s with Beatnik characters like Allan Ginsberg and Jack Kerouac. They are a new generation escaping ostensibly smothering bourgeoisie life and looking for a higher level of consciousness, but in reality they are libertines using their intelligence to achieve their desires. They prefer not to work, are into drugs like LSD, are bisexually promiscuous and are utterly irresponsible individuals. They set the moral tone for the late democratic period to come with its hippies, drugs, sex and rock and roll. America's early natural morality involving the social contract, work, reward for effort and capitalism starts withering away under the aegis of relative morality in late democracy.

With democracy's evolution, peace gradually loses its appeal and America becomes more violent. It engages in more destructive wars. The Civil War, World War I, World War II and the Korean War turn America into a warrior nation. With these wars, ugly politics and loss of democratic compass, contention ensues that demagogues exploit. They come from both sides of the aisle, like Joseph McCarthy and his black lists and Huey Long denouncing the rich and banks. The seeds have been planted in mature American democracy for

258

the divisiveness to come. The contestants come to be called liberal Democrats and conservative Republicans, but time will show that a divide has grown much deeper.

LATE

In the 1960s, America entered its last stage of democracy. The nature of democracy changed dramatically. The core ideals of freedom, equality and justice change, America is superintended by a powerful central government, morality has lost its bearings and American society is rife with divisiveness. Democracy is different.

Its change is most evident in the law. With its unmooring the law from morality the unjust unequal treatment of women and minorities in early democracy becomes acceptable with other minorities in late democracy. Governments begin hiring and contracting preference policies, universities begin accepting students based on their race or gender rather than merit, and the 1964 Civil Rights Act creates protected classes based on race, color, religion, national origin and sex, as well as other laws based on age, pregnancy, citizenship, familial status, disability, veteran and genetic information. Government embarks on a variety of programs to advance some of these sects' interests at the detriment of others, and any semblance of equal treatment under the law is ignored. Affirmative action laws follow that require preference to protected classes so a medical student named Allan P. Bakke is denied entrance in favor of a less qualified minority applicant. Early America's meritocracy is replaced by positivistic policy, and injustice is the result. Under the emerging feminist movement, federal law mandates women's inclusion in sports under Title IX regardless of interest or cost. Women supported by the law demand equality in sports but wink at the universities that accept more women than men under preferential treatment laws. The equality envisioned by late democracy can only be achieved with a double standard.

Economically, the law embraces unequal taxation that supports the inevitable change in rights. Rights are no longer protective but rather demand obligations from others. Most significantly, the natural foundations of law established in early democracy become a hindrance, which brings about non-originalist judges who reinterpret them in order to align the law with progressive governmental policy. In late mature democracy, a stifling and enervating politically correct progressive fog descends on America that preaches collectivism and vilifies the rugged individual. It is a smothering demand to conform to progressive policies. It is a fog brought on by the tyrannical blue state majority that has had their political way in social and economic issues. The red states, which remain repositories of early democracy, are increasingly stifled. America also becomes more assertive and belligerent, engaging in almost continuous wars. The Vietnam War, Iraq War, and Afghanistan War, as well as ongoing conflicts in the Middle East, make America a warring nation. Positive law, inequitable taxation, progressive policies and wars naturally bring contention, which breeds a new crop of demagogues in late democracy. Richard Reich attacks the rich producers, and Senator Charles Rangel inflames race relations. Statesmen leaders like George Washington and Abraham Lincoln fade from the ideologically divided political scene.

DEMOCRACY IN AMERICA

Democracy has a predictable cycle, which has been played out in history and is being played out in America. The characteristics of that cycle in America previously described were the mere non-fatal manifestations, but the six fatal reasons, some of which were mentioned by Tocqueville, are working their destructive ways today. It is indeed ironic how in each case true democracy concomitantly and gradually brought the very forces that destroy it. It is now time to describe the six fatal reasons why democracy is failing in America.

LOSS OF FREEDOM

Americans are losing freedom. Every one of the ironic reasons democracy takes freedom is occurring in contemporary America. The largest, most powerful and richest centralized government in the world increasingly controls all aspects of citizens' lives, and they find themselves increasingly caught in a web of devised artificial rules and regulations promulgated by legislators and faceless Washington bureaucrats. Governmental regulations have exploded over the last one hundred years, filling volumes and showing no sign of abating. What was small government in early democracy is now ubiquitous government on the municipal, county, state and federal levels in late democracy. The old world politics and lack of freedom that the immigrants were fleeing is emerging anew. Few today celebrate true freedom, and many seek security. A public safety net has become sacrosanct, which includes a myriad of governmental welfare and entitlement programs. The New Deal, Great Society and Obamacare have worked their charm and created a vast army of dependent citizens. The new political mantra has become socialism's demand, "to each their need," and citizens' highest priority has become "don't touch my Medicare." Socialism, the child of once-reviled communism, has become acceptable. The Socialist Party of America no longer needs to put up a candidate for president, because the mainstream Democratic Party is offering a socialist candidate of its own—Sanders. The American zeitgeist has changed. The social weal, which was once the rights to life, liberty and property, has become the rights to life and security. Happiness has become living securely, and with this change, security has eclipsed freedom.

In order to pay for the ever-expanding safety net, federal government debt has ballooned and become unsustainable. Americans no longer think prudentially or in terms of Jefferson's admonition that one generation has no right to financially encumber another. Now they believe need should be met at any cost, and in Bill Clinton's sacred pact

261

between generations. With this, future generations have been saddled with debt, which diminishes their freedom. Meeting need has become the zeitgeist, and its message is disseminated daily by politicians and the media. Tocqueville and Fukuyama were right in observing that in the natural tension between freedom and equality, societies love equality more than freedom. In America, equality has eclipsed freedom and metamorphosed into a paranoid demand for parity in all respects. The battlefields are many: race, gender, wealth, age, religion and sexual orientation, and the battles are bloody and indecisive—they only plant the seeds of deferred discord.

American law now panders to this new zeitgeist, like The Hughes Court did in 1937 in its age. Because the law now endeavors to codify and make permanent equality in all respects, it has become the object of perpetual scorn and in the process debased. The very concept of merit under affirmative action laws has abrogated the fundamental doctrine of equal treatment under the law. With this, some citizens gain and others lose, and citizens' freedoms are curtailed. With this, American law has become just a social fact and detached from morality, so, as the assassin's creed demands, everything is permitted. Indeed, the very concept of what constitutes a right under the law has turned 180 degrees. Where rights once constrained for freedom, they now compel for security and take freedom. The issue of non-originalist judges making decisions based on all things considered and their easy off-handed reinterpretation of the Constitution could only arise when the law succumbs to the whim of the times. Americans have lost a degree of freedom due to unpredictability, like the jailed marijuana user convicted under past laws existing in a society that has decriminalized its use.

American law has changed protected sects into privileged sects, thus taking the freedom from non-protected and non-privileged sects. The law has become importune and now tells individuals whom they can sell their house to, whom

262

employers can hire and fire, and whom restaurants can serve — any sign that says "we reserve the right to refuse business to anyone" has become illegal. Under late democracy, American law is taking individual freedom. The liberal effort to remake human nature through law always presents two new problems when one is ostensibly solved, and the consequence is a repressed cold anger that surfaces often in late democracy.

Early Americans embraced the right to own property because it represented freedom — the freedom to own something. Under the aegis of equality, the freedom to own became envy of those who own too much, which has lead to a zeitgeist that demands any disparity of wealth be corrected. With this, the tables turn, and property, which once represented freedom, now represents anarchist socialist Pierre-Joseph Proudhon's theft. With this change, interminable laws have been promulgated, regulating and redistributing property in innumerable ways that assail the very concept of private ownership. Tax laws in America take more property from those that own it, and government mandates how businesses must allocate it. For many, property in the form of paper money represents freedom, so the government naturally embarks on a program of printing it so all can be "free." But specie is not the same as property, so in late American democracy, the federal government is forced into a delicate balancing act, trying to meet citizens' demand for money on one hand and inflation on the other, and Frédéric Bastiat's ambiguity is the result. The government prints currency to make everyone equal, but doing so only debases the currency, which makes everyone equal in poverty. Indeed, there is no freedom in poverty and there is no freedom to get rich. Democracy diminishes the freedom to own property.

America has seen a tectonic shift under the aegis of democracy from individualism to collectivism, and with it, the reverence for individual liberty. The early American rugged individual is gone, but its illusion remains in the name of autonomy. Many think they are free because they have autonomy, but they are not. Autonomy exists within a controlling system, whereas freedom means to be free of the system. Freedom is far more liberating, exciting and dangerous than autonomy. For example, America is predictably becoming a medically socialized nation in which patients have the autonomy to keep their medical records confidential but not the freedom to opt out of the system. The autonomous patient has a small degree of control but is caught in an over-controlling web of rules that has taken away true freedom. It is like being a toad in a drainage ditch with the "freedom" to swim around until the farmer opens a valve and drains it.

Today, collectivism and the emphasis on human interdependency is the theme, and the result has been to average Americans, diminish merit and assault enterprise, which together are turning Americans into jellyfish. Virtue and success no longer come from character but rather what the loudest politicians and their political parties, as well as ivory tower university intellectuals, tell us. The individual is increasingly being valued only to the extent that they conform to the group's opinions. We see this smothering conformity today, with overarching imperatives like diversity and inclusiveness, that marginalizes the individualistic nonconformists. If a business does not bake a cake for a same-sex couple or hire a handicapped person due to their handicap, it is berated and fined under law. The owners have lost the power of choice and, with it, freedom.

Individualism made America great, and history tells us that under it citizens do not retreat into themselves at the expense of the common good, as Tocqueville feared. Contrariwise, individualism harnessed the talents and abilities of thousands of early Americans who created, built, produced and imagined. Adam Smith was right, Andrew Carnegie and Bill Gates have done more to enhance and expand the social weal than the collective central economic planning in any collectivist communist country.

James Madison was also wrong. He was concerned that the tyranny of the majority would result in faction in democracy. He feared that the prominent party would trample the rules of justice and oppress the minority. He thought the causes of faction could not be removed in democracy, so it was necessary to control the effects. His solution was a representative democracy whereby representatives guarding the public weal would mitigate faction. It would also proliferate sects, making each less able to pervade the body whole. Time and late democracy have proven Madison wrong. National parties like the Republican and Democratic parties today have emerged in which representatives tow their party line and have become so powerful that smaller parties have been made irrelevant because they have no influence. These mega-parties are the united majorities of people today who, as Madison feared, trample the rules of justice and take minorities' freedoms.

The Democratic Party, a majority party, has, over the last one hundred years, advanced the Richard M. Weaver's God-word progressive, which is the source of many minorities' loss of liberties today. In my state of Oregon, for example, the Democratic Party has held unassailable power for decades, and the result is laws that favor public employee unions and are inimical to business. Its Tweed-like control of Oregon's largest city, Portland, tyrannizes smaller Oregon cities and rural inhabitants with, for example, state environmental laws that ruin their economies and take their freedom. In spite of Madison's solution, which was representative democracy, the tyranny of the majority and its ability to diminish freedom is alive and well in late American democracy.

The political ideal for freedom was attained in early American democracy, the tenets of which are embodied in America's birth certificates and were enhanced in 1865 with the Thirteenth Amendment abolishing slavery and in 1919 with the Nineteenth Amendment granting women the right to vote. This ideal is failing because there exists hidden forces in the very nature of democracy that militate against freedom. Unlike its free origins, America has become a nation where the reasons why freedom should be curtailed outweigh the reasons why we should be free, and the result is anger, contention and divisiveness.

INEQUALITY

Like freedom, Americans are losing equality. Democracy is a political system that is trying to solve an unsolvable equation involving freedom, equality and nature. Each part of the equation opposes the others; freedom does not exist in nature and does not bring equality, equality does not exist in nature and often takes freedom, and nature offers neither freedom nor equality. Fukuyama's concern over how democracy can reconcile liberty and equality arises because nature bats last — we are truly only equal in death when we curl up like a fetus and return to whence we came. Political systems work the equation differently, but when they move to solve one part, problems inevitably arise in another. Consequently, the optimal political system is one that achieves averaged compromises. But, as we have seen as democracy ages, it becomes increasingly resistant to any Solonian compromise. Instead, it jiggles the equation increasingly in favor of equality in all respects. With this, a myriad of problems arise that are manifest in late American democracy, which have been discussed throughout this book. The equation is only being skewed in America today.

American law in late democracy is a consequence of this skewered equation. It dispenses inequality with progressive taxation, under which 25 percent of American earners pay 84 percent and 1 percent pays 37 percent of all federal income taxes; government hiring policies that favor minorities; government policies that preference contracts to minorities;

Small Business Administration loans that give preference to economically disadvantaged minority-owned businesses; and affirmative action laws that give preference based on gender, minority status, sexual orientation and handicap in jobs and universities. Under the aegis of positive law, in late democracy, rights have become positive, purporting to grant equality only by dispensing inequality. The student's right to higher education has become another's debt when many default on their student loans. It is now acceptable to many Americans that the law embraces inequality and discrimination and abandons the fundamental principle of equal treatment under the law. It is indeed ironic that early American democratic laws dispensed inequality, mature democracy largely corrected them and late American democracy reintroduced them — inequality is being built back into the law with America's approval. To make matters worse, because the law is abandoning these fundamental principles, it is increasingly coming under attack from both sides of the aisle and, in the process, debased. The rule of fair law is corroding in late American democracy. The right and only solution is for the law to be neutral, bias free and blindly treat everyone equally.

In contrast to its idealistic roots, America has become a socialistic nation, and democracy is the reason why. The majority poor have driven the natural lifecycle of democracy described in chapter five, and America is now predictably in its late stage. The Fabian socialists have done their job well as Nietzschian slave morality prevails under the aegis of Christianity. The New Deal, Great Society and Obamacare in their myopic progressive vision to meet need have changed America's root zeitgeist from freedom, justice and equality to a social safety net, tax-the-rich mentality, and a utilitarian morality that dispenses inequality. With this, they have successfully altered the political equation in favor of equality in all respects, introduced intolerance, and initiated innumerable pejorative consequences manifest in America today. Democracy has brought inequality to America.

America has embraced a divisive philosophy. Socialism is not a unifying political philosophy but rather divides into proletariat and bourgeoisie and poor and rich. It engenders an "us versus them" mentality in total contrast to America's incipient unifying ideals of freedom, political equality and justice for all. Now, due to the advent of socialism in 2011 one half of all Americans receive benefits from one or more government programs, and 34 percent receive federal welfare benefits according to the United States Census Bureau. Unlike its roots, America now has a vast dependent class of citizens, many of whom pay no taxes. At the other end of the spectrum, Federal income taxes in 2015 on a few are as high as 39.6 percent which taken with all other taxes (Social Security, state taxes, county taxes, city taxes and business taxes, not to mention estate taxes) can easily exceed over half of one's income. To feed the dependant, government's rapacious need for money has become insatiable. America has set up a double standard in which the majority poor is treated differently than the minority producers. Inequality in benefits and taxation has been built into the system, and the war between rich and poor in democracy presaged by Tocqueville is being intensified today.

We see this contest everywhere, as the distinction between producer and consumer blurs. On one hand we have the unremitting demand to tax individuals, property and businesses, redistribute wealth, vilify corporations as welfare recipients and diminish the right to own property. On the other is the mainstream business middle class Tea Party, wholesale defeat of congressional Democrats who supported Obamacare and the Republican Party's repeated threat to shut down the federal government.

In chapter three the historic argument that democracy would bring tyranny by the uneducated poor stealing from the rich was evaluated meritless unless the underclass' demands became excessive. Socialism in America today indicates that their demands do become excessive and, when given the power of the majority due to democracy, they steal from others, just as the rich nobles in seventeenth-century France did from the peasants. Poignantly, it seems that whoever gains power dispenses inequality, and in America today it is the poor.

Tocqueville's foreboding was right, democracies do tend to socialism, the political struggle in democracy is ultimately between the have and have-nots and property is the great battlefield. It is a war being played out today in America. This war exists in stark contrast to early American democracy. Adams, in *The Federalist Papers*, wrote that the first object of government was the protection of different and unequal faculties of acquiring property, and the Founding Fathers, who were concerned that the many would steal from the few, limited suffrage to property holding and taxpaying citizens in the Constitution so they could not. Under socialism this has changed, and today any disparity of wealth is vile. Indeed, many Americans today think the very disparity of ownership of property is itself inequality.

There are three aspects of property: how it is acquired, used and disbursed. Early democracy's emphasis on freedom cared little about how it was used and disbursed but was intensely interested in how it was acquired. Most early Americans admired property and aspired to accumulate it because they had the opportunity to do so. The economic systems of their European homelands offered little opportunity to acquire it. In contrast, today most Americans are more interested in how property is dispersed and indifferent to how it is used and acquired. It does not matter to them that Gates earned his wealth but only that it ought to be redistributed. The results of this adulterated view are laws and policies in late democracy that treat those who earned their property differently than others. Their property becomes subject to taxes, mandates, restrictions and obligations designed for them alone. They are treated unequally under the aegis of democratically inspired socialism.

The relationship between inequality in late democratic America and morality has been discussed at length elsewhere in this book and thus will only be briefly summarized here. Early America's principles were based on the ideas of Thomas Hobbes and John Locke, which embodied the social contract moral theory. It was in all citizens' interests to form compacts not to steal from one another, and one of the purposes of government was to enforce this compact or the right to own property. The result is freedom and political equality but not necessarily equality in all respects. The nature of democracy changes this into utility, which brings relative morality and the assassin's creed of nothing true and everything permitted. Parenthetically, we see this moral code ensconced in America today, with sex and violence ubiquitously permitted everywhere. It is the resulting moral positivism that enables injustice to individuals. Examples of this in America's current laws and policies as well as attitudes are scattered throughout this book. It is this natural moral process of democracy that enables it to treat people differently, bringing inequality.

One depressingly poignant example of this new late democratic morality is its willingness to treat future generations unequally. The idea of paying one's way in life and settling one's debts has disappeared from the American landscape. Today, under the mantra of utility and happiness for the most, Americans are enjoying unearned benefits future generations must pay for with indifference. They are in effect treating future generations unequally by mortgaging their futures for their own benefit. This selfishness is one of late democracy's worst characteristics.

Many no doubt believe the assertion that socialism brings inequality absurd. They would rightfully claim that it equalizes wealth and brings egalitarianism. What they fail to understand is that socialism brings an artificial form of

270

equality that imparts inequality. It is this structural inequality built into law occurring in America today when taken to excess that angers citizens — it is a structural inequality that has been the bane of past civilizations. Early democracy offered equality, and late democracy in America supplanted by socialism offers only security in exchange for freedom and true equality.

It turns out Tocqueville was justified in being skeptical of democracy's inability to curb the demand for equality at the expense of freedom. In late American democracy, the demand has only intensified with little prospect of compromise. Indeed, in 2015 demagogic socialist Democrat presidential candidate Bernie Sanders demands free higher education for all, free universal healthcare and expanded Social Security benefits. His socialistic platform is not about compromise but rather pushing equality in all respects further. He is doing so with many Americans approval — as of this writing 23 percent of Americans were in favor of his platform. Equality has eclipsed freedom, and inequality to some is increasing for many individuals and minorities. Like the loss of freedom, the inequality late democracy dispenses only results in the divisiveness we see in America today.

INJUSTICE

Reinhold Niebuhr's statement that man's inclination to injustice makes democracy necessary is true only as far as it goes because it does not take into account late democracy's corruption of the concept of justice with social justice. Throughout this book, democracy's suppression of freedom over equality, the emerging belief in equal in all respects, advancing socialism, the change from natural to positive law and its adoption of utilitarian morality militate against universal justice. These forces in democracy jiggle the ultimately unsolvable political equation to one uncompromising extreme that invariably treats some citizens unjustly.

Based on 240 years of American history, it appears that democracy follows an ineluctable process, a kind of cause and effect sequence that changes the concept of what it means to be just. This section will endeavor to describe this sequence. Many no doubt will celebrate the evolution, calling it progressive and just. The important question, however, is whether it brings injustice. If citizens are treated unjustly, they will forever oppose the new political equation, resist and not cooperate. Indeed, it was Aristotle who wrote that revolutions occur in constitutional states when the constitution itself permits the lack of justice. This is not a formula for any political system to be the end of history.

Perhaps the origin of the problem with justice begins with the transformation of political equality and equal opportunity in early democracy to absolute in late democracy. In chapter three, the historic charge against democracy that it was too abstract was discounted on the condition the abstractness did not stray too far from nature and lose touch with reality. It appears now that the ideal of equality in democracy does evolve into an unrealistic abstraction that ignores natural abilities, promulgates laws that incite anger and resentment and ultimately satisfies nobody.

In order to bring about an exceedingly abstract and unnatural equality that does not comport with nature, to continue the thread, the law has to be bent. The manifestation of this bending has been the transformation of American law from natural to positive. The law has to be just a social fact or just what the judges do because in nature we are not equal. In order to bring about what policies are desired in democracy, reality has to be manipulated and transmogrified, often by non-originalist judges. So, in late American democracy we see the convoluted consequences of the Fourteenth Amendment, the passage of the Sixteenth Amendment that enables socialism, the abrogation of the Commerce Clause in the 1930s and a woman's right to abortion legalized under the banner of privacy and not justice.

272

Positive law must arise to enforce Protagorean late democratic policies.

With the law detached from morality and just a social fact justified under positive jurisprudence it is only natural that the free-floating concept of social justice emerges. The idea of social justice is a relatively new one. Some cite its beginnings in the 1840s when a Jesuit priest named Luigi Taparelli coined the term that spread with that era's revolutions. In America, the term was used by Supreme Court Justice Louis Brandeis and in the jurisprudential writings of Roscoe Pound. In the early twentieth century, organized labor increasingly used the term, which came to maturity in the writings of John Rawls in the 1970s. Significantly, it is only in late democracy that the novel idea of social justice appears.

So what exactly is social justice? Various sources describe it as public education, immigration reform, equality for homosexuals, economic justice for poor and working families, a woman's right to equal pay, diversity, the right to equitable treatment, human rights, equal opportunity, equality, the fair allocation of a community's resources and the right not to be discriminated against based on gender, sexuality, religion, political affiliations, age, race, belief, disability, location, social class or socioeconomic circumstances. Social justice is a potpourri of wishes and desires individuals or sects that are not equal in all respects espouse, hence its natural occurrence in late democracy. It does not bring justice to all but only those sects claiming justice. It does not account for ability, effort, industry or personal responsibility, all of which it derides as characteristics and concepts enabling inequalities in society. It is an ineffable, protean and capricious conceptual *tabula rasa* on which anyone can write. It occurs in late democracies in order to turn the law into a force that will bring equality in all respects, which it does through positive rights.

Social justice is not inherently wrong—all citizens should have the right to equality. However, democracy-inspired social justice, as the thread continues, naturally turns negative rights into positive rights that harness the power of the law to achieve equality in all respects. Recall the invocation of negative rights derived from Locke in early American democracy. They were intended to prevent government from interfering with citizens' freedom. Now, under positive rights the government practices reverse discrimination and requires some citizens to pay for positive rights. Recall from chapter three one of the arguments against democracy was that it brings positive rights, which was discounted as one of its fatal flaws unless the definition of what constitutes a right changes. It now appears that the definition does change, positive rights do ascend in democracy, and injustice does ensue to some; thus, it is a flaw that makes democracy just one more thesis in the dialectic of history.

It should be noted that some wrongfully believe the Constitution does contain some positive rights, such as the right to legal representation. The Constitution does rightfully provide for this, but, like the right to life, it does not require others to pay for it. What is a negative right becomes reinterpreted by some as a positive right in late democracy.

The Christmas list of positive rights is fathomless. They cannot be completely delineated, measured or described. They are like parasites with voracious appetites that hosts forever need to feed. These positive rights began in America's mature democratic stage and unabatedly advanced in her late stage. In her early late stage, the positive right advancement rung was universal healthcare. Many Americans came to believe they have a right to healthcare and they turned to the government and the law to bring it about. It was an epic battle waged in 2009 and 2010, and Obamacare was the result.

This section is about justice, so the question now becomes: does justice demand citizens have the positive right to healthcare? On a deeper level, the question is whether one person has a moral obligation to insure another lives? Certainly, Christianity with its ethic of being thy brother's keeper would preach that there is such an obligation. But this question is about morality and not religion. The question is whether there exists a morality that truly dispenses justice that obligates the coercive power of government be used to force some to provide healthcare to others. The thread will now naturally invoke the previously discussed social contract and utilitarian moral theories, which will end with Rawls's theory of justice.

In chapter eight on injustice and ten on relative morality, it was argued that early American democracy was based on the social contract, which is a moral theory that dispenses justice." The simple compacts humans make based on their self-interests in order to live better lives are clear, real, immediate and consistent; result in morality; end in justice; and promote human safety and happiness. A central role of the state is to enforce these simple compacts. The social contract does not morally support universal healthcare for a variety of reasons. It should be mentioned here that this perspective is derived from Hobbes. Some contend that alternate versions of the contract theory from thinkers like Locke, Jean-Jacque Rousseau, Rawls and David Gauthier do justify positive rights and thus support universal healthcare. This issue is beyond the scope of this book. My opinion is that their interpretations do not support positive rights, sometimes corrupt Hobbes's theory and sometimes endeavor to usurp it for utilitarian means. This last point will be explained in more detail later in this section with Rawls.

First, the social contract does not support universal healthcare because the contract is voluntary and based on self-interest, so many people would not support it. Many would think it is in their interests not to participate. They could be young and healthy, they may prefer other ways to maintain their health, or they may simply not want to pay for it. Thus, the only way to implement universal healthcare is by coercion, but this would break the voluntary nature of the contract. If coercion is necessary, then universal healthcare is not supported by the social contract theory.

Second, some claim universal healthcare is akin to social services like fire, police, roads, sewers, and national parks. But this is not the case. Clearly, people would voluntarily support some services because it is in their interests to do so. It is in everyone's interests to have sewers because without them the individual runs the real risk of illness. But it is not necessarily in everyone's self-interest to have national parks, subsidized housing or universal healthcare. Many, for example, would think national parks are nice, but they may never visit them and thus do not want to pay for them. The same holds for universal healthcare for the reasons mentioned previously, many would not support it because it is not in their interests.

Finally, the social contract involves negative rights, whereas universal healthcare imparts a positive one. The social contact would negatively prohibit anyone from interfering with a citizen's right to healthcare, but it would not positively obligate others to provide it. Generally, universal healthcare imposes a positive obligation that is not in many citizens' interests. Many would not voluntarily agree to it. Thus, the social contract does not establish the moral right to require that one ensures another survives; thus, the universal right to healthcare. Poignantly, Obamacare would never have passed in early American democracy.

In contrast, utilitarianism does support universal healthcare. The romantic aspiration of happiness for the most would require a society to distribute healthcare in such a way that brings the best health for the most. Recall that in chapters eight and ten, it was argued that democracy naturally adopts utility, and the positive right to healthcare is the consequence. So, the necessary thread of injustice in democracy in the case of universal healthcare arrives at its dénouement in late American democracy; with no moral imperative and no mutually agreed to compact, some are forced against their interests to provide for others' health. There is no fairness or justice to them in this late democratic positivistic policy. To continue my previous point, Obamacare only emerged in late American utilitarian democracy.

Because the social contract brings justice, proponents of utility endeavor to usurp and reengineer it in a way to support utility. The National Education Association, for example, cites the social contract to support its utilitarian objectives, and Rawls, a Harvard philosophy professor, used it to develop a theory of justice. His imaginative theory is a contemporary example of the corruption by democracy of the social contract theory recast as utility. Let us examine it in light of healthcare.

His theory begins with two principles of justice. First, each person is to have an equal right to the most extensive scheme of basic liberties compatible with others. Second, social and economic inequalities are to be arranged so that they are both reasonably expected to be in everyone's advantage. From this, Rawls proposes a social contract where from an original position no one knows their place in society or their natural abilities because they are accidents of nature. He calls this the veil of ignorance. Under such circumstances he argues that individuals would choose a system of justice that establishes the requirement that if one person gains, then others gain. This he calls the difference principle, which allows some to gain as long as the worst off benefit. Under this theory, universal healthcare would ostensibly be just as long as the worst off, or those who need healthcare, benefit.

Does Rawls's theory of justice justify universal healthcare? It does not for numerous reasons. First, the veil of ignorance is unrealistic. Rawls's theory is based on the assumption that people will make choices in ignorance. It is a theory that only works by requiring people to be ignorant of their choices. They cannot know, for example, their social position or abilities, and they are expected to make decisions about justice without this knowledge. This is unrealistic because people will know their social position and abilities, and, more importantly, many would wisely choose not to make a decision in ignorance. Given the choice, most would simply wait until they have more information before they made a decision. With knowledge of their inabilities, the least advantaged would agree with Rawls's theory and become the privileged least advantaged, and if they are one of the advantaged, they will not agree to make decisions in ignorance and thus gain by not being hampered by the difference principle. Either way both win by not making a decision under the veil of ignorance. Significantly, it is difficult to understand how justice derives from ignorance.

Some point out that the purpose of the veil is to eliminate biases that are not morally relevant to justice. But natural abilities are not accidents of nature that must ignored as biases — rather, they are real, should be celebrated and must be accounted for in any theory of justice. It is indeed strange to think that we must eliminate any bias toward Albert Einstein's intelligence in such a way to handicap it so the less intelligent could benefit. Justice ought not demand Einstein be ignorant of his unique ability or handicap him.

Second, Rawls's theory violates individual freedom because requiring individuals to make decisions under a veil of ignorance does not respect individual choice. Under normal circumstances, people have a range of choices, but his veil of ignorance artificially limits those choices. For example, assume a heart patient needs surgery and there are many disadvantaged people in need in the hospital. Under Rawls's theory, under universal healthcare, a doctor might offer only less expensive options to the heart patient so to free up medical resources for the least advantaged. The heart patient's right to freely decide on treatment has been violated. Some claim this is an unfair criticism because Rawls is addressing macro societal issues, but if any such macro theory of justice commits micro injustice to individuals, it is not a true theory of justice. Recall from chapter eight that utility does permit injustice to individuals.

Three, his theory imposes a positive healthcare right that obligates some, thus violating their rights, such as the right to keep their property. In the case of Obamacare, broader coverage was mandated for more people that raised many individuals' premiums, and if citizens fail to carry health insurance, they are fined by the government. Unlike utility, the social contract would never allow for these injustices to some.

Four, Rawls's theory offers no comprehensive explanation of what constitutes being the least advantaged. It could be proposed, for example that everyone in America who makes less that $200,000 a year is least advantaged. This would create many least advantaged and few advantaged. It would, in effect, be socialism, where healthcare would be paid for by a very few able for many in need. It would be a healthcare system where each is to pay according to his ability and receive healthcare according to his need. This is a key socialistic tenet, which we have seen democracy naturally adopts with its emphasis on security over freedom. Finally, Rawls's theory violates one of Immanuel Kant's deontological moral imperatives, which is to treat people as ends and not means. His theory is imbued with ways people are treated as means, including the veil of ignorance, robbing their natural abilities, which have become accidents of nature, and being one of the able in socialism. Rawls's theory does not support universal healthcare, takes freedom and imparts injustice.

Contrariwise, some claim that if personal choice were the highest good, then there would be no political systems or healthcare. Some cite theories outside the liberal tradition, such as communitarianism, that would. A challenge to this view is beyond the scope of this book, but it should be noted that history tells us communism fails; it imparts injustice and is one of those Protagorian metaphysical systems that Jonathan Swift's flappers were intended to dispose.

Rawls's theory of justice is a natural product of democracy's evolution. Justice is sought in imagined utopias that exist only as long as some artificial human-devised overarching controlling entity like government enforces them. Such political systems too often dispense injustice and are foreign to early American democracy based on a social contract that arose naturally and did impart justice.

Unfortunately for Niebuhr, the law in late democratic America is not imparting justice. It failed because there exist too many natural forces in democracy that hinder justice, including the overemphasis on equality, the advent of positive law, the reinterpretation of justice as social justice, the emergence of positive rights such as the right to healthcare and the moral segue from the social contract to utility. Democracy naturally brings these irresistible juggernauts that even the legal profession, which Tocqueville believed was the most powerful existing security against the excesses of democracy and its proclivity to impart injustice, failed to prevent.

Mentioned earlier, two essential requirements for just laws are the rule of law and equal treatment under the law. Regarding the former, Adams insisted that government be bounded by fixed laws. However, we have seen that American late democracy under positivistic law finesses this principle. Equal treatment under the law is also essential but again this principle has become adulterated under positive law. Violation of these two principles coupled with a utilitarian morality, has enabled social justice that is not a universal justice.

American laws' proclivity to treat people unequally is particularly iniquitous. Following is a brief excerpt from my book *On Law* explaining why:

> Legal discrimination for social policy or opinion
> occurs in a democracy. Discrimination has become
> a political tool [in America] where race is protect-
> ed but property is not. It is illegal to discriminate

against a certain ethnicity, but it is legal to discriminate against a high earner with progressive taxation.

Equal protection under the law is a fundamental requirement for any just legal system. Historically, it meant that all citizens must stand equal before the law and that justice must be blind to wealth, color, rank or privilege. This is justice under the law.

Preferential treatment...is intended to correct certain societal injustices. Some believe there exists a compelling state reason for laws to prefer some citizens over others. However, these idealistic and lofty kinds of laws are wrong because they imbed injustice in the law. The claim to a past injustice is not limited to any one person or sect. Preferential treatment laws themselves cause stereotypes, violate individual rights, violate equal treatment under the law and build discrimination into the law.

When the law becomes non-neutral, it reverts to its antiquated form of coercion by a sovereign— which in a democracy is the majority. The only consequences must be loss of respect for the law and social discord, which we see in [late American] democracy.

Mark Levin, in *Men in Black*, provided an example of legal discrimination today in America. The Fourteenth Amendment to the Constitution prohibits all state discrimination based on race without exception. It proclaims equal treatment under the law for all. However, in the Regents of University of California v. Bakke case (and extended cases), the Supreme Court allowed discrimination and violated this critical foundation for just law. In brief, it has ruled that if there is a compelling state reason with a narrowly tailored university acceptance application process that achieves diversity, the University of California could discriminate based on race. Dissenting justices noted that diversity has never been a compelling state interest to initiate discrimination in the law and observed that there appeared to be no diversity programs for Christian fundamentalists, Muslims and Orthodox Jews. Unequal treatment under the law has been sanctioned by America's highest court.

With the diminution of these critical foundations of justice, expedience is one natural result—it becomes more important to do what works than what is just. Examples of this are found throughout American law today. A plethora of land-use laws limit the use of property and sometimes take it without compensation, environmental laws penalize the deep pockets and not what caused contamination, gender laws protect one sex while preferential treatment laws discriminate against another, sex laws bring guilt with no regard to intent, affirmative action laws favor one ethnicity while discriminating against another, such as in the case of Bakke, tax laws tax some citizens at higher rates and proportionately more than others, wealth redistribution laws bring benefits to some and not others and, with the abandonment of the Commerce Clause, the federal government is free to control all aspects of commerce for the benefit of some at the detriment of others. American law is so imbued with expedience in late democracy, most fail to see the just forest through the expedient obscuring trees.

Two salient manifestations of expedient justice today are strict liability laws and overcriminalization. Justice demands that a perpetrator's intent be weighed so any punishment is proportional to the level of their wickedness. This is mens rea, or intent. Premeditated murder, for example, is punished more severely than accidental manslaughter. On the continuum of degrees of intent, at one extreme are strict liability laws, where intent is not considered; one is guilty if they committed the crime. It does not matter, for example, whether an older man who had sex with an underage girl thoroughly vetted her age, the only relevant fact is that he slept with her, which makes him guilty. This is strict liability and the number of such laws has been increasing in late American democracy.

The replacement of a *mens rea* requirement with strict liability in federal law is harshly and unjustly criminalizing many activities. For example, diverting a backed-up sewage system, abandoning a snowmobile in a blizzard, digging up arrowheads and packing frozen lobsters in plastic bags rather than paper are strict liability laws requiring federal prosecution. These new levels of punishment are a consequence of policy ascending over justice and being enforced through strict liability, and the result is too often injustice to the individual.

Another example of policy trumping justice for the sake of expedience is overcriminalization. At America's inception, there were only about twenty federal crimes. Today, it is estimated that Congress enacted approximately 450 new crimes between 2000 and 2007, or between fifty and sixty new crime laws per year. Further, federal code now has about 4,500 statutory federal crimes and between one hundred thousand and three hundred thousand federal regulations. How could any one citizen possibly know each of these laws and regulations? It appears that in America, one legacy of democracy is to create more laws with harsher penalties in order to bring about unrealistic political objectives. Its laws are increasingly based on expedience, and injustice is often the result.

Much was said about ends and means in chapter eight on injustice. Ends trump means — with just ends, means are not unjust. Early democracy had principled ends to which the means were or became subordinate. True justice is an end and not a mean, so in a just legal system, means are not unjust. However, as democracy ages, this changes as means ascend and become justified for innumerable desired ends. The concept of justice in late American democracy as an end has been so adulterated with social justice that innumerable unjust means can be employed to ostensibly justify an end, which for many appears just.

The important democratic ideals of freedom and equality were discussed earlier. It was mentioned that Fukuyama was concerned that there is no fixed point of agreement between them. This loss of a fixed point is evident in America today, where equality and security are ends valued over freedom, and the results are unjust means that have been described in this section and throughout this book. With the ascension of means, many of the unjust problem characteristics and consequences of late democracy that naturally arise can be seen in America today. With justice as a front, equality has become power, and especially the power to achieve security, merit and responsibility have become words for inequality; morality has become relative and little more than fashion or opinion; and expedience has replaced equal treatment under the law. With these developments, rights enshrined in the Constitution shielding individuals against the power of government have faded under the majority's hegemony. There are consequences to these developments in late democracy, and anger and resentment are two that lead to democracy's ultimate undoing, which is divisiveness.

CONCENTRATION OF POWER

Jefferson believed that history does not teach us but rather only warns us, and one such warning must be the concentration of governmental power, which is inimical and ultimately fatal to democracy. Tocqueville warned of concentrated power in democracy that suppresses liberty, and George Orwell, in *1984*, famously described an omnipresent, controlling, manipulative and surveilling Big Brother government that punished individualism and took liberty. Early democracy heeded Jefferson, Tocqueville and Orwell's warnings and embraced limited government. In America, it followed Jefferson's advice with a federal government that governed little and was unattractive of notice. Indeed, one animating factor for both the French and American Revolutions was escape from the tyranny concentrated governmental power enables.

This has all changed in late American democracy. Unlike its roots it could be argued that the American federal government today is the greatest concentration of governmental power ever seen in history, far surpassing some historic regimes like ancient Rome. After the Cold War ended with the Soviet Union in 1991, America emerged as the world's only standing superpower. Unlike past regimes, the American federal government's power is global, with military bases and troops in seventy-four countries all over the world. In 2015, it spent almost $600 billion on defense, which is more than the next seven countries combined. It consumes more than a fifth of the nation's income and has over 2,600,000 employees. As previously mentioned, it has promulgated over 4,500 federal laws dealing with crime and perhaps as many three hundred thousand federal regulations. Some estimate that there are over two thousand federal departments regulating all aspects of Americans' lives. The United States gathers intelligence on Americans through the Central Intelligence Agency, conducts surveillance through the National Security Agency (Tocqueville wrote that surveillance is an obsession with central governments) and enforces its power through a multitude of agencies, including the Federal Bureau of Investigation. The American federal government has become Big Brother.

There are five reasons democracy will fail in America due to concentrated power in the federal government. They are high taxes; perpetuating one policy for all; the tyrannical majority that superintends federal power, which takes freedom; the loss of local control and vigor; and the potential for a dictator.

In order to pay for this, leviathan's social and military spending taxes have become oppressive for the most productive Americans. On the federal level, they are taxed with federal income taxes, capital gains taxes and perhaps corporate taxes, to name just a few. On the state level, these taxes are often reproduced and added to with sales taxes. The county level adds real estate taxes, and city taxes include just about anything. It is not unreasonable to say that, after considering all sources of taxes, some Americans are paying over 50 percent of their income in taxes. Recall that one reason for the decline of the Roman Empire and the central cause of the French Revolution was over-taxation. Some no doubt would argue that things are different today because, under the aegis of socialism, the able producers should pay high taxes. What they fail to understand is that it is an inequitable tax system that sews the same discord that oppressed the Romans and infuriated the French.

Over-taxation is an important point because once it is ensconced it remains and usually grows. Under socialism, the demand for more redistribution of wealth, bigger government to implement it and higher taxes to achieve it only grows, as the concentration of government takes on a life of its own, like a parasite devouring its host.

The second reason is federal centralized authority making decisions for all. In a pluralistic society, there is more freedom because sects can establish their own policies, but when the federal Congress passes legislation, it often usurps local laws, traditions, beliefs and ways of living. Prohibition, Obamacare and numerous environmental laws could be examples. The same happens with the judicial branch. The Supreme Court legalizes same-sex marriage and abortion for all at the horror of many individuals' conscience and religious groups' beliefs.

Allied with this is the concern that the majority of voters in American democracy superintend the federal centralized power. The federal government and its policies mirror the majority's views, to which the minorities are slaves. It is Tocqueville's tyranny of the majority enforced by the federal government. The majority is free, for example, to pass federal laws that bring taxes that are beneficial to them and not to others. The majority poor, for example, vote to tax the rich at higher income rates to maintain their federal benefits. All of these policies and laws are enforced by an army of faceless federal bureaucrats that are increasingly controlling of all aspects of Americans' lives.

It is intuitively true that when governmental power is centralized, local communities lose their vitality, which is the fourth reason. Today in America, a citizen suggests that a school program ought to be changed in such a way, and the inevitable response is that it against federal law. Another citizen suggests a location for a new park, and again the answer too often is that federal law prohibits building in that location because it is a habitat for some endangered animal. Local control is usurped by the central government; citizens become resigned because they have no control over federal law, and they stop trying to imaginatively improve their community. This happens repeatedly throughout the nation, and the result is resignation, loss of incentive and imagination, dependence, and ultimately the decay of community spirit.

In America today there are federal mandates for drinking water, effluent standards, hazardous waste disposal, obligations for local medical care, obligations for localities to pay for employee healthcare and educational standards. The controversial Common Core State Standards Initiative, for example, establishes standard tests for all public schools, so the battleground over what constitutes a proper education moves to the bureaucracy of Washington and out of the hands of local educators and parents. The result is a federal government's national policies dictating how local communities are to educate their children and live their lives. With no control of their future, they become vapid, dependent and lifeless entities.

The final and perhaps most serious reason concentrated governmental power harms democracy is that it creates an entity a future president could use to bring dictatorship. In chapter nine, various presidential powers were described, including executive orders that could be used to implement a president's policies and circumvent the democratic process. Barack Obama, for example, used them in gun control, for amnesty to illegal immigrants, to increase the federal minimum wage, to overturn welfare reform, in ordering the Justice Department to stop enforcing the Defense of Marriage Act and unilaterally declaring Bristol Bay, Alaska off-limits to oil and gas exploration. Agree or disagree with his actions, when a president says, as did Obama, that he will act without Congress if they do not act themselves and in the process bypass the democratic process, democracy is at risk. It is not so unrealistic to envision an extreme future president frustrated by Congress turning to executive powers to achieve his or her ends.

If eternal recurrence is true, history teaches us that concentrated power in government can be fatal to government. In chapter nine and in this chapter, three reasons have been given; they are high taxation, loss of local control and the potential for dictatorship. Both ancient Rome under emperors and seventeenth-century France under kings had inordinate concentrated governmental control, and both failed. In Rome, any semblance of a balance of power under a republic was eliminated when the executive or imperial branch overarched the senate and judiciary. It is tempting to compare the rise and fall of Rome to American history. The early Roman Republic, for example, could be compared in many ways with America's first one hundred years. Both experienced the struggle for freedom and wariness of government, and both were expansive in nature. What is more striking are the innumerable parallels between the Roman Empire, or the period from 31 BCE to 493 CE, and America in the twentieth century. In each period, there is an increasing presence of a military and projection of power. Today, America has a vast military establishment that is stationed in virtually all parts of the globe. In both periods, there is increasing wealth. America in the twentieth century has grown to be one of the richest nations in the world. Finally, both periods experienced the increasing centralization of government along with a burgeoning bureaucracy. America today has an unprecedented, powerful and centralized government that has, to a very large extent, usurped states' rights.

Also extraordinary are the similarities of early Roman and American attitudes toward government. Early on, both displayed a healthy distrust of centralized and unaccountable government. The Roman constitution of the early third century BCE showed suspicion of all government. It involved checks and balances within government between magistrates, tribunes, legislatures, administrations and the judiciary. Frank C. Bourne wrote in his *History of the Romans* (paraphrased) that all the branches of the government served to check one another. Similarly, America's Founding Fathers imbued in the Constitution (particularly in the Bill of Rights) limitations on the federal government, checks and balances, and limits to governmental power over individual freedom. But in both cases, this distrust of centralized power faded, and both evolved into massive central powers. Like ancient Rome, America today is experiencing big and unaccountable centralized government and an expanding bureaucracy to administer its laws. It is disconcerting that two countries built originally on Jeffersonian republican ideals gradually fade with the exigencies of circumstances.

France before the French Revolution also had centralized power under monarchial kings. Mentioned earlier, it had become prosperous due to manufacturing, which enabled the government to become the largest spender, employer and debtor. Indeed, it was the oppressive and hated *taille* tax used to support the government that was one of the leading causes of the peasants' revolt.

The obvious correlation is that excessive taxation is needed to support large centralized government. In the case of Rome and France, it was to support a bureaucracy and military, and in contemporary America, it is to support bureaucracy, military and social wealth redistribution policies. As discussed earlier, in Rome, Diocletian would simply establish a national budget and then levy whatever tax satisfied it, irrespective of actual production. To garner these taxes' fixed amounts, farmers were harassed and legally tied to farming.

American centralized government today taxes excessively, issues mandates requiring others to pay and penalizes those who refuse. A citizen is fined, for example, for not having health insurance. If history is a teacher, it tells us under these circumstances, citizens either quit like the farmers did in ancient Rome or rebel like the French peasants did in the late 1700s.

History also tells us that centralized power saps local control and enervates communities. Described earlier, it was the growth of the Roman bureaucratic empire with its high taxes and imperious policies that usurped local municipal responsibility. Citizens became enfeebled, unable to act and, as Bourne wrote, useless and parasitic. Bourne continued with the observation that (paraphrased) it is rather disheartening to reflect that the very interest of the central government in the happiness and well-being of those towns lead to a paternalistic bureaucracy that ultimately inundated the sense of municipal responsibility and pride in local traditions and emasculated their vigor. Similar to ancient Rome, as was mentioned in chapter nine, Tocqueville wrote about the democratic change in French thinking due to the French Revolution. Under this new way, people began thinking the best governmental system consisted of all powerful government bureaucracies that took control on behalf of the state of men's private lives. That governmental system ultimately ended in dictatorship.

We see the same thing happening in America today under the aegis of centralized federal power. With the loss of the original American independent ethic, citizens are increasingly looking to Washington for solutions. With this, federal power is increasingly controlling all aspects of Americans' lives in education, health, the environment, safety and security. There exist today massive federal bureaucracies that implement innumerable laws and policies that increasingly regulate all aspects of citizens' lives. Many Americans today look to centralized power not only for their sustenance but also how to act. It would seem that democracy cannot last long when its citizens become so enfeebled.

Finally, history warns us that concentrated governmental power gives the potential dictator the means to become one. Augustus and Napoleon were able to become emperor/dictators because there existed a central power to bring it about. Under a weak central power diffused by states' rights, as in early American democracy, Washington, Jefferson or Madison did not have the means to become dictators. Today, under the aegis of perhaps the most powerful government ever, one extremist president using his or her vast array of powers has the means to become 1984's superintendent of Big Brother.

Concentrated governmental power is ultimately fatal to all political systems, including democracy. It dispenses singular one-made-for-all policies, suppresses local vitality, brings high taxes, limits freedom and enables dictatorships and possible tyranny. In America today, Obamacare, legalized abortion and same-sex marriage incite anger in many American citizens. Government mandates and high taxes further give rise to the Tea Party movement that vigorously opposes central government's political hegemony. Centralized power has not brought consensus or peace to American politics — only discord and divisiveness.

RELATIVE MORALITY

What better example of the consequences of relative morality could be found than in the Beatnik and Hippies movements of the late 1950s and '60s in late American democracy? Utilitarianism had replaced the social contract, so now nothing is true and everything is permitted. Aristotle and Tocqueville were right, in democracy everyone gains license to do as they please, and the only moral measure becomes one's own happiness. All other American gypsy movements, such as the speakeasies under Prohibition in the 1920s, pale in comparison.

It was a time of sex, drugs and rock and roll. It was the time to do your own thing, live for the day and eschew convention. It began with self-consumed, hedonistic and dissipated characters like Kerouac and Ginsberg in the 1950s. Barry Miles, in his biography *Jack Kerouac: King of the Beats*, described Kerouac as a self-destructive personality who was coldhearted, obdurate and callous. He was bisexual, anti-Semitic, racist, childish, irresponsible, selfish and self-centered. He was an alcoholic and drug addict. He was an immoral individual always seeking freedom, unconcerned with others, seeking new pleasures and avoiding responsibility. He escaped to Mexico to avoid paying child support. He was a sexist who believed women should be kept in their place. He lived a bohemian life of escape as an insensitive, selfish and cowardly dreamer. He wrote *On the Road*, which is a stream of consciousness novel about freedom, male bonding, feelings, spontaneity and intuition. It is the kind of hedonistic book bereft of any moral teachings that only the literati in late democracy would laud. Kerouac lived with his mother the last part of his life in an alcoholic haze and died at age forty-seven from cirrhosis of the liver.

The hippie movement of the 1960s was a broader and deeper movement that mined the minimal limits of how we ought to treat one another and set the stage for the age of relative morality in America. Jay Stevens, in his book *Storming Heaven*, described sophisticated reborn Kerouacs like Aldous Huxley and Timothy Leary and pranksters like Ken Kesey, deep into drugs like LSD. It was the apex of relative morality's time symbolized by dissipated and irresponsible youth in Haight-Ashbury doing as they please in their pursuit of happiness.

Stevens described communal crash pads where you lost your clothes, virginity and old values and a sixteen-year-old girl, new from the Midwest, who got repeatedly raped. He described the ubiquitous use of drugs, where on a given day roughly half the people in San Francisco's Haight-Ashbury were tripping, had been tripping or were about to trip. At one point, San Francisco General Hospital was treating an average of 750 drug panic reactions a month. Most were pampered adolescent kids who had enjoyed rich upbringings and decided it was all crap. They were seeking an unrealistic other world that always receded as they approached. They were trying to create a workable map of anarchic reality that never worked.

They were impressionable youths who passionately defended their lifestyle and beliefs. One such belief was socialism, and the mystical idea that whatever was needed would be provided. Capitalism and money were evil. Predictably, the hippies were always short of money and the necessities of life, so when they went to San Francisco General Hospital for a drug overdose, it was the California taxpayers who paid their bills.

Interestingly, Stevens described their culture as status oriented, with hierarchies of prestige despite their rhetoric of no leaders. With their passionate insistence that they are the wave of the future, intolerance emerged and hardened against those who would not conform. Some described their culture as perfect for fascism. Indeed, in the later days of the Haight, the dominant mood was anger, and violence was the result. The Diggers began carrying guns, and numerous riots broke out, with kids throwing stones, pavement and Molotov cocktails. Unsurprisingly, divisiveness was one consequence of the hippie movement.

Many of the consequences of late democracy described in the '60s are manifest in America today; America today is a macrocosm of the '60s without the long hair and beads. Certainly, many of the destructive characteristics described can be found in most societies, but they have been magnified in late American democracy due to relative morality. America has reached the natural dénouement of utilitarianism. Ubiquitous sex in the media, promiscuity, teenage pregnancies, adultery, strip clubs and internet pornography are just a few examples. The attenuation of the institution of marriage is perhaps one of the most damaging. Half of American marriages fail, divorce is rampant, mothers are raising children in fatherless families in poverty and unwed mothers and illegitimacy are common. Utility in sex has ascended, the Playboy philosophy of sex has prevailed, birth control has become abortion and same-sex marriage has been legalized. Any moral code that was intended to prevent such circumstances has been discarded.

Past societies have had mind-altering drugs like alcohol, but America has become a drug culture with heroin, LSD, meth, ecstasy, STP and Venus. It is only a natural consequence that marijuana is legalized. America has become a wealthy nation that has enabled indulgence, pleasure and decadence with problems it papers over with money. Rather than face reality, Americans are escaping it like the hippies of the '60s, with unrealistic expectations. Untethered from truth, Americans in late democracy expect equality in all respects, which requires politically correct social norms and liberal education to teach that human differences are due to nurture and not nature. With nurture alone as its guide, true causal relationships have become obfuscated, such as promiscuity, divorce and unsupported children, and the only solution is an unremitting demand for more governmental services that bring bigger government, higher taxes and debt. The unrealistic specter of socialism has also arrived with 2016 Democratic candidates Sanders and Martin O'Malley promising to bring happiness to the most by having the government satiate bottomless need. Like the hippies of the '60s, many Americans have come to believe whatever is needed will be provided.

Early America embraced a melting pot, but with relative morality and nurture alone as the guide, this has been supplanted with diversity in late America that celebrates different cultures. Like equality, now all cultures are equally good, whether or not they are. Predictably, different cultures have arisen that passionately celebrate their differences, fragmentation has begun and balkanization is rising, as sects' ideologies intolerantly harden, just like in the late '60s counterculture. The hippies were intolerant of nonconformists, just like many Americans have become intolerant of non-democratic ideas. Free speech is lauded as an ideal, but when a southern state hoists the Confederate flag or a Midwest town inscribes a biblical phrase on a building, the people become intolerant. Freedom of speech and religion are acceptable only when they propound skewed late democratic ideology.

It is only natural that the late '60s permissive hippie culture became intolerant and ended in violence. Similarly, under utility and the assassin's creed, America has become a culture of violence. Columbine, Springfield, Aurora, Chardon High School, the Boston Marathon, and San Bernardino are just a few examples of a culture of violence due to the loss of true morality. Society has become paralyzed because its late democratic utilitarian ideology masks the true problems; all it can do is assail the Second Amendment. Masks blind, and with blinkered views, the majority in late democracy stumbles into its final and fatal phase, which is divisiveness. Like Haight-Ashbury, American progressive democracy has seen many advances, each of which has added an iota to an underground cauldron of burning anger, resentment and vindictiveness. Today, we see this volcanic cauldron's eruptions periodically, such as the Tea Party, opposition of Obamacare and the unusual support of renegade Donald Trump for president. The majority is again paralyzed and can only feebly label such events as barbarian, extreme and radical, but, again, it is incapable of addressing the true causes.

One final consequence of relative morality in America today is in law. This topic has been discussed in detail throughout this book and is resurrected here only briefly because it is so important. The law in late American democracy has become politicized. It has become contradictory and is often capricious due to the majority's acceptance of unjust means. The rule of law in late democracy is threatened, the law treats people unequally and negative rights embodied in the Bill of Rights are becoming positive. Unjust laws are ultimately fatal to any society.

Fukuyama's assertion that morality involves a distinction between better and worse has been lost in America's current climate of relative morality. It has become the unhealthy society Nietzsche predicted because it has no horizon or accepted values and beliefs. It is a moral zeitgeist without foundation or privileged perspectives rather than one that coherently coalesces opinions and sentiments. It is like a free-floating capricious relativistic bubble that only mirrors majority opinion and not truth. The 1960s' indulgent pleasure-seeking morality bereft of any right or wrong is American relative morality today.

Democracy has caused America to lose her moral compass, and one consequence is injustice, which inevitably leads to divisiveness. One only need to survey the newspapers in late American democracy to see that discord and divisiveness have become chronic. Divisiveness is democracy's Achilles heel, and it will be discussed next.

DIVISIVENESS

America in the early twentieth century is deeply divided. There is anger, accusation, bitterness, fractionalization, charges, counter-charges, resentment and hatred. Anger daily permeates the media, venom is spewed by our politicians and violence is ubiquitous. This anger has hardened into intolerant and irresolvable positions that have become blind to compromise. America has become a country permeated with divisiveness. This is not a single-issue divisiveness but rather one that represents deep philosophic differences about the nature of the world, how we ought to live, the nature of man, the constitution of justice, the function of government and what it means to be free. It is a fundamental collision over what it is to be human.

This is a kind of divisive internal strife that occurred in ancient democracies like Athens, republican Rome, northern Italy and France before they failed. It is also the kind of faction that many historic thinkers have warned against. Plato, Aristotle, Tocqueville, Madison, Hobbes and Edward Gibbon are just a few who believed democracy brought chaos, instability, faction and contention. It is the kind of divisiveness that cannot resolve the differences Fukuyama presaged. History warned us that democracy will bring divisiveness, and it is here now writ large. Divisiveness was a flaw of democracy dismissed in chapter three unless it leads to turbulence and contention; it has and thus will be the scribe that writes democracy in America's epitaph.

Democracy enables magnified perceived injustices, which results in resentment and anger from just about everyone. In democracy, everyone has a gripe because it unleashes unquenchable human desires from all sides of the isle. The poor, rich, white, black, minority, endowed, unendowed, handicapped, man, woman, city dweller, country citizen, heterosexual and homosexual—all find reasons for being wronged. Democracy is like a petri dish that grows dissention bacteria. The grocery list democracy naturally develops is endless. Some claim loss of freedom, others, loss of security; some claim excessive taxation and loss of property, while others claim greed of the rich and the disparity of wealth. Some claim inequality, while others champion merit and ability. Some claim socialism is good because it satisfies need, others claim it steals from the able; one envisions a safety net, and the other theft through progressive taxation. Some think justice means to treat people fairly and be left alone, and another to correct past and present societal injustices. Some believe law that is written and agreed to is sacrosanct while others see the law as fluid, correcting societally induced injustices. With this, some naturally consent to inequality under the law, which others find reprehensible and debasing to the law. Some see rights as addressing need, while others see them as a defense against government. Some embrace governmental power because it is the vehicle that can make human society better, while others see it only as tyranny. Some see this governmental power used positively, bringing long-needed solutions to human problems, while others see it as loss of freedom due to the tyranny of the majority in democracy. Some believe morality is happiness for the most, while others view it as adhering to compacts like not stealing and keeping your word. With the new ethic of universal happiness some think indulging in sex and drugs is acceptable, while others concerned with consequences decry immorality and decay. And everyone has unrealistic aspirations, which bend their lens of reality to fit their personal desires. The inevitable result is contention and divisiveness.

Exacerbating these circumstances is the mantra for diversity, which democracy naturally brings about. The ethic of a melting pot in early American democracy has changed to a call for diversity in late American democracy. This is a key fatal change in American democracy that heralds the disintegration of its cohesive social norms. Diversity intensifies faction both of which Fukuyama warned were weaknesses of democracy. American media today is rife with new grievances from some sect demanding redress: Black Lives Matter, the Occupy movement, justice for illegal immigrants, the rights of homeless people, the plight of Islamic people, the pay gap between women and men and prejudice against just about everyone. The pockets of divergent interests and demands have grown exponentially in America and show no signs of abating. America's roots have changed under the aegis of democracy from can-do, rugged individualism, self-reliance, free enterprise and optimistic attitudes to complaining and blaming. American culture is increasingly being defined by its opposites and not commonalities, has fewer similar propositions about what constitutes a good society, what is right is now being defined from outpost positions and our *grundnorms*, or transcendent fundamental norms involving freedom, and justice and equality are shattering. Americans today agree on little. Americans have become, as Weaver described, free-floating experimenters without faith in our birth certificates. We now question everything, like the Flagellants of fourteenth-century France and the hippies of Haight-Ashbury of the '60s. As experimenters, Americans have become untethered from reality and the true concepts of what it means to be free. America is losing it cohesiveness, and divisiveness is the result.

Certainly all ages have cultural differences, but America's divisiveness today is broad and deep. There exist innumerable fundamental individual, sectional and cultural/philosophic ongoing differences, many of which appear to be beyond resolve. Due to democracy's freedom and permissive utility, individuals naturally have disparate attitudes on human sexuality and mores that regulate human sexual behavior. Libertines champion the Playboy sexual permissive philosophy, the '60s writ large, while others recoil at free condoms at school, premarital sex, teenage pregnancy, adultery and children born out of wedlock. Abortion remains a chronic source of divisiveness, with ongoing protests and interminable legal battles. For the pro-choicers, Planned Parenthood dispensing birth control and performing abortions is right, while the right-to-lifers see abortion as murder and a convenient method for the licentious. Vast differences exist in opinions over who should have sex with whom. On one side are the traditionalists believing in heterosexuality, where marriage is between a man and a woman, and on the other the non-traditionalists, including those who are lesbian, bisexual, gay, and transgender, who believe homosexuality and same-sex marriage is acceptable. There existed a vast divide on the issue of same-sex marriage that was ostensibly settled by the Supreme Court in 2015, but internecine warfare continues, as many judges refuse to issue licenses to same-sex couples on religious grounds.

Sectional differences are outstanding in contemporary America. The South has remained rebellious and sullen for a hundred and fifty years. Only recently has it reluctantly and with defiance taken down the Confederate flag, and it continues to smolder under the boot of the Fourteenth Amendment. Southern radio is replete with admonitions to secede from the union. Indeed, if succession were legal, Texas might well succeed from the union. Some Texans have said that it is time for their conservative state and liberal New Hampshire go their separate ways. Secession movements occur regularly throughout America.

One only need look at a map of the red and blue states' voting patterns to realize how divided America is by section. The costal blue Democratic states are in constant tension with the central red Republican states. For example, in the 2000 presidential election (excluding Washington D.C.), thirty states voted red and twenty blue, in 2004 thirty-one red and nineteen blue, in 2008 twenty-two red and twenty-eight blue and in 2012 twenty-four red and twenty-six blue. For these four elections, states voted red 107 times and blue ninety-three times, which is 53.5 percent red and 46.5 percent blue. America is almost evenly divided.

Finally, there exists an ongoing division between urban and rural dwellers. The urbanites blithely pass state laws involving water rights, timber and grazing that negatively impact rural citizens. The results are devastating to rural dwellers, and they have a feeling of being tyrannized by urban centers. The consequence is ongoing smoldering resentment. In 2016,

300

a group of citizen militiamen forcefully occupied the federally owned Malheur Wildlife Refuge in Oregon, demanding the return of federal lands to the ranchers and farmers.

One could dismiss these individual and sectional divisions as commonplace — every society has some degree of divisiveness. What cannot be dismissed, however, are the deep cultural zeitgeists that exist today; contemporary America is two cultures living side by side in a silent but fatal war. Politically, the two parties have parity, and many elections are evenly split, which is an example of this equal divide. Philosophically, conservatives and liberals have their own ideas and agendas, with little in common. One side believes in individualism, self-reliance and strength while the other believes in collectivism and welfarism (or the need to be thy brother's keeper and a social safety net to secure the weak). One side emphasizes responsibility and accountability, while the other derides them as methods of enslavement. One side believes our character is molded largely by nature, while the other emphasizes environment and nurture. Morally, one side emphasizes the social contract, need to adhere to compacts and virtue, while the other, utility and the need to bring happiness to the most.

The most conspicuous setting of this contest is being played out in politics. In the federal legislative branch, these two worldviews collide, and the result is gridlock. The Republicans and Democrats disagree on innumerable issues, like federal debt, healthcare and the very role of government. Congress has battled over the issue of debt in the form of balanced budget amendments since 1936 with little success. In 1985, Congress passed the Balanced Budget and Emergency Deficit Control Act (known as the Gramm-Rudman-Hollings Act), which was intended to produce a balanced budget by 1991 but did not. In 1986 Congress came close to passing a balanced budget, but it was defeated in the Senate by just one vote. In 1987, Congress revised the law and adopted higher deficit levels, supposedly bringing a balanced budget

301

by 1993, but again it did not. In 1990, and again in 1993, Congress revised and extended these targets, which postponed a balanced budget indefinitely. The House considered a balanced budget amendment twice in 1994 but failed. In 2010, there was a bruising, close fight over the Affordable Healthcare Act that continued until a decision was made by the Supreme Court in 2012 that it was legal. Since then, more than sixty efforts have been initiated by Congress to rescind the law. Healthcare remains an ongoing internecine battle in American politics. The role of government in citizens' lives has been a core lightning rod issue between the contestants. One side believes government hinders freedom, while the other wants it to bring security. Throughout the twentieth century, this battle has been waged over and over in the New Deal, Great Society and now Obamacare.

These two worldviews naturally result in different economic systems. One favors capitalism, competition and profit. It sees its system as free enterprise that brings wealth and opportunity. The other favors socialism that mandates "from each their ability, to each their need" and the state control of the means of production. The former views the latter as theft, and the latter views the former as greedy. Under these worldviews, one naturally sees businesses as job- and wealth-creating entities, while the other reviles the disparity of wealth and greedy corporations. Socialist presidential candidate Sanders, for example, demands in his blog that American corporate greed must end. It is only natural then that one side believes taxation is too high and favors a flat tax, while the other believes some should be taxed more and advocates a steep progressive tax. It is also only natural then that for one entitlement is a right and for the other a burden. Mandates that require businesses to pay for employees' health insurance, laws that force individuals to pay for unwanted health insurance coverage and enforced minimum wages are all seen by them as theft. Indeed, one views Social Security as an inviolate entitled right, while the other just getting back what they paid in.

The point of all this is to demonstrate the consequences of America's two zeitgeists being played out in politics today. Perhaps the most significant consequence is the threat to shut down the federal government. This occurred under President Gerald Ford once for ten days; five times under Jimmy Carter, each lasting between lasting eight to eighteen days; a few times under Ronald Regan; twice under Clinton lasting five and twenty-one days; and once, lasting sixteen days, in 2013 under Obama over Obamacare. Anarchy is a significant, real and dangerous manifestation of divisiveness in America today.

One worldview naturally inclines to positive law because it is believed to be the vehicle that corrects past wrongs and improves society. Such a view often deemphasizes the rule of law and equal treatment under the law, which the other worldview that inclines to natural law finds intolerable. The former sees affirmative action and protected group laws as justice and the latter as tyrannical injustice. We see this contest played out today in America in the congressional process of electing Supreme Court justices. The contentious nominations of Samuel Alito and Clarence Thomas and the rejections of Abe Fortas, Harrold Carswell and Robert Bork are examples. As a result of this dichotomy, law has increasingly become the arbiter of politics. Its function is to determine winners and losers so as one zeitgeist prevails a cadre of resentful losers stung by perceived injustice ensues. The result has been increased divisiveness.

The ancient battles between the sexes and races are magnified in democracy. It was mentioned earlier that one of democracy's great strengths is to bring justice and equality to all. This, however, was a strength of early democracy, and as it ossifies with age, these virtues become lost as feminists and minorities demand that law remediate past wrongs. One side sees the University of California Davis School of Medicine's rejection of Bakke in favor of a less qualified minority as justice and protected classes as ending discrimination while the other side sees only injustice and the perpetuation of discrimination. The list of enhanced divisions grows as democracy ages, theists enter politics, the far right battles secularists over issues like abortion and education and institutions begin diversity programs that others believe fracture society. The consequence of these divisions in America today is constant, unremitting tension, increasingly acerbic disputes and divisiveness.

This divisiveness is the primary reason democracy fails. Recall that one condition required for democracy is civil society outside of government — democracy cannot exist in anarchy. Due to these divisive issues, that civility is disappearing in America. Today, underground anger erupts regularly on all sides. Don't touch my Medicare, Martin Luther King, Jr.'s 1965 march on Selma, Black Lives Matter, the Occupy movement, the 2009 Tea Party movement, and militants occupying the Malheur National Wildlife property are just a few that join the long ranks of historic enduring grievances, like the Southern states resentment of the Fourteenth Amendment, resentment of the Sixteenth Amendment and higher taxes, anger over the federal debt caused in part by Johnson's Great Society, as well as contemporary anger over the dictates of Obamacare and the Supreme Court's decision legalizing same-sex marriage. The results in late democracy are occasional flares of anger, resistance, non-cooperation and a lingering air of potential rebellion and ultimately revolution. It is not one side becoming extremist but rather all sides. These are the circumstances that enable demagogues who exacerbate existing divisions by pandering to sects' grievances.

The 2016 race for president of the United States is one example. Two leading candidates are socialist Democrat Sanders on the left and billionaire Republican Trump on the right. These are not statesmen seeking compromise, a middle ground or any Solonian mean but rather extremists endeavoring to advance their ideological agenda and become president by pandering to the fears, prejudices and emotions of angry citizens, which are caused by late democracy. It is

304

precisely one of these kinds of individuals who could become America's Napoleon. A new frustrated president of their ilk faced with rising contentiousness, resistance, and violence, hindered by gridlock in Congress, could commence the process of bypassing democracy's inertia by issuing proclamations, executive orders and, if necessary, national security decision directives in order to achieve his or her objectives. Americans themselves, fearful of the rising consequences of divisiveness could sadly acquiesce, which would be the last nail that seals democracy's coffin.

Fukuyama predicted that democracy would be the end of history by resolving issues, but the divisiveness seen in America today would indicate that he is wrong. It appears the age-old master-and-slave struggle he refers to is alive and well in contemporary America. To support his thesis, Fukuyama invoked famous German idealist philosopher Georg Wilhelm Friedrich Hegel, who believed freedom was the end of human history. An alternate reading of Hegel's *Phenomenology of Spirit* could be that America is watching the unfolding of truth through a dialectic of thesis (early democracy) and its negations to antithesis (late democracy) that results in a new synthesis (which could be something other than democracy or balkanization) which would be a new thesis that continues the dialectic. In other words, democracy is just one political synthesis in a long chain of dialectical synthesis. The divisiveness described in this section is merely the negations of the thesis that leads to the antithesis and ultimately synthesis. It could be just another conceptual perspective with a successor view that accounts for its limitations. For Hegel, if democracy were the final absolute synthesis or notion of the evolution of human political development, there would be no negations, contradictions or divisiveness — but there are.

Unlike Fukuyama's thesis, the divisiveness we see in America today would indicate that the former masters are not placated with comfortable bourgeoisie life. Rather, they

305

become intolerant of democracy and exit the system, like those sketched by philosopher Rand in *Atlas Shrugged*; they no longer cooperate with the system; or they pick up the sword again and violently rebel. Similarly, it would appear that the former slaves are not satisfied with democracy and resist, rebel, protest and occasionally commit violent acts. Democracy is not the end of history because divisiveness tells us the Hegelian dialectic is not finished.

It is the cauldron of underground anger that drives the disillusionment and frustration on all sides in late American democracy. This fuels divisiveness, which results in the loss of civility. Civility, a prerequisite for democracy to exist, is fading in America — and with it democracy's two-hundred-year experiment.

CONCLUSION

It is interesting to speculate why democracy ultimately fails. I believe it fails because people cannot handle freedom. The object of any political philosophy is human happiness, and democracy promised to bring it with justice, equality and freedom. Democracy achieved historic advancements in justice and equality, but it ultimately fails with freedom because people are incapable of achieving the responsibility that maintains it.

Jean-Paul Sartre believed that freedom entails responsibility. Democracy brings the freedom but does not teach the responsibility. Indeed, George Bernard Shaw believed that many are incapable of shouldering the responsibility of the freedom democracy brings. Georg Wilhelm Friedrich Hegel may be right that humans' greatest aspiration is freedom but democracy apparently is not the political philosophy that brings it.

For freedom to exist, reason must prevail. Only reason forces one to look beyond personal interests to the whole. It is from this perspective that responsibility to others is born, as well as the realization that happiness does not come from indulging the passions. Freedom and the happiness it brings ultimately emerge through reason controlling passion.

This is not a new thought. Benedict de Spinoza, in *Ethics*, stressed the need for reason to master passion in order to achieve inner freedom, which means achieving outer freedom entails mastering inner passions. Reason is the schoolmaster that enables humans to understand, consider consequences and form true judgments. It is what brings virtue, high-mindedness, clear ideas and the courage that enable humans to control their emotions. Reason enables freedom. Samuel Johnson wrote *An Account of the Life of Mr. Richard Savage*, in which he described a certain Mr. Savage as an unhappy man with an irregular and dissipated manner of life that made him a slave to every passion. He was not the master of his own emotions; thus, his temper was dominated by his passions, which made his life uncertain and capricious. Without reason superintending his passions, his life was spent avoiding bill collectors, seeking pleasure and being unhappy.

Democracy does not constrain passion; rather, it releases it. Democracy exhorts us to maximize our happiness—it is a virtual explosion of passion over reason. It does not tell people how to be coolly reasoned but rather how to achieve happiness through impassioned utilitarianism. Indeed, Francis Fukuyama himself wrote that [verbatim] the ability of liberal democratic societies to establish and sustain themselves on a rational basis over the long term is open to some doubt. Many of the consequences of this were described in chapter eleven on divisiveness and twelve on democracy in America. Emotionalism, anger, contentiousness, licentiousness and the inability to compromise are a few examples. Democracy does breed chaos without rationality that leads to disorder and decay. Due to this defect, the sad truth is that as democracies

308

age, self-rule becomes increasingly difficult, which we see manifest in America today.

One need only contrast utility with contractarianism to appreciate this. Utility's happiness for the most removes restraint and unleashes passion, whereas the social contract requires individuals to accept mutual compacts that constrain their self-interests. Reason explains to the thinking person that their interests are better served by honoring voluntary agreements that limit their rights. The former morality usurps reason in order to achieve happiness, whereas the latter enlists reason to achieve freedom and happiness.

David Hume explained this defect of democracy when he wrote that reason is the slave of the passions. Reason's propensity to proceed in a methodical manner does not appeal to those seeking to gratify pleasure. Consequently, most Americans are slaves to their passions, which impedes their judgment, causes them to be controlled by fortune, robs them of being their own masters and blinds their minds. They have become Johnson's Mr. Savage.

When human passion is unleashed by democracy, an ineluctable sequence of events ensues. Passion becomes zeal, single-mindedness prevails, and people become less willing to compromise; the result is intolerance. Tocqueville believed democracy legitimizes unrestrained passion, and Edward Gibbon wrote that one reason for society's decline is excessive zeal—two famous historians citing a historic cause and its consequence. This is an often unrecognized and somewhat curious twist of history that Gibbon described—when passion becomes zeal, societies begin to fail.

French philosopher Albert Camus explained why this happens. Camus was trying to explain one of history's great paradoxes, which is that if people are more good than bad, then why do they do more evil acts than good ones? His answer was that when human freedom becomes an unlimited demand for liberty, such as in democracy, the result is tyranny. It becomes tyranny because with unlimited freedom people have a propensity to go to the extremes of absolutism or nihilism. In democracies, majorities espouse absolutes, and oppressed minorities vote for nihilism. The hegemonic majority zealously prefers the democratic system to retain their prerogatives while the minority is increasingly willing to wager democracy for some better system that may bring freedom. It is the absolutes that cause evil, while the nihilists sit back and do nothing to prevent evil. We see the absolutes naturally segue into zeal, and the inability to compromise and intolerance are the consequences—citizens become increasingly indifferent to others' concerns, circumstances, aspirations and freedom. Citizens become callously single-minded, and a kind of unreflective herd mentality ensues. It is Gibbon's zeal that leads to single-mindedness, which caused past societies to fail. It is what lead to their acidic disputes that we see reproduced in America today.

With zeal, citizens' views harden into uncompromising positions. Zeal and the single-mindedness it engenders turns people inward, focusing on their self-interests, which is a mindset that causes them to see differences rather than commonalities. Freedom in democracy has this inclination to celebrate and enhance our differences rather than our similarities. The current fashion of diversity in America is one example. Unlike the ruthless competition that Adam Smith told us moderates capitalism, democracy has no similar moderating counterbalance to the tyrannical majority. Early American democracy did have checks on majority rule, but these have eroded over time, and hegemonic uncompromising tyranny of the majority has ensued. The majority and minority's differences have become increasingly difficult to adjudicate in late American democracy.

Democracy forgets history—it forgets the advice from great moderating thinkers. Solon said there must exist a balance between the rich and poor for a successful society, Aristotle advocated finding a mean, and English historian Thomas Babington Macaulay advised the upper and lower classes to steer a middle course between despotism and anarchy. Compromise avoids antagonism, brings the greatest good, enables civilization and preserves democracy.

But as democracy ages, it finds it increasingly difficult to bring compromise, or to find the mean between extremes, due to intolerance. In chapter three, it was asserted that excessive zeal is not necessarily fatal unless it turns into intolerance. Unfortunately, it has in late American democracy, and today we find the hardened polar beliefs of capitalism, socialism, freedom and equality ensconced. The advocates' views are ardent, unwilling to compromise and increasingly intolerant of the other. Divisiveness is the only conceivable outcome of this intolerance and it is the same intolerance that stalked ancient Athens and Rome — and more recently France and America.

Fukuyama and Hegel were wrong — passion overruling reason drives the cycles of history and prevents any new synthesis of freedom. R. G. Collingwood was right — history is the story of human passion, and trying to predict it ignores human will. Passion, zeal, single-mindedness, and uncompromising intolerance brings the divisiveness that makes democracy only one failed form of government among many, and not the end of history.

History tells us that the occurrence of democracy in America is rare and will be short. Certainly, only time can tell us for sure if it will endure, but if history is any teacher, it would appear that democracy in America will follow the same fate as past political systems and perish.

SOURCES

The information and ideas for this book came from a variety of sources, including my education, Wikipedia and Google. Most of it, however, came from books I have read. Some of them are as follows: Francis Fukuyama's *The End of History and the Last Man*, which is cited throughout this book. In the introduction, I used E. H. Gombrich's *Art and Illusion*. In chapter two on the history of democracy, I gathered some information on ancient democracies from Plutarch's *The Rise and Fall of Athens* and Thucydides *The Peloponnesian War*. For modern democracy, I relied heavily on Alexis de Tocqueville's *The Old Regime and the French Revolution* and *Democracy in America*, as well as Christopher Hibbert's *The Days of the French Revolution* and Stendhal's *Life of Napoleon*. I was influenced by some of historian Barbara W. Tuchman's books, including *The First Salute* and *A Distant Mirror: The*

Calamitous 14th Century. I refer to Tocqueville's thoughts on democracy throughout this book.

Many of the arguments presented in chapter three on the historic arguments against democracy were garnered from biographies of famous individuals, such as Dumas Malone's *The Sage of Monticello*, as well as *The Great Quotations* compiled by George Seldes. Because Fukuyama often cited Georg Wilhelm Friedrich Hegel to support his theory, I used Hegel's *The Phenomenology of Spirit*, which I have studied. Many of my criticisms of his theory were derived from famous historian R. G. Collingswood's *The Idea of History*. For the cycles of democracy, I was influenced by numerous historians who are cited in the book, but particularly by Edward Gibbon's *The History of the Decline and Fall of the Roman Empire*. A few thoughts were garnered from Jared Diamond's *Guns, Germs and Steel*, which provided information on early societies and the reasons for their evolution, and David McCullough's *The Great Bridge*, due to his wonderful description of John A. Roebling and his desire to make the most of himself in free democratic America. For ancient criticisms, I relied on Plato's *Republic* and some of Cicero's writings. For more recent criticisms, I used *The Federalist Papers*, in particular *No. 10*, by James Madison, as well as *The Philosophy of Law* by Raymond Wacks.

For chapter four I referred often again to Fukuyama's book, as well as to historian Arnold J. Toynbee's *A Study of History*. On the cycles of history in chapter five, I used many sources, including Marnie Hughes-Warrington's *Fifty Key Thinkers in History* and Ralph Waldo Emerson's *Self-Reliance*, as well as some of the sources of arguments fatal to history described in chapter three. I also consulted various sources on the history of democracy, as well as some historians and philosophers of history, such as Christopher Russett's *The Days of the French Revolution*.

For section three on the reasons democracy fails, I relied on innumerable sources. On freedom, many ideas came from

James Buchan's *Frozen Desire: The Meaning of Money* and E. O. Wilson's *Sociobiology: The New Synthesis*. On inequality, I used my own book *Socialism in America* and the sources I had used to write it, including *The Communist Manifesto*, Harry W. Laidler's *History of Socialism*, Karl Popper's *The Open Society and its Enemies* and Thomas Robert Malthus's *An Essay on the Principle of Population*. I also referenced Friedrich Nietzsche's *On the Genealogy of Morality* as well as Roderick T. Long's reproduction of the Bastiat-Proudhon Debate. In my discussion on injustice and the law, as well as on affirmative action, I used numerous sources including my own book *On Law* and Mark Levin's *Men in Black*.

On the concentration of power, I used many sources. Information on the Roman Empire's concentration of government came from a history paper I wrote on the subject. My principal sources for that paper were Frank C. Bourne's *The History of the Romans*, Samuel Dill's *Roman Society from Nero to Marcus Aurelius*, A. H. M. Jones's *The Later Roman Empire 284–602*, Rodney Stark's *The Rise of Christianity* and Chester Starr's *The Roman Empire*.

Also, some information was derived from my 2010 spring term class lecture notes on the Roman Empire taught by Professor Gary Ferngren at Oregon State University. My information on executive privilege came mostly from Phillip Cooper's *By Order of the President: The Use and Abuse of Executive Direct Action*. I also used *The Irony of Democracy* by Thomas R. Dye and L. Harmon Zeigler and referenced Paul Johnson's *Modern Times*. My chapter on relative morality was mostly from memory, but I had fun using Jonathan Swift's *Gulliver's Travels*. In chapter eleven on divisiveness, I used numerous sources, including Aristotle's *Politics*.

Throughout this book, I used various sources, such as my book *A Reference Guide to Stoicism*, John Locke's *Two Treatises on Government* (and in particular his second treatise), Carl L. Becker's *The Declaration of Independence*, Kenneth Minogue's *Politics*, Richard M. Weaver's *The Ethics of Rhetoric*, Friedrich

Hayek's *The Road to Serfdom* and *The Constitution of Liberty* and John Stewart *Mill's On Liberty*.

Much of the information in my chapter on democracy in America came from my knowledge and observations. I did reference Andrew Carnegie's *The Gospel of Wealth*, as well as the ancient Greek philosopher Solon. For the '60s section, I used Jay Stevens's *Storming Heaven* and Barry Miles's biography *Jack Kerouac: King of the Beats*. In the section on relative morality, I referenced John Rawls's *A Theory of Justice* and Robert Nozick's response *Anarchy, State, and Utopia*. In this chapter, I also referred to Ayn Rand's *Atlas Shrugged*.

In the conclusion, I used David Hume's *Treatise on Human Nature* and Benedict de Spinoza's *Ethics* regarding reason and passion. I also referred to some of Samuel Johnson's writing from Oxford's *Samuel Johnson: A Critical Edition of the Major Works*, edited by Sir John Frank Kermode.

About the Author

John Bowman lives in Portland, Oregon, where he raised three daughters with his wife Kathy. He is the author of numerous books on philosophy, real estate, politics, sports, words, Stoicism and humor.

He received a Bachelor of Arts degree in 1973 from Whitman College, a Bachelor of Arts degree in philosophy in 1993 from Portland State University and a Master of Interdisciplinary Studies degree in philosophy and history in 2010 from Oregon State University. His master's thesis, titled *Stoicism, Enkrasia and Happiness*, surveyed the ancient philosophy of Stoicism and particularly the famous Roman Stoic Seneca. A complete list of his books follows.

The author welcomes reader's comments, observations and rebuttals. His books and biography can be viewed on his website at www.johnlbowman.com, comments can be sent via his blog at WWW.JOHNLBOWMAN.COM/BLOG/ or he can be reached by e-mailed at JLBREALTOR@QUEST.NET.

OTHER BOOKS
by John L. Bowman

- Reflections on Man and the Human Condition
- Selected Topics in Philosophy
- Nobody's Perfect
- How to Succeed in Commercial Real Estate
- Socialism in America
- God's Lecture
- A Reader's Companion
- Stoicism, Enkrasia and Happiness
- Aegean Summer
- The Art of Volleyball Hitting
- Graduate School
- Provocative and Contemplative Quotations
- On Law
- A Reference Guide to Stoicism
- A Reader's Companion II

www.ingramcontent.com/pod-product-compliance
Lightning Source LLC
Chambersburg PA
CBHW072049020426
42334CB00017B/1444